# The
# Single-Camera
# Director

## Second Edition

A student's guide to the artistic and technical elements of single-camera television production spanning the pre-production, production, and post-production phases and emphasizing the role of the director.

by
Mark N. Herlinger

Second Edition

Updated July 2004
Printed in the United States of America
ISBN: 0-9647401-3-3

Published by:
Western Media Products
P.O. Box 591, Denver, CO 80201
www.media-products.com
800-232-8902

# About the author:

Mark Herlinger holds a B.A. in radio-TV-film from the University of Michigan and an M.A. in journalism from the University of Colorado.

Since 1981 he has directed documentaries, public affairs programs, talk shows, educational and entertainment programs. He has received regional Emmy awards for directing and his productions have been broadcast regionally and nationally.

Since 1985, he has taught single-camera television at the Metropolitan State College of Denver and the University of Colorado. He is currently an adjunct faculty at the School of Journalism and Mass Communication at the University of Colorado, Boulder.

Since 1988, he has been in business as an independent producer and media publisher, creating broadcast and corporate video and multi-media presentations.

# Acknowledgements:

The author gratefully acknowledges the following for technical assistance:

| | |
|---|---|
| *Design*: | A. B. Forster, Chuck Thornton |
| *Illustrations*: | Chuck Thornton (chapters 4 & 15), John Boak (chapter 8 storyboard characters) |
| *Photography*: | Mark Herlinger |
| *Production*: | Janet Roucis |
| *Copy Editing*: | Teresa Herlinger (edition 1), Allison St. Claire (edition 2) |
| *Consultation*: | Wayne E. Brenengen, CEAVCO Audio-Visual Company |
| | George Guiette, Denver Dubbing |
| | Scott Forbes, CEAVCO Audio-Visual Company |
| | Stuart Keene, Freelance Videographer |
| | Todd Mueller, Computer Animator, Colorado Studios |
| | Jerry Schneider, Film/Video Equipment Services |
| | Darrel Wong, Ph.D., Voice Recording and Research Center |
| | Denver Center for the Performing Arts |
| *Photo subjects*: | Bob Amend, Jamil Anglin, Jed Brunk, Mark Camacho, Tom Craig, |
| | Allison Donnely, Darren Gonzales, Ronald Green, |
| | Raymond Hill, Jennifer Johnson, Stuart Keene, |
| | Julie Krivanek, Chad Ogburn, Jason Oliver, Elena Salazar |

# Contents

# SECTION V

## POST-PRODUCTION

# SECTION VI

## EXERCISES

# Introduction

The world of television has become a technological whirlwind. The tools of the trade are becoming available to more and more people in all aspects of business. Hardware and software breakthroughs are happening constantly. Whereas once there were one or two broadcast videotape formats and no consumer formats, today the formats and associated terms are confusing at best: HDTV, Motion JPEG, MPEG-2, DVCam, DVC Pro, Digi-Beta, Digital Hi-8, firewire, serial digital interface, DVD-R—it's enough to make anyone lose sight of the fact that television is not just a technical phenomenon but also an art form and a storytelling medium.

It's no easy task to pay equal attention to both the creative side of TV and the technical. But someone has to do it. The person assigned to this task is the TV director. The director stands at the juncture between story ideas and widgets and must know how best to use the widgets to bring the ideas to life. So, by understating the role of the director, we understand the TV production process as a whole.

TV production students are often expected to direct television projects. To help get them off to a good start, this book illuminates the thought processes required to direct a TV show. The following lessons will help one learn to think, plan, and evaluate the TV production process. Scenarios will apply to both broadcast news and corporate video production.

While equipment may change yearly, directorial principles that guide the way to piece a story together, the way to frame a shot, the way to coach actors transcend time and equipment updates. For example, the art of shooting various angles and piecing them together so that the scene has a logical flow without any continuity breaks is a timeless and essential skill. Knowing how to condense action and how to move people quickly through time and space are also fundamental to the art of directing. These and many other artistic principles are covered in this book.

Therefore the TV student should not feel bad if his or her department does not have the latest and greatest widgets. These widgets are likely to become outdated during the student's tenure at the university. It's far better to expect a good introduction to the principles of directing—these transcend all makes and models of cameras, recorders, and editors.

At the same time, it's certainly important to understand the technical tools of the trade and the context in which they are used. This book covers equipment and its proper use, including: camera operation, lighting, audio, graphics, and linear and non-linear editing. Specific makes and models are not emphasized as these are likely to change. Rather, this book covers basic trends in the industry along with a directorial context in which to understand them.

Along the way, this book will also acknowledge and clarify differences between traditional and modern aspects of TV technology with emphasis on the two most significant technical recent trends in the TV industry: the move from analog to digital recording formats and the move from linear to non-linear editing systems.

So get ready to learn the process of TV directing for the single camera production. And remember that facts alone can be confusing. Context is the key to understanding. Therefore, a main feature of this book is the frequent use of contextual examples that allow the reader to wrap his or her mind around the TV production process, to see how the pieces fit together, and to make sound decisions at each step along the way.

# 1

# Overview: A Real World Application

The following scenario is one example of a single-camera video director at work.

After several fatal accidents at its mill sites around the country, the Regis Lumber Company decided to create an educational video program on equipment safety. This video program will become required viewing for employees at all sites worldwide.

The production will cost the company close to $45,000. But, in light of lawsuits, medical, and insurance costs, the executives decide that the price of creating an effective educational presentation is worthwhile.

A TV production company is called and a proposal requested. A TV producer from the company is put in charge of developing the proposal which includes a treatment and a budget.

As soon as the proposal is approved by the lumber company, a contract is signed. The preproduction phase gets underway immediately. A writer is hired to research and write a script. The writer meets with company officials to discuss content and required teaching points. Next, a TV director is hired to craft the show and maintain artistic and technical control. The director sits in on the initial discussions and works closely with the writer. The writer and director tour the factory and begin envisioning scenes. They explore suitable places to do the shooting.

The script calls for some dramatic vignettes that will require actors. The director initiates the audition process and also begins organizing the necessary crew and equipment for the shooting.

In the production phase, all the scenes are videotaped at the lumber mill. The shoot will last three days, two days for the dramatic vignettes using the "masterscene" style of shooting, and one day for shooting comments from company executives using the "interview" style of shooting. The team will also shoot some specific training procedures using the "demonstration" style of shooting. In each case, the director will call for numerous takes—repetitions of the same scene—to get a variety of angles and to get the best performances out of the actors and company employees. By shooting various angles and framings, the director creates the illusion that there were three or more cameras at the scene instead of only one.

When the shooting is finished, the director will proceed to the post-production phase, otherwise known as "editing." The director will work closely with an editor who pieces the scenes together using a non-linear computer-based editing system. Much more footage will have been shot than actually needed. But this abundance of footage allows the director and the editor to make choices about which takes were best and which angles to use. Selected scenes will be digitized into a computer editing system and the editor will begin to select them, arranging them in order.

The director knows that the factory executives will need to approve the program. In fact, they will likely ask for changes once they see the show in its edited form. It seems no matter how many times they review the script, some problems won't catch the clients' eye until they see them on the screen.

So, the director will first create a "rough cut" of the program, piecing all the elements together, enough to give a good sense of how the program flows, but without spending a lot of time fine-tuning everything.

Once changes have been made and a rough cut has been approved, the post-production phase can continue. A narrator will be selected and recorded. Music themes will be chosen from a music library of prerecorded music. Titles and graphics will be created. A computer animator will make animation to show scenes that could not easily be shot on location—for example, the internal workings of certain machines.

The final product will have more than 150 edits and many different scenes and camera angles. But all scenes at the mill will have been shot with a single camera.

The last part of the post-production phase is distribution. In this case, the program will be distributed in the form of VHS cassette copies, labeled, packaged in an attractive four-color cover, and sent to the training offices of the mill's locations around the country to be shown at training sessions of thousands of employees. As more and more personal computers are sold with DVD drives installed, the company executives request that the the show be available on DVD as well.

This story is just one example of how single-camera field production works. It offers a sense of everyone's role and the many procedural steps from beginning to end.

In this example, the product will never be broadcast on television. Instead, it will be distributed privately within the company. But a similar process would take place for television news, documentary, and special interest programs for broadcast. Breaking news may require a more spontaneous response with less time to prepare. The crew may be smaller. The director and camera operator may be the same person. But the goal is the same—to capture a story on location using one camera, then bring it back to the editing room and edit various shots and angles to make it look as if several cameras were used. The rest of this book will explain these steps in detail and give you a working knowledge of the single-camera production process and the role of the director.

Theoretically, it would be nice to have multiple cameras at all the locations in order to get many shots and angles at once. In some productions, that is exactly what happens. Multi-camera productions involve two or more cameras capturing various angles of a scene simultaneously, usually in a TV studio, but also on location at sporting events and other live events. With a multi-camera set-up, the TV director can select between the various cameras using a video switcher console with rows of buttons and fader bars. By switching instantly between cameras, the editing occurs as the action happens.

In contrast, single-camera production scenes are shot first and edited later. All the footage is shot with one camera and the shots are assembled, arranged and rearranged in an editing studio.

Some productions lend themselves more readily to single or multi-camera production. For example, talk shows and live sports events lend themselves perfectly to multi-camera production. Documentaries, hard news stories, news features, training programs and commercials are a few examples of programs that are typically shot on location using a single camera.

(1.1) Multi-camera directing. The director watches numerous camera monitors and makes immediate decisions about shot selection.

(1.2) Single-camera directing. The director and crew gather footage to be edited later.

For many projects, like the lumber mill safety program, a multi-camera production would be impractical. It would be too much trouble, requiring too much equipment and too many crew people. Further, the multi-camera process forces immediate editing decisions upon the director that can be made at a more leisurely pace later in the editing room. In a case like this, the typical choice is to shoot all scenes with one camera and edit later.

In this book we'll explore the single camera process as it applies to a variety of industrial and news applications. We'll focus on the director because this person, more than anyone else on the team, needs to understand the production process both technically and aesthetically. By looking at the process through the director's eyes, we'll not only learn the "what" but also the "how" and the "why." We'll not only learn the basics about TV production, but we'll think about the director's considerations at each step in the process, thus helping it all come together and make sense.

Terminology is highlighted throughout the book by **bold italics** and listed in the index. Let's begin with some terms that describe the single-camera process:

## EFP/ENG

The most common industry term for single-camera TV production is **EFP**, which stands for **Electronic Field Production**. EFP refers to any production in which a TV crew takes a camera on location and records footage on videotape to be edited later.

Another term used in the industry is **ENG** which stands for **Electronic News Gathering**. The two terms—ENG and EFP—are used somewhat interchangeably, although ENG is commonly used in the context of TV news.

The ENG team from a TV news station, usually a small crew of two or three, is dispatched by the station assignment desk when breaking news occurs. In order to be small in number, the team doubles up on responsibilities. One person may act as both director and camera operator. Another is both writer and reporter. A third may help with lighting and audio. In short order, the ENG team must write the script, shoot the story, and edit a final product to be ready for broadcast a few hours later that day. The finished edited story is referred to as a **news package**.

On the other hand, the EFP team can take more time and often has the benefit of a larger crew: producer, director, camera, audio, lighting, make-up, production assistant, etc. A documentary, TV commercial, or training program may take several weeks or months to complete.

In summary, ENG productions such as news packages, are shot and edited quickly, perhaps in just a few hours using a small crew. EFP productions, which encompass almost anything other than hard news, may take weeks or months to plan, write, shoot, and edit.

## PRE-PRODUCTION, PRODUCTION, POST-PRODUCTION

The TV industry organizes any video production process according to three major phases:
1) *pre-production*
2) *production*
3) *post-production*

Pre-production covers: conceptualization, planning, budgeting, site-surveying, hiring of crew, acquiring necessary equipment—everything that occurs right up to the day of the actual shoot.

Production covers the shooting process: set-up on location, lighting, audio, coaching talent, and taping or filming all the necessary scenes.

Post-production covers the editing: logging all the footage, revising the script to reflect any changes made while shooting, recording narration, adding music, and piecing all the scenes together using a video editing system.

This book will present the single-camera process from beginning to end according to these three phases of production.

## WHAT LIES AHEAD

Section 1 of this book provides background and perspective on the history of television and how the TV process has evolved.

Section 2 covers aesthetic principles about the TV medium, principles that every director should understand.

Sections 3, 4, and 5 cover the three stages of the process: pre-production, production, and post-production.

Section 6 contains a set of exercises to use as class assignments. The exercises offer the chance to practice the skills covered in this book.

At the end of chapters, you'll find a shaded box like this with the title:

**A REAL WORLD APPLICATION, CONTINUED:**

In these sections throughout the book, you'll find a continuing update about the TV production going on at the Regis Lumber Mill. These brief chapter postscripts are meant to summarize and apply the principles covered in each of the chapters and to give yet another example of how the director thinks and acts through the entire single-camera production process.

# 2

# What is a Director?

When you were a child, did you ever play house? Did you perform puppet shows for your parents? Skits at school? Talent shows at camp? Did you build model space ships and stage intergalactic battle scenes?

If you did any of these, then you were already a director because you decided what went where and who would say what and when. If, after creating your presentation, you looked upon the finished work with pride and proclaimed, "It is good," then you already experienced the joy and satisfaction of directing.

It doesn't matter what the medium was—puppet show, skit, or talent show. What mattered was that you wanted to create. You wanted to shape and mold the presentation, and you enjoyed both being in charge and working in collaboration with the others involved.

Today, you may be exploring the field of television and those same impulses are at work. As with any endeavor, some try it for awhile, some make a living at it, and some achieve greatness. What makes one director better than another may be a combination of training, innate talent, and luck. In any case, the conversion from childhood impulses into professional pursuits is ideally accompanied by a grounding in the technical knowledge of the medium and enhanced by an experience of life that yields perspective and something to say.

Although we may hear more about directors during the Academy Awards than at any other time of the year, there are film and TV directors working in many different capacities throughout the industry who get less attention. Every situation comedy, TV movie, news show, corporate training video, sporting event, infomercial, or in-store point-of-purchase video display has had someone behind the scenes acting as director.

Today, the technology of video production has become affordable to a wide variety of businesses. Only a few decades ago, TV production was largely in the hands of local TV stations, major networks, and a few large production companies. With the expansion and diversification of television production, there is an ever-increasing need for TV directors. Corporations are producing their own video productions for training and marketing. The multiplication of cable TV channels has also increased the need for TV programs and people to direct them. Production companies come in all shapes and sizes from huge corporations to small independent producers and directors working out of their homes.

What if your goal is not necessarily to be a director? What if you want to be a camera operator? Or an audio engineer? Whatever your intent, it will help if you understand the director's job. The whole crew works best when the members understand each other's roles. In this book, all crew positions will be explained.

## WHY HAVE A DIRECTOR?

A television production needs a director for the same reason that a symphony orchestra needs a conductor. Whenever an ensemble gathers to perform, someone is needed to act as visionary, coordinator, organizer, and leader.

The symphony conductor does much more than dictate the tempo by waving the wand. Prior to the rehearsal process, the conductor studies the material and develops an artistic vision for the performance. The TV director does the same for a television program.

## QUALITIES OF A DIRECTOR

A fascinating characteristic of the TV production process is the way in which two vastly different spheres of influence come together to produce a program: concept and technology. The production has a conceptual element—the thoughts and emotions that make up the subject matter. And, the production has a technical element—the camera, the recording deck, the lights, the staging, and the special effects. The director must coordinate the two worlds of concept and technology. This is true for both TV and film.

In our physical world, any art form has its technical component. A painter must have paints and a canvas. A sculptor must have a foundry to melt bronze or a kiln set to the proper temperature to bake clay. A musician must have a properly constructed and tuned instrument. Each artist must understand the technology on which they depend.

In television production, however, there is an amazing and intense blend of high technology with artistry, arguably more than in any other art form. Those who choose to direct television should realize that they will have to understand both worlds. Thus, an interest in things technical as well as things creative is a good personality profile for the TV director.

That does not mean all directors share the same level of interest in technology. Some directors are known mostly for their sensitivity in working with actors. They may direct situation comedies or serious dramas, paying more attention to drama than to technology. Other directors may be known for technical wizardry and may gravitate toward product commercials or science fiction programs that require complex special effects. Others directors may be journalistic and prefer working on documentaries and news stories. But each must be aware of both the artistic and technical nature of the TV medium.

Being well organized is another necessary quality for any director. In fact, all members of the production team should have a good organizational sense. If people are unable to meet deadlines, keep track of time, keep track of lists of things to do, then the production falls apart and time and money are wasted. So, if you fancy yourself an artist who wants no part of logistical concerns, then you might choose a more solitary pursuit, one that allows you to work at your own pace. However, with TV production, people and materials need to be coordinated and the production needs to run as close to schedule as possible. A disorganized director spells disaster for the production.

Every director has a different personal style. Some like to give performers and crew very specific instructions step by step along the way. Other directors are inclined to give general instructions and let the others have more creative leeway. Either personal style is fine as long as the director can effectively execute the production and keep the crew working together as a team.

You may find that your own style makes you more suitable for directing a certain type of program. An investigative documentary, for example, may require a much more assertive style of directing than a romantic drama, which, in some cases, may require a delicate sensitivity and ability to communicate subtle nuances to the actors.

## THE PRODUCER

In the profession of television and film, there is another authority on hand besides the director—the *producer*. People often wonder what the difference is between the producer and director. Part of the answer is simple   the producer has authority over the director and therefore takes an even greater responsibility for questions and problems relating to the production.

The more complicated part of the answer is that the producer's and director's areas of responsibility often overlap. You may encounter different balances of power between producers and a directors. In some cases, the producer will give the director many specific guidelines about the artistic execution of the program. In other cases, the director will have leeway to make his or her own judgment calls.

In general, however, the producer is responsible for the overall concept of the show as well as logistical and financial concerns. The director is responsible for the actual execution of the production.

*Executive producers* have overall authority for TV or film productions. They can hire and fire. They establish budgets and make sure those budgets are met. Other producer roles include the *creative producer* who is involved in the writing or conceptualizing of the story and *line producer* who is onsite at the production, making sure everything is going according to plan.

In the TV and film industries, you will find some situations in which the producer and the director are viewed as completely discrete jobs. Yet, in other situations, even major Hollywood releases, you will find one person credited as both producer and director. In TV news, a reporter may act as both producer and director of a field story. The age old truth prevails—there are absolutely no absolutes. The roles of producer and director will always be in search of a clearer distinction.

## REALIZING THE POTENTIAL OF TELEVISION

Have you ever watched a TV show or film and thought that the book version was better? In other situations, you may have liked the movie version better. So, can any story translate to any medium? Why not? Provided that the director realizes the potential of that medium and makes the most of it.

To appreciate the characteristics of a medium such as TV, consider what it was like when television was brand new technology and directors had to figure out what to do with this new form. Historically, film preceded TV, and theater preceded film. Each of these genres tries to tell stories to an audience, yet each has unique attributes. A director may choose one genre over another because of his or her fascination with those attributes. For example, the theater stage forces the director to create all time and space illusions using the same physical space. That challenge may compel a director to work in the theater. A television director may be compelled by the ability to reach a mass audience very quickly from many locations. A film director may be compelled by seeing the finished product on a large screen.

A challenge facing early filmmakers was to break away from the conventions of the theater stage in which the viewer sees the performance from one angle. Some film directors experimented with variety of angles and points of view, the pace of the program, and the use of special effects. Their films looked quite different than theater performances.

Other early films, however, look much like theater performances, as seen from the audience perspective. These films presented long unedited scenes in which the actors performed much as they would on stage and the camera did little else but watch.

Whether the film looks like a theater presentation is not an issue of right or wrong, good or bad. Rather, it's an issue of exploring the abilities of the medium and deciding how best to work with it to produce the given subject matter. The director should consider whether or not he or she is taking advantage of the unique abilities of that medium.

So, here's a mental exercise. Consider what the unique attributes are of each medium: theater, film, television. Try this as a way to focus your understanding of what you hope to accomplish with television and what will make a subject translate well in television rather than in another form.

Compare your ideas with the following assertions:

1) Theater offers the chance to see a live performance. For some viewers, that experience is most compelling.

2) Film and television are very similar in that they present recorded and edited sound and picture on a two-dimensional screen. Both offer the ability to manipulate shots through editing, thus moving the viewer anywhere in an instant. Both offer close-ups, something theater can't do.

3) Film offers a larger projection and better resolution than television.

4) Television offers instant playback, the ability to broadcast through the airwaves, and the ability to do instantaneous editing via multiple cameras routed through a switcher, such as for a live sporting event.

5) TV is a close-up medium. Because TV sets are relatively small, and TV resolution is relatively poor, images look best close up.

As you think of other distinguishing characteristics, you'll focus your attention on the medium in which you wish to direct and consider how you would maximize its potential.

## TELEVISION VERSUS FILM

How does the director choose whether to pursue television or film? First, by understanding the differences between the media and what kinds of productions are typically produced in each medium.

Film has always been a better looking medium than television. Film's resolution is better, thus it can be projected much larger and maintain good picture quality.

TV has always been a practical medium, offering speed and instant access to the world through broadcasting. TV has found its own set of practical uses including news gathering, documentary production, sports and nightly home entertainment.

Even though film has better resolution than video, either medium can look good or bad depending on the skills and resources applied to a production. When comparing film to television, it's easy to make the mistake of comparing characteristics of the genres themselves when the comparison should be between production budgets. For example, comparing a $15,000 video production to a $15,000,000 feature film is more of a comparison of production budgets rather than of the media's inherent qualities.

However, assuming that the same budget is spent on both media, that both productions are equally well lit, equally well shot, the film, by its technical nature, will yield a higher resolution image.

TV picture quality is improving every year. A video picture in the United States has traditionally been a 4:3 (almost square) format composed of 525 scan lines. The *High Definition Television* format doubles the number of scan lines and widens the picture to a 16:9 ratio which looks a lot like a 35 mm movie in miniature. As video resolution improves, it can be projected on large screens with better results. In fact, some feature films are already being made in video.

## SUMMARY

So how can one best summarize the role of a TV director? In any medium, he or she is a leader and visionary. But in TV, the director's most distinguishing quality is that he or she must be the liaison between the technical world and the conceptual world. Nobody is more responsible for understanding both worlds and acting as the diplomat to bring them both together than the director. A good director will speak both languages.

Directors choose the media that attract them. Some will choose film, some theater, some graphic design, and some television. Within the field of television are many styles, some technical, some dramatic, and some journalistic.

Directing is about asserting creative ideas and making them work well on the screen. This book will present many rules and principles to help you make your ideas come to life. Learn the rules. But also realize that rules are made to learn and then break. For example, you may set out to light your subject according to a textbook method, only to discover that the light looks better if you depart from the textbook rule. With experience, you will decide when to use the rules, when to ignore them, and when to improve upon them.

3

## From Analog to Digital

It's helpful for the director to have an overview of the technical trends in the TV industry—a sense of where we've been and where we are headed. This chapter will highlight some of the important milestones and trends in TV technology. We'll pay particular attention to the evolution from the analog recording method to the newer digital method.

In the scope of technological history, both television and film are recent inventions, evolving within a few decades of one another. A crude form of television was introduced in 1884 when Paul Nipkow applied for a patent on his mechanical image scanning device. It used a spinning disc full of holes through which a light was projected. The movie business developed faster. By, 1895, French brothers August and Louis Lumiere were marketing the first viable movie camera and projection system and inviting the public to view their films.

Television had to wait decades for public consumption. In 1927, American Philo Farnsworth applied for a patent on an electronic scanning system—the prototype of today's TV set. Actual TV broadcasting began in Germany with coverage of the 1936 Olympics and in the United States with the 1939 coverage of the New York World's Fair opening and an address by President Roosevelt. NBC began commercial broadcasting in 1941.

TV was only a live transmission medium. Images went directly from the camera to the transmitter. There was no video storage mechanism—only a crude configuration known as *kinescope* in which a film camera was aimed at a TV screen to record the image. Videotape didn't exist yet.

Videotape recording was attempted in the early 1950s. The first commercial videotape player/recorder was the Ampex VP-1000 introduced at the 1956 National Association of Broadcaster's convention. The advent of videotape bifurcated the TV production process. Two distinct methods were now available: the multi-camera style which is typically used in a studio and is often live transmission, and the single-camera style which is typically used for any production that requires mobility and requires a recording medium. To this day, both styles are used, sometimes separately, sometimes in conjunction with each other.

The evolution of television production technology can be characterized by four major trends:

1) a move toward lighter weight and easily portable equipment
2) a move toward more automated and durable equipment
3) a move from analog signal processing to digital signal processing
4) a move from linear editing to non-linear editing

## LIGHTER WEIGHT

Size and weight of TV equipment were major obstacles. At first, TV cameras were too big and heavy to handle. Videotape recorders were equally tedious to move. Remote productions in the 1960s took a team of engineers and production personnel to lift huge pieces of equipment into buses or trucks. Engineers had to spend enormous amounts of time setting up all the equipment once it reached its destination. Over the years, equipment has become more portable and easier to maintain.

## AUTOMATION AND DURABILITY

Today, many of the professional video camera's functions are automated, computerized and require minimal attention. Cameras are compact and relatively lightweight compared with earlier models. They have much greater tolerances for sudden movement and intense light.

By contrast, early TV cameras were less automated and extremely vulnerable. Older cameras had no zoom lenses. Instead, they were equipped with a turret of fixed focal length lenses that had to be dialed in one at a time. Electronic settings in older cameras were so delicate that engineers had to go through an extensive list of setup and alignment functions to get the cameras ready for each production.

Inside the older broadcast video camera, an image is focused on the surfaces of three extremely sensitive glass pick-up tubes which convert light signals into electrical energy. These tubes are so fragile that they are damaged by intense light, they fall out of alignment easily, and cost thousands of dollars to replace. In the late 1980s, the charge couple device (CCD) was introduced—a fancy name for a light-sensitive computer chip—which replaced tubes and eliminated problems associated with them. The chip can withstand intense light and won't fall out of alignment.

(3.1) Older camera use pick-up tubes to convert light into electricity.

(3.2) Newer camera uses CCD chips.

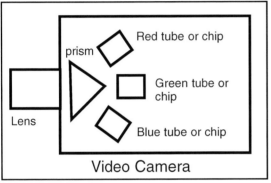

(3.3) Inside the camera, a prism splits light into three primary colors, red, green, and blue. The light from each color goes to one of three tubes or chips.

Today's cameras offer internal menu options—seen in the view-finder—for quick in-the-field modifications of color, light levels, and picture clarity. These settings used to require engineers, screwdrivers and oscilloscopes to adjust. Newer cameras come with electronic **setup cards** which plug into a given camera, memorize setup information—color, black levels, etc.—and can then be plugged into other cameras, instantly recalling the same parameters.

## VIDEOTAPE FORMATS

Cameras and videotape decks are two separate pieces of equipment that have evolved independently. Thus, a video camera is only that piece of equipment which produces an image. The videotape recorder stores the image. The term *format*, when applied to videotape, refers to specifications of the videotape and its associated electronic recording system. Camera characteristics may be examined separately.

This chapter will highlight some of the important milestones in videotape format development. Since there are more than thirty different formats from broadcast to industrial to consumer grade, not all formats will be discussed in detail. In the next few pages, we will cover some important milestones in the broadcast videotape format evolution. For a full list of videotape formats, see figure 3.9.

(3.4) Two-inch "Quad" VTR

When videotape first became available, the format was physically huge by today's standards—a two-inch wide tape format spooled on a heavy reel that weighed as much as an encyclopedia. A record/playback machine was the size of a kitchen stove. No one even considered toting one around, except by installing one on a television remote truck with full crew. This tape format was known as *two-inch* because of its tape width or *quadruplex* because of its four electromagnetic heads that spun on a drum to read and record the tape signal. Since the tape machines were so heavy, they were bound to stay in studios or trucks. The two-inch videotape format was not always interchangeable among two-inch machines and could only be read by the electromagnetic heads that originally recorded the signal. Thus, playing a tape on another VTR sometimes required physically transplanting the electromagnetic head assembly to the other machine.

In the meantime, portability was left to the 16 millimeter film medium. Film was used as a news gathering medium for TV because film cameras were easy to transport. The film was shot, processed, and either transferred to videotape or loaded on a film projector aimed directly into a TV camera to be incorporated into a live broadcast. TV stations had film editing rooms for the cutting and splicing of news story footage. News reels were shot on film and flown back to the networks for the next day's newscasts. The expression "Film at 11:00," was literally true. Single-camera video field production would have to wait for lighter, more portable formats before it could become widely used.

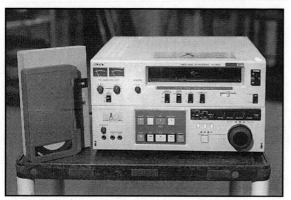

(3.5) The 3/4" U-Matic Portable VTR

## THE 3/4-INCH U-MATIC

In 1972, the Sony Corporation introduced a new broadcast quality format that made video portable—the *3/4-inch cassette* format. This format was also known as *U-MATIC* or *helical*, which referred to the method by which the tape is diagonally wrapped around a spinning drum containing the electromagnetic heads. The new format came in two versions: a large studio-size deck using 60-minute long cassettes and a small portable version using "mini" 20-minute cassettes. The portable 3/4-inch U-MATIC videotape recorder is about the size of a small suitcase and is carried over the shoulder or toted on a cart.

Cameras were becoming more portable as well. So together, smaller cameras along with the portable 3/4-inch U-MATIC VTR revolutionized the news gathering business. Electronic News Gathering (ENG) could now replace film as a newsgathering format. EFP productions benefitted too as portable video became used in a variety of corporate and industrial productions on location.

The new portable video had obvious advantages over film. It could be seen instantly. No more need to waste precious film stock. Overseas footage could be transmitted via satellite.

Even though the camera and recorder had become lighter weight, they were still too large to lump together as a single unit. Cameras and record decks were separate units and had to be linked by cables. Thus, a camera operator was closely followed by a cable-linked assistant carrying the 3/4-inch recording deck.

As video formats developed, the challenge was to improve signal quality while reducing weight and size. The 3/4-inch U-MATIC format was portable but the picture quality was inferior to the traditional two-inch format. The industry still needed something more portable than two-inch tape but better quality than 3/4-inch.

(3.6) The one-inch reel-to-reel VTR

## THE ONE-INCH REEL FORMAT

In 1976, the Sony corporation introduced the *one-inch reel-to-reel* format also known as *one-inch Type C*. Engineers had figured out a way to achieve two-inch quality on a tape half the size.

Like the 3/4-inch format, the one-inch machine was made in both the large studio machine and the smaller portable version. Although both versions were larger and heavier than their 3/4-inch counterparts, the one inch tape's picture quality was far superior. Now, high quality documentaries, commercials, and entertainment programs could be videotaped on location without sacrificing quality. But the weight was still a problem, requiring at least two people, one holding the camera and the other holding the heavy tape deck. Newsgatherers, in need of easy mobility, were not inclined to use the one-inch portable format. Instead, it was used for more elaborate productions with more crew to help handle the equipment.

The one-inch format featured *dynamic tracking*, a feature by which the spinning tape heads can read a clean signal off a videotape that moves at any speed within a range of 300% forward speed to 100% reverse speed. Dynamic tracking heads can also read a paused tape, generating a clean still frame. Although other formats had attempted dynamic tracking, the one-inch format was the first to find commercial success. Hence, features such as the "slow motion instant replay" were easily accomplished from the VTR.

## BETACAM AND M-II:
## PROFESSIONAL HALF-INCH CASSETTE FORMATS

In 1984, weight was substantially reduced by the introduction of the professional half-inch cassette format by both Sony and Panasonic. With professional half-inch tape, engineers again demonstrated a way to make video more portable while preserving quality.

*BetaCam*, the name the Sony corporation gave its new professional half-inch tape, was originally released as a 20-minute mini-cassette. Later versions of the BetaCam format increased in size and length to 30-minute mini-cassettes and full-size cassettes holding 60 and 90-minute tape lengths.

(3.7) Sony's BetaCam format (left), Panasonic's M-II format (right).

(3.8) Camcorder—BetaCam VTR on board a broadcast quality camera.

It took years for the public to realize that Sony's professional BetaCam, used by TV stations and production companies, is vastly different than the consumer BetaMax. The cassettes are the same size. But the BetaCam electronics are far superior and the price is substantially more than home equipment. Where a home BetaMax camcorder might have cost less than a thousand dollars, professional Sony BetaCam recorders have been priced from twenty to fifty thousand dollars.

The professional BetaCam nearly matches the one-inch signal quality, and the BetaCam weight is profoundly lighter. In fact, the Beta decks are so light and compact and the cameras have also become so light that the two are now often merged into one unit. The portable BetaCam on the back of a camera became known as the *camcorder*. With a BetaCam deck mounted on a camera, the operator could finally act independently without a second person cabled close behind.

At the same time BetaCam became available, the Panasonic corporation developed its own version of the professional half-inch called *M-II*. Sony's BetaCam and Panasonic's M-II were similar in application but incompatible by design. A BetaCam tape could not be played in an M-II system and vice versa. This was unusual for the TV industry. Traditionally, different companies made compatible tape machines of the same format. For example, a one-inch format machine might have been produced by Ampex or by Sony and either could play the same tape. Not so with M-II and BetaCam.

The incompatibility between Sony's half-inch Beta product and Panasonic's M-II product forced a showdown to see whose version would take hold in the industry. Interestingly, the same showdown occurred between the two companies over the consumer half-inch formats: BetaMax and VHS. Panasonic won the consumer war with its VHS format. However, on the professional level, Sony won with professional BetaCam. BetaCam quickly became the dominant half-inch format acquired by TV stations and production companies. Panasonic's M-II is still on the market, but to a much lesser degree. Most TV stations use BetaCam. For several years, NBC adopted M-II and most of its affiliates were using the format, but they finally realized the futility of staying with a format that hardly anyone else was using.

## COMPOSITE VERSUS COMPONENT

BetaCam was the first format to introduce the *component* method of signal processing, offering an better alternative to the traditional composite video signal. The *composite* video signal is a single video output from the camera or VTR, the kind you would expect to see on a home VCR or camcorder. However, video engineers found that splitting the signal into three components of the overall signal produced

## TAPE AND FILE RECORDING FORMATS
*(founding company in parenthesis)*

### Analog tape, consumer grade
1/2-inch EIAJ open reel
8mm (Sony)
1/4-inch (RCA)
VHS, half-inch (Panasonic/JVC)
BetaMax, half-inch (Sony)

### Analog tape, industrial grade
3/4-inch U-matic (Sony)
3/4-inch U-Matic SP (Sony)
S-VHS, half inch (Panasonic/JVC)
Hi-8 (consortium)

### Analog tape, broadcast grade
BetaCam, 1/2-inch (Sony)
BetaCam SP, 1/2-inch (Sony)
M-II (Panasonic)
Two-inch quad, open reel (Ampex)
One-inch Type C, open reel (Sony)

### Digital tape, consumer grade
DV (consortium)
Digital 8 (Sony)

### Digital tape, industrial grade
DVCAM or D7 (Sony)
DVCPRO (Panasonic)

### Digital tape, broadcast grade
D-1 (Sony)
DCT (Ampex)
D-2 (Sony)
D-3 (Panasonic)
Digital BetaCam (Sony)
D-5 (Panasonic)
BetaCam SX (Sony)
Digital S or D9 (JVC)

### Analog File Format
LV-Laservision Disc (Pioneer)

### Digital File Format
AVI (IBM)
QuickTime (Apple)
CD-I(interactive) (Pioneer)
CD-V(video) (consortium)
Motion JPEG (consortium)
MPEG (consortium)
MPEG-2 (consortium)
DV (tape and file format)

### High Definition Television
1125/60, analog (Sony)
1250/50, analog (Thomson)
HD-D5, digital, (Panasonic)
HDCAM, digital (Sony)

(3.9) Videotape and computer-based video recording formats. Some of these formats are now obsolete and hardly used. Notice that the digital file formats are not ranked according to consumer, industrial, and broadcast quality grades. With digital file formats, quality is a function of sampling rate. Motion JPEG, for example, can be sampled at a low or a high rate producing either consumer or broadcast quality.

a picture with less video noise, hence better resolution. The component method breaks the video signal down into separate light and color information.

Today, most industrial and broadcast cameras offer various ways to output a video signal. Analog video can be output in three ways, listed by order of quality: component output (three-signal output, characterized by three separate wires or one multi-pin cable), a composite port (characterized by one combined signal BNC or RCA-style plug), and *S-video*, also called "*Y/C*" (characterized by a small multi-pin cable). Digital video has made popular two additional types of wire connections: the *serial-digital interface (SDI)* connector and the *firewire* connector.

## UPGRADING THE ANALOG FORMATS

The older videotape formats such as one-inch, BetaCam, 3/4-inch, 8mm, and VHS are all analog formats. Some of these formats got reintroduced in a metal tape version called "SP" which stands for "superior performance." For example, BetaCam upgraded to BetaCam SP. Three-quarter inch upgraded to 3/4-inch SP. Even the consumer grade VHS upgraded to S-VHS. Eight millimeter upgraded to Hi-8. In each case, the tape format is still analog.

## DIGITAL TAPE FORMATS: DIGITAL BETACAM and DVCAM

New videotape formats have been introduced that use digital recording technology instead of analog. A digital recording employs a fundamentally different way to encode the video and audio signals onto a recording medium. Sony introduced a new digital version of the BetaCam format called *Digital BetaCam*. The tape is the same size, but the recording mechanism lays down a digital signal on the tape instead of an analog signal. Today, both the older analog BetaCam SP and the newer more expensive Digital BetaCam are available. Sony also offers other broadcast quality digital videotape formats called D-1 and D-2 which are expensive and found in some professional edit suites.

In the constant search for smaller and lighter weight equipment, the *DV format* was introduced—Sony features the *DVCAM* format and Panasonic features the *DVCPRO* format for professionals. Meanwhile, the consumer version of this format is referred to as *mini-DV* using a very small cassette containing a shorter length of this 1/4-inch wide tape. These purely digital formats do not have the same level of resolution as BetaCam due to the need for compression in order to fit a signal on such a small tape. However, the portability, the picture quality, and the menu options that digital technology offers make the DV formats increasingly popular.

## DIGITAL FILE FORMATS

As video gets recorded onto media other than tape—computer hard drives and computer discs—some new formats are referred to as digital file formats rather than videotape formats. Some examples of these would include: AVI, QuickTime, Motion JPEG and MPEG. These formats are most commonly used for video playback on a computer. Notice in figure 3.9 that the DV format is listed both as a videotape format and as a digital file format. This is a unique situation in which a tape format stores video in a manner completely compatible with a computer video file. Unlike other formats, the DV can be transferred from tape to computer without any intermediate processing.

## TAPE STORAGE VERSUS HARD DRIVE STORAGE

As video equipment becomes more durable and automated, there has been an ongoing weak link in the technology—the videotape itself. The flimsy tape can be all too easily wrinkled, twisted, bent, gnarled, caught, cut, ripped, torn, scratched, and otherwise ruined. Digital recording does not cure the problem completely, partly because some digital formats still record to tape, and because other digital recordings go to computer hard drives which are also susceptible to surface damage. Nonetheless, you can expect to see fewer videotape and more computer-based formats—disks and hard drives. In the computer environment, the video signal is not subjected to the physical abuse that videotape experiences as it wends its way through the many moving parts of a videotape machine.

## ANALOG TO DIGITAL

Television equipment is becoming increasingly based on a *digital* recording method. What does digital mean? How does it apply to the equipment you use? The following is a simple technical overview of digital recording to help you understand the difference between digital and analog methods of encoding sound and picture.

Recording a sound or picture has always required some sort of encoding process. In other words, the recorded signal must represent a picture or sound on a recording medium such as tape. The volume, the brightness, the colors of a scene, and all the other nuances that we see and hear in a given scene must be represented by some sort of electromagnetic code. When the tape is played back, the video or audio gets decoded back into the pictures and sounds they represent.

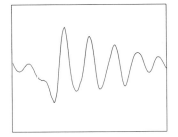
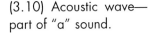

(3.10) Acoustic wave— part of "a" sound.

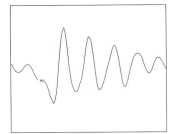

(3.11) Analog signal. A microphone vibrates to induce a similar pattern into electrical current.

| 1100, 1111, 0000, 0011, 0101 |
| 1111, 1010, 0010, 0101, 0010 |
| 0000, 0101, 1010, 1110, 0000 |
| 1010, 0101, 1000, 0001, 0011 |
| 0010, 1001, 1010, 0010, 0000 |
| 0010, 1010, 1111, 1110, 1111 |
| 0010, 0100, 0100, 1001, 1010 |

(3.12) Digital signal. Each characteristic of the acoustic wave is converted to binary code.

The traditional method of encoding is called *analog*. Analog means "analogous" or "similar." In audio, acoustic patterns in the air—sound waves—get encoded by inducing similar or analogous electronic wave patterns through a microphone. In video, light wave patterns get encoded by inducing similar or analogous electronic wave patterns via the camera's pickup tubes or CCDs.

Let's use an audio example. When someone speaks into a microphone, the vocal cords modulate the air to reflect the changes in sounds. These fluctuating pressure waves hit the element in a microphone and produce an analogous modulation of electronic wave patterns to be stored on tape in a magnetic form. Figure 3.10 represents the sound wave of one spoken syllable—a portion of the vowel sound "a." It shows the fluctuations in the voice that are required to make this sound. Figure 3.11 shows the same signal as an electronic wave form. The microphone receives the sound and mimics the pattern fluctuations in an electronic wave pattern. Figure 3.12 shows that the same voice pattern can be recorded as a digital signal. This time, a digital recorder samples the sound wave and converts it into a string of binary number codes to represent all the minute fluctuations in the signal.

Traditionally, all radio and TV electronic signal processing used an analog encoding method. Now, one-by-one, aspects of both audio and video are being reintroduced in digital versions. That simply means that the encoding process has changed. For a familiar example, the audio industry made a significant change when it released the compact disc. The music on a CD is encoded by numbers instead of by analog wave patterns.

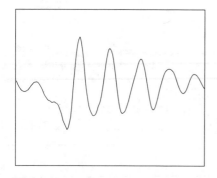

(3.13) This graph shows the original analog signal.

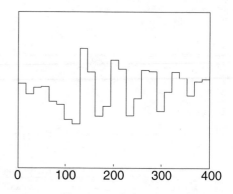

(3.14) This graph shows a digital sampling rate of every eighth point on a 400 point sampling scale.

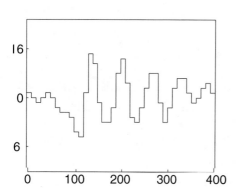

(3.15) This graph shows a digital sampling rate of every fourth point on a 400-point sampling scale—a higher frequency and a closer resemblance to the initial analog signal.

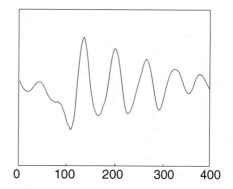

(3.16) This graph shows a digital sampling rate of every second point on a 400-point sampling scale—a higher frequency yet and a much closer resemblance to the initial analog signal.

Digital encoding converts an audio or video signal into numbers that can be stored in a computer environment. In audio, every frequency and sound characteristic can be represented by groups of numbers. When the sound gets encoded, numbers are assigned to each new change in the sound. These encodings happen thousands of times per second. The encoded numbers can then be decoded. As the decoder recognizes groups of numbers, it will reproduce the sounds that they represent. In video, the same encoding process by numbers applies to qualities of light and color.

Let's examine the digital process in more detail. The conversion from analog to digital has two basic steps: sampling frequency and quantization.

## SAMPLING FREQUENCY

The digital audio or video recorder tries to convert all analog information into digits. But the recorder cannot work fast enough to process the infinite detail of the analog signal. So it takes a periodic electronic *sample*. In actuality, these samples occur extremely close together, thousands of times per second. Different processors use different sampling rates. The more frequent the sampling, the better the digital recording matches the look or sound of the original analog signal.

The best quality will come from the highest sampling rates. You may notice, for example, that a digital audiotape recorder (DAT) offers a choice of sampling rates— 11025, 22050, 44100, 44116, or 48000 Hertz (cycles per second). If you understand why a higher frequency sampling rate yields a higher quality sound reproduction, you can select the highest quality that is compatible with your studio's technical capabilities. Higher sampling rates mean more information to store, thus larger computer files.

## QUANTIZATION

The other aspect of digitization that affects quality is called *quantization*. Quantization involves assigning a digital value to each sample point along the way. That value will eventually be recorded as a binary number in the computer and used to recreate a specific sound or picture later when the signal is played back.

The digitizing encoder cannot code infinite values. It must draw upon a finite set of values and try to match each sampled point with the closest value. For the sake of explanation, let's say a certain sound element has a true value of 11. The digitizing computer may code the sound or picture element to the computer's nearest preset value, which might be a 10. In fact, any value that the computer recognizes in the 8-12 value range may be automatically coded as a 10, hence a slight compromise of rounding up or down from the original value. If the digital processor has only a few preset values to draw upon, then the digital recording of the analog signal will be coarse and crude. The more values available, the more clearly and closely the digital recording will approximate the original sound or picture.

Here's the same explanation again, using a familiar analogy. When you were in elementary school, some children had boxes of eight Crayolas. Some had sixteen. Some had sixty-four. But some had the Mega Crayola Box of colors. Let's assume that all students could color at the same speed (the same sampling rate), but some had more color choices than others.

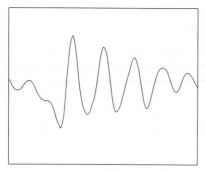

(3.17) The initial analog signal will be sampled and quantized.

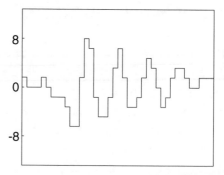

(3.18) Four bit quantization is done at 16 value levels. In reality, this would be an unacceptably low and crude quantization level, not yielding enough detail.

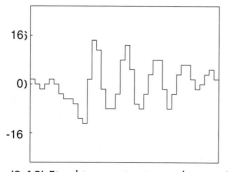

(3.19) Five bit quantization is done at 32 levels. Notice how the digital signal more closely resembles the analog signal.

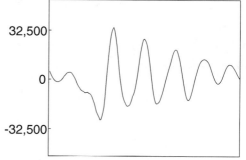

(3.20) Sixteen-bit quantization uses 65,000 value levels. The digitized signal closely resembles the original analog because there are so many more values from which to recreate the sound.

The same is true in quantizing of an analog signal. If an analog signal is the color lavender, but all you have is an eight-crayon box, then the digitizer looks for the closest preset value among the eight choices, in this case blue. However, if the digitizer has a greater number of quantization levels available, such as the 64-crayon box, then likely it can find a purple—a closer match. But if the digitizer has thousands of preset values available, then it can likely find the exact shade of lavender.

The number of quantization levels is the number of value choices available. These quantization levels are referred to as *bits*. A simple exponent formula says that 4-bit quantization is $2^4$ or 16 values. Five-bit quantization is $2^5$ or 32 values. Sixteen-bit quantization is $2^{16}$ or 65,000 values. Figures 3.17 through 3.20 show a comparison of bit levels.

## ADVANTAGES AND DISADVANTAGES OF DIGITAL PROCESSING

1) Digital produces a cleaner signal. In the traditional analog system, the process is subject to extraneous magnetic signals on the tape that get reproduced as noise and hiss. Digital processing substantially reduces this problem with better error correction and error concealment.

2) Any tape format is subject to stretching over time. The analog decoding suffers when the tape stretches, producing a distortion known as "wow" or "flutter." The digital signal can withstand a much greater amount of tape distortion before it is unable to decode the digits.

3) Digital information is easier to store, recall, and manipulate using the computer. That's because every setting has a specific numeric value that can be recorded, altered, or updated. Numbers become the universal language for precise values assigned to sounds and pictures. So, for example, animation that used to be done by hand could only be modified or manipulated by the artist in a painstaking frame-by-frame process. Animation based on digital information in a computer can be manipulated and modified by changing numerical values. Computers can reproduce sounds and pictures according to these numerical values. Precise changes can be made by simply changing a set of numbers, thus saving hundreds of hours of manual re-creation.

4) In analog recording, every copy from one tape to another degrades the signal a little bit at a time. Since making analog copies involves mimicking the original signal, the copies are never quite as precise as the original. Digital decoding does not depend on mimicking. Instead, it relies on decoding a set of numbers which can be done over and over with almost no loss in the signal quality.

What are the disadvantages? Today, most would say "no disadvantages." However, when audio first became digital, critics argued that the digital method of encoding could not be as detailed and precise as analog. They argued that analog reflected more nuances and that digital was too crude in its sampling of sound.

The digital sampling process has improved greatly since the early criticism. Technically, digital sampling is not as precise as an analog copy, but the differences are often too minute to notice. The advantages make the digital process worthwhile.

## STORAGE REQUIREMENTS

A digital signal can either be recorded onto a tape or onto a computer hard drive. The problem is storage capacity. Tape as a storage medium is convenient because tapes are relatively cheap and limitless. Computer hard drives are more costly minute-for-minute but offer the advantage of a random access environment for instant location of video clips.

Here's an example to illustrate why the computer storage issue is such a challenge. Let's take a sentence, "I like split pea soup with toast." That takes about 2 seconds to read aloud.

Typing that sentence in a word processor may require only about 30 bytes of computer storage. The same sentence stored as a digital audio file might require about 60,000 bytes. Digitizing a video picture of someone saying the sentence along with the audio portion of the signal could require about two million bytes of storage space.

So imagine, if two seconds of live video requires two million bytes of space, then a half-hour TV show, which would run 1800 seconds, would require 900 times that amount of storage, or 1.8 billion bytes.

## COMPRESSION

A prevalent misconception is that digital is always the preferred choice. Digital recording methods are not always better than analog methods. In order to store massive amounts of digital information, computers use various levels of *compression*. Compression is an algorithm that makes a computer's capacity to hold information more efficient. The more compression is used, the worse the picture quality. Therefore, it is good to be aware of how much compression occurs in any system you use such as a non-linear editing system or a tape recording format.

Compression works by finding sound or picture information with similar qualities, then using one bit of information to represent numerous similar bits of information within the same frame or from neighboring frames, thus cutting down on the amount of data that must be processed in the computer. For example, if a scene shows clear blue sky, then the need for blue pixels will be numerous throughout portions of the picture as well as from frame to frame of a given scene. The compression formulas figure out ways to re-use certain blue sky pixels to represent the ones that follow. As

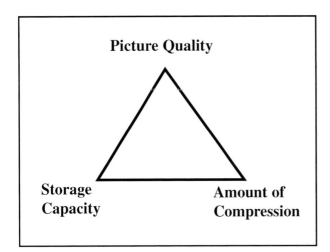

(3.21) This graph helps explain the relationship between picture quality, amount of compression required, and storage capacity in any digital recording. The rule is: If any two items are high in value, then the third item must be low in value. For example, if you choose high picture quality and high storage capacity, then low compression is needed.

you might imagine, this is a compromise and at some point, as the compression increases, the picture loses detail and becomes jagged, pixel-like, or block-like.

You choose the amount of compression, either by choosing a system based on its inherent compression ratio, or by choosing a system that lets you vary the compression rate. You might choose to store an hour of poor quality video rather than ten minutes of good quality, thanks to the extreme compression. At times storage space is more important than quality. Other times, you may choose a lower compression rate in exchange for better quality.

The need for extreme compression diminishes as larger storage devices become available. For example, 20 gigabytes of hard drive storage can hold about an hour of broadcast quality video at a fairly low compression ratio. A few years ago, a 20-gigabyte hard drive connected to a personal computer was unheard of. Today, it is already dwarfed by hard drive arrays that hold up to a terabyte of information.

With increasing computer storage capacity, the future of videotape is being debated. Tapes are is still the cheapest and most convenient way to store many hours of either analog or digitally recorded video. But as the technology completely converts to digital recording and as hard drive storage capacities increase, videotape will become less important. For example, many TV stations are playing back their commercial breaks off large computer hard drives called *video file servers*. These players are simply huge hard drives that can sequence the commercials and play them over and over. No videotape is needed and the process is highly automated.

As computers can process greater amounts of information at faster speeds, the need to compress diminishes. Some of the leading non-linear editor manufacturers are now making non-linear systems that do not compress the video at all.

## LINEAR TO NON LINEAR VIDEO EDITING

Digital processing has had a huge impact on video editing. Initially, videotape was physically cut and spliced like film—an awkward process since the person doing the editing could not hold up the tape to see where frames begin and end. In video, the image is stored as a magnetic field, similar to audio tape. The video editing process became purely electronic—a function of pushing buttons instead of cutting tape.

The traditional drawback of electronic editing has been the fact that one tape gets electronically copied or cloned onto another tape. As mentioned, analog copies have some inherent quality loss. An edited video program, which is made up of scenes copied onto a master tape from other tapes, is not quite as high resolution as the original footage. This inherent drop in quality is called *generation loss.* Digital technology largely alleviates this age-old analog problem. With digital editing, there is far less generation loss. Numbers passed back and forth do not deteriorate the way the analog signal does.

Traditional editing systems have been *linear* in nature, sequencing a series of scenes from one set of tapes onto a master tape. Newer *non-linear* editing systems do not send scenes to a videotape at first, but rather to a computer hard drive where the scenes can be manipulated in a random access environment similar to word processing. When editing is completed in the computer environment, the show is "printed" back to videotape similar to the way a word processing document is printed to paper.

Traditional linear editing systems have three basic components: a *playback machine (player)*, a *record machine (recorder)*, and an *edit controller.* The playback machine is loaded with the original footage. The recorder is loaded with a new tape on which to create an edited master program. Scenes are then cloned off the player machine in the desired order and replicated on the record machine. The original source tape is unchanged. The new tape—the edit master—contains a composite of all the chosen scenes. Thus, the editing process is basically a sophisticated copying process. The edit controller is a keyboard used to locate and enter precise points on the videotapes where edits should occur. The edit controller initiates the starting and stopping of each edit.

Since linear editing is a method of precisely copying scenes from one tape to another, the job of the edit controller is to determine exactly where frames of video start, since they are not visible to the eye. In order to perform a clean edit, the transition must occur precisely between frames of video which are indicated by electromagnetic information on the videotape. The editing machines sense exactly where frames begin and end.

This method of electronic editing is called linear editing because all the scenes that make up an edited program are put down on a tape in a linear progression starting with the first shot and moving on. Therefore, it makes sense to try to build a show in order of shots from beginning to end. Once a series of scenes is edited onto a new tape, that order cannot be changed without re-editing subsequent scenes.

By contrast, non-linear editing, which made its debut in the late 1980s and grew dramatically throughout the 1990s, eliminates the problem of reediting scenes in order to resequence them. First, all original footage from videotape must be transferred or digitized into the computer environment. Then, scenes can be sequenced and resequenced by clicking and dragging icons.

Non-linear editing is to linear editing what the word processor is to the typewriter. The non-linear concept is based on the idea that all information is held in the computer environment while revisions are made. As long as the information is in this random access state, anything can be modified, moved, lengthened, or shortened before being "printed" to videotape.

### *Will non-linear editing systems completely replace linear systems?*

TV companies have major investments in traditional linear videotape systems such as the one-inch and BetaCam formats. A company is likely to acquire non-linear editing in addition to its linear system, offering clients both options. Linear editing has advantages. Time is saved at the outset by avoiding the need to first digitize all the original footage. And linear editing offers compression-free editing whereas all but the most expensive non-linear editors use some degree of compression. Non-linear systems are limited by the amount of video information they can store on their hard drives. Video requires massive amounts of computer storage space. For lengthy productions that use many hours of raw footage, non-linear systems can be impractical. Linear editing may never disappear completely, but as computer storage and speed increases, there will be no reason not to edit in a non-linear environment.

## CONCLUSION

Many think that anything digital automatically means better quality. That is not true. Digital recording has many advantages, but the quality is only better than analog if the sampling rate and quantization is high and if the system design is of high quality. Otherwise, good analog recordings can be of equally high quality.

As seen in figure 3.9, some videotape formats are digital and some are analog. Just because a video recording is on a tape does not automatically indicate that it is analog or digital. Tape can hold either type of recording. You must be familiar with the system you are using to know whether its encoding process is digital or analog.

So, how do you know whether a video system is analog or digital? Chances are the answer is "both." In many situations, some components of the system are digital and some are analog. For example, a production company may own a digital camera which records to an analog VTR. Then, the video is digitized into a non-linear editor and finally output onto an analog tape.

Here are some helpful hints. Computers only process digital information. So, any video actually stored on a computer is digital. Remember, though, that just because there is a computer in the editing room doesn't mean that the video signal is necessarily recorded on the computer drives. Many analog videotape format editing systems employ computers for certain aspects of the process such as edit controlling, edit list management, and graphic design. Is the computer actually processing and storing the video signal? If not, the video may be analog. Also, remember that just because video is on tape doesn't mean it is analog. Many digital formats record onto tape.

As a director, you are constantly facing choices, many of them technical. Do I edit with a linear or non-linear system? Is my equipment digital or analog? Composite or component? What tape format should I use? What sampling frequency do I digitize my audio for DVD? Which is better, MPEG-1 or MPEG-2 and why? You don't have to be an engineer to answer these questions. If you know enough to ask the right questions, you can make good technical choices as you shoot and edit video.

# Section II

The television director, as both technician and artist, should understand the nature of the medium. This section introduces you to ideas about the building blocks of video and the creation of moving pictures.

Specifically, the following four chapters will discuss:

• The Frame—the smallest unit of a moving picture

• Resolution—the attribute by which we describe picture quality.

• Three-dimensionality—the challenge of creating a 3-dimensional world using a 2-dimensional medium.

• Composition—considerations about where to place the camera and how to place subjects within the camera's field of view.

# 4

# The Frame

Throughout history, people have found ways to create static images, from the ancient caveman's drawing on the walls of his livingroom to modern four-color digital printing. From painting to sculpture, Polaroids to X-rays, Xeroxes to ultrasounds, people have been compelled to record and retain images.

But one thing we have never been able to do is record movement.

With this statement, the reader is shocked. "Of course we can record movement! We do it all the time with the film camera and the video camera."

But is that really true? Consider the film medium. Hold up a strip of 16mm film to the light and what do you see? A series of individual frames. No movement.

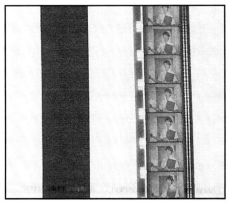

(4.1) Strip of videotape (left); strip of 16mm film (right).

Similarly, video is recorded magnetically as a series of individual frames. In video, the frame is defined as a scan of the TV screen that starts at the top of the screen, scans hundreds of lines to the bottom of the screen before starting over again.

In neither medium is the recorded image a fluid movement. Why? For the same reason that we don't travel at the speed of light—it's a method that we simply haven't conceived. All we have is the ability to use a series of frames to simulate movement.

How does a series of frames simulate movement? Consider the set of flip cards you may have played with as a child: perhaps cards depicting a doggy moving its head back and forth, or a couple dancing the Fox Trot. Flipping through the cards creates movement. Flipping slowly creates a jerky motion. Flipping quickly creates smoother movement.

(4.2) Individual frames in sequence create the illusion of movement

When the eye sees the cards flip by, each image is sent to the brain via the optic nerve. Each individual image is noted by the brain. But the remarkable part is that the brain lets each image linger for a fraction of a moment. We call this phenomenon *persistence of vision*. The image persists in the brain very briefly after the eye no longer sees the image.

If the cards flip slowly, the time between each card lasts longer than the persistence of image in the brain. The brain notices the end of one image and the beginning of the next, hence a gap in between and a perception of stopping/starting. However, if the cards flip quickly enough, the brain is still retaining one image while the next one comes into view. The images meld together. The result is a simulated movement.

How fast must the cards flip? Experiments show that the necessary minimum speed is sixteen frames per second. Any frame rate that exceeds sixteen frames per second will assure a good illusion of motion. Thomas Edison first standarized film projection at 40 frames per second (fps). The Lumiere brothers reduced that number to 16 fps. The film industry eventually standardized film speed at 24 fps. The video industry standardized at 30 fps because of its numerical compatibility with the 60-cycle alternating electrical current system in the United States, insuring a cleaner picture, freer of electronic disturbances.

Technically, the *frame* can be viewed as the smallest unit of motion in the film or video medium. Frames are the building blocks of either medium. When editing, these building blocks (frames) become important considerations. An edit from one scene to another must occur after the end of one frame and before the beginning of the next frame.

When editing a film, for example, physical cuts are made between frames. The ends of frames are glued to the beginning of other frames. In video, the cutting is electronic. In either case, the important thing is to maintain whole frames, to avoid editing in the middle of frames.

## MEASUREMENT

The frame becomes the unit of measurement for film and video. For example, the length of a transition such as a wipe or dissolve is measured in frames as well as seconds of elapsed time. If a dissolve lasts one second and there are 30 frames per second in video, then the dissolve spans 30 frames. At the outset of the 30-frame span, the new image begins to fade in while the old image begins to fade out. By the fifteenth frame of the 30-frame span, both images are at a cross-point, 50% intensity each. By the last few frames in the 30-frame span, the new image is almost fully faded in and the old image is about to disappear.

## CLOCK TIME

Cameras and VTRs offer clock displays to measure the running time of a video playback or recording. The clock time shows Hours, Minutes, Seconds, and Frames.

```
02:33:24:12
 H   M   S   F
```

(4.3) Time code shown in hours, minutes, seconds, and frames.

Note the following clock time display: This clock-time number identifies a frame of video located at 2 hours, 33 minutes, 24 seconds, and 12 frames. The Seconds column will advance every time the Frames column reaches 30 (*30 frames = 1 second of video*).

## TIME CODE OR CONTROL TRACK TIMER?

Clock time may be generated in two ways: by ***control track*** and by ***time code***.

1) Control track is a steady electronic pulse common to all VTRs. Control track serves to regulate the constant rate of VTR playback and recording. Some clock time readouts simply advance their numbers as long as they see control track on the tape. The numbers are arbitrary. They simply indicate that a video signal (always accompanied by control track) is present on the tape. You can zero or reset these numbers anytime you wish.

2) Time code generated clock numbers look exactly the same as control track numbers. However, in this case, the clock time is actually recorded on a separate track on the videotape, thus permanently assigning numbers to every frame of the tape. A time code track is a feature that comes with some videotape decks and is common on all high-end industrial and broadcast equipment. Time code is always preferable

to the control track counter feature because the numbers stay constant. Computer editors depend on time code to find locations on videotapes. For example, a two-second dissolve may begin at 2:02:24:10 and end at 2:02:26:10. Or a 1.5 second dissolve might begin at 2:02:24:10 and end at 2:02:25:25. The computer controller keeps track of locations on the tape by referencing the time code numbers.

Time code and clock time are hard to distinguish because their readouts look identical. The only difference is that one is a recorded signal on the tape and the other is an arbitrary counter. A handy rule-of-thumb is this: If you can hit a reset button to zero the numbers while a tape is paying, then you're looking at a control track readout.

## SCAN LINES AND FIELDS

(4.4) TV image composed of scan lines.

Let's look more closely at the physical makeup of frames. The film frame is a photographic slide or transparency. A strip of film is like a series of still slides in a row. As film is shot, it's just like exposing many individual photographic slides. When the film is projected, the "slides" are rapidly illuminated one at a time.

In video, a frame is created by a constant series of electronic *scan lines*. The scanner sweeps across the screen, row by row, until the entire screen has been scanned. Then, the scanner begins again.

TV engineers found that the TV image looked smoothest if the scanning was done in two sweeps per frame: all the odd lines first, then all the even lines. Each sweep is known as a *field*. Thus, one frame is composed of field #1—all the odd scan lines, followed by field #2—all the even scan lines. Two fields = 1 frame. 30 frames = 1 second of video. The field/frame distinction is important. A field is really only half the picture.

The process of scanning two fields for each frame is called *interlacing*. Its purpose was to reduce flicker in the picture. Interlacing is less common on today's monitors. Most computer monitors, for example, are not interlaced.

How many scan lines are there in video? The answer depends on what country you are in or what format you are watching. The United States standard set by the NTSC (National Television Standards Committee) uses 525 scan lines. However a new U.S. standard called HDTV (High Definition Television) doubles the number of scan lines. In other countries, you may find the NTSC standard or either of two other incompatible formats known as PAL (Phase Alternate Line), which uses 625 scan lines and is common in many European countries, and SECAM (Sequential Color with Memory), standardized in Russia and France, which also uses 625 scan lines.

## FRAME APPLICATION

With the technical understanding of the frame in mind, now you can consider movement as a series of individual frames. How does an image change from frame to frame as an action takes place? How many frames does it take for an action to happen? What if no movement occurs? What if the camera moves? Any of the following variations may occur:

1) The subject stays identical from frame to frame—no movement, no change. The viewer sees this as a still picture. Time passes as the sequence of frames progresses, 30 per second, but there is no change on the screen. The result is a static or a still shot.

2) The subject moves. For example, a person walks through the scene. Each frame in the sequence shows a slight advancement of the person's body position, although the framing of the picture does not change. The camera remains motionless.

3) The subject changes due to camera movement. The subject may or may not be moving, but the camera does a tilt, pan, etc., and the viewer sees a frame-by-frame change corresponding to the camera movement.

4) The scene changes due to an editing transition from scene to scene. A transition in video or film from scene to scene can be a:
• Cut
• Dissolve
• Fade
• Wipe

Let's consider each of these basic transitions in the context of their basic units— frames.

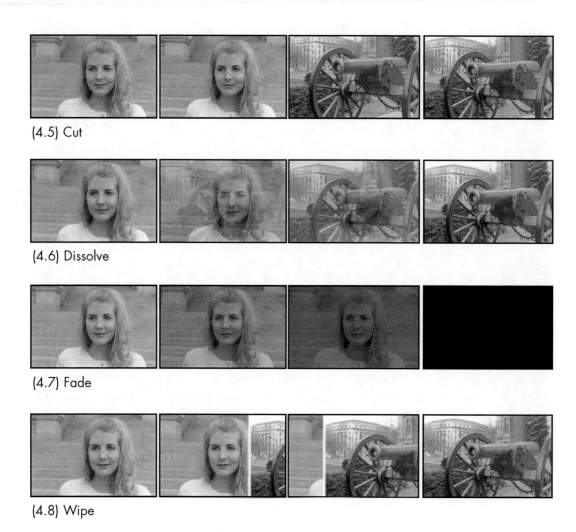

(4.5) Cut

(4.6) Dissolve

(4.7) Fade

(4.8) Wipe

## CUT

The fastest transition in film or video is called a ***cut***, which is an immediate transition between scenes, ending a scene on one frame and beginning the new scene on the next frame. In the case of film, that means making scene changes between individual photographic images. In the case of video, it means making scene changes after one series of TV scan lines is complete, which constitutes the completion of a frame, and before the next scan series begins.

## DISSOLVES, FADES, WIPES

Whereas a cut is an instantaneous transition between frames, a dissolve, fade, or wipe takes longer and spans the length of several frames. For example, a dissolve is a transition in which one image fades away as another image simultaneously fades in. During the period of dissolve, overlapping images are seen in the same frame. One series of frames from video source A must fade out while another series of frames from video source B must fade in. These two simultaneous fades are super-imposed over each other, creating a transition we call a dissolve.

## DIGITAL WIPES

When wipes were first invented, they had no benefit of computerized manipulation, so they were 2-dimensional—a line moving across the screen to reveal a new picture, or an enlarging or diminishing circle. Today, computer digital manipulation allows the wipe to perform 3-dimensional moves in real time—page curls, cube rotations, squeezes, and pushes. When a wipe is controlled by a digital processor, we call it a *digital wipe* or a *digital video effect (DVE)*.

---

**A REAL WORLD APPLICATION, CONTINUED:**

The director assigned to the lumber mill project, introduced in chapter 1, knows that the frame is the basic building block of his craft. He will consider the frame both practically and aesthetically.

From a practical standpoint, he knows that the preferable way to edit his videotape is by using a time-code-based editing system with an edit controller that can electronically see where one frame ends and another begins, thus assuring clean cuts between scenes. He will measure transitions by number of frames. In the editing room, he will choose transition rates according to frame counts. He may ask for a 20-frame fade-up, a 30-frame dissolve, or a 45-frame wipe from scene to scene.

He also knows that frames can be numbered, identified, and logged according to the time code numbers that were originally recorded on tape while shooting. His assistant will take notes during the shooting process, logging scenes according to time code numbers for easy reference later. Since the time code clock can be set manually before recording, the crew resets the time code for each new videotape shot. Tape #1 begins with a time code number 1:00:00:00; tape #2 gets reset to number 2:00:00:00. Thus, hour numbers correspond to tape numbers, a handy housekeeping trick for ease in tape identification later while editing.

---

# 5

## Picture Quality and Resolution

Have you ever taken a photographic negative to a shoddy one-hour developing store and found that the finished print looked quite awful? Maybe it was fuzzy looking, washed out, too blue, or streaks and scratches covered the picture.

Then, you took the same negative to a much better lab, perhaps a custom photo lab, and the print you got back looked beautiful, ten times crisper and cleaner than the first. The colors were accurate.

What can you say about the difference between the two results? Obviously, one is a better quality job than the other. In other words, the resolution of one printing was better than the other.

The word *resolution* means transformation. An idea can be resolved. A musical chord can be resolved. So can an image. A photographed image undergoes transformation as it gets processed. Once it has completed the process, the question is: how good does it look? How well did it resolve? How closely does the new image resemble the original subject?

Good resolution means a reproduction that has all the detail and clarity of the original. Poor resolution means that the image is lacking in clarity or detail.

The same term—resolution—applies to any area of graphics, including video. In fact, achieving good resolution is the technical bottom line for any aspect of TV or film production. It's the concept we use to evaluate cameras, recording decks, lenses, computer graphics, videotape formats, and more. Good resolution is what makes one camera worth more than another.

For a better understanding of resolution, let's consider a familiar instrument—the human eye. The eye, along with the brain, attempts to resolve any image that it sees. Ideally, the image in your brain closely resembles the subject that you see. But many obstacles can compromise the quality of the resolution. For example, suppose you are myopic (near-sighted). The image may be out of focus.

What if you wear glasses but the glasses are dirty? The image won't be clear. And even if the glasses are clean, the glass or the plastic in the lens adds another layer for the image to pass through and there is a small measurable amount of distortion. What if your eye has a cataract, a cloudy covering of the lens? Then the image will be clouded. What if the image is viewed in dim light? Detail could be missing in a shadowy darkness. Images might appear as silhouettes. What if you are color blind? The colors could be altered. What if the image is seen in a fog, or a heavy rain? Again, the image can be distorted by obstacles passing between your eyes and the subject.

In any of these examples, the image that resolves in the brain is compromised because of some sort of disturbance. The resolution is not as good as it could be.

Then, there is the question of the eye's natural ability to see even when everything is working perfectly. The eye, as wonderful as it is, has limitations. It can only see certain colors in the light spectrum. It can't see infrared, gamma rays, x-rays, or ultraviolet. It can't see as well at night. And it has a limited field or angle of view. Any subject that exceeds the limitations of the human eye may not be resolved, even if the eye is working at 100% capacity.

Compared with the human eye, the video camera is even more susceptible to problems and limitations. The camera will fail to resolve an image in situations where the eye can. One of your technical concerns, as director, is to minimize the limitations wherever possible and try to maintain high resolution in your production. If you begin by understanding that the camera cannot see as well as the eye and by learning the camera's limitations, you can plan for situations that help maximize the camera's ability.

Some aspects of resolution may be beyond your control, such as the quality of the equipment you are using. A $50,000 camera will produce a higher resolution than a $1,000 camera, but you may have no choice other than to use the cheaper camera.

But there are many areas that you can control. In other words, do not discount the need to think about resolution just because you are stuck with a cheap camera. In fact, the cheap camera needs your help even more than the expensive camera in order to create quality images.

As a director, you want to have as much technical understanding as possible to assist you when you make various choices about equipment selection, lighting, videotape format, etc. The more you understand about the limitations of your equipment, the better you will be at maximizing the quality of your pictures—maximizing your pictures' resolution.

Perfect resolution is not always the desired goal. There may be situations in which the director prefers a picture that looks grainy or a little bit soft in focus such as a romantic scene or a music video clip. Maybe you want the image to be black and white, even though the original was in color. Maybe you want it to look like a scratchy old movie. The importance is that these decisions are by design and not by equipment limitations.

No camera can resolve the real world perfectly—a two-dimensional medium that falls far short of the human eye cannot replicate a three-dimensional world. But some cameras have much better resolution characteristics than others. The best cameras will have the best resolution. Manufacturers are always striving to increase the resolution capabilities of any camera, VTR, or graphics system.

## PRINCIPLES THAT AFFECT RESOLUTION

Resolution is affected at many points in the TV production process. Here are a few examples.

**Resolution Principle #1: Film and video can be evaluated by the inherent method by which the picture is reproduced.**

What are the building blocks that make up a frame? The finer and more detailed the building blocks, the better the resolution.

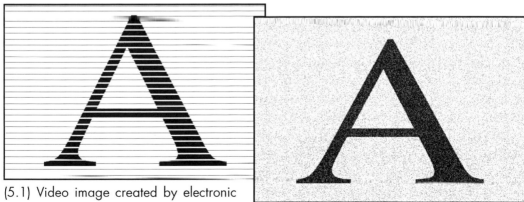

(5.1) Video image created by electronic scan lines

(5.2) Film image created by light-sensitive chemical molecules.

In video, a frame is composed of scan lines. Each scan line is composed of pixels. A pixel is one unit of information in the scan line that can each be individually assigned color and brightness levels. A traditional 525 scan line TV image is composed of about 360,000 pixels.

In film, an image is composed of millions of light-sensitive molecules. Each molecule individually reacts to light and color, many times the resolution of even 360,000 pixels.

The real world displays infinite detail. Every object in nature has shape, color, and texture. Sometimes the detail is very small and complex, such as the grains of sand on a beach, or the fur on a cat's back. In order to reproduce the image with good resolution, the medium must have building blocks to reconstruct the image that are small and fine enough to represent the detail of the original image.

Imagine that you have a supply of small squares or tiles with which to make a mosaic. If the squares are large and the selection of colors is limited, then the image you create will be very coarse. You may successfully recreate the image of a square brown box on a solid blue background. But what about the grains of sand on a beach, each a slightly different shade and shape? Your limited selection of oversized tiles won't allow you to recreate such fine detail. However, if you had extremely small tiles in a wide variety of colors, then you would have the building blocks necessary to recreate a very detailed image. These principles apply to any visual art form. In each case, you must consider what the building blocks are for that medium.

Film can reproduce extremely fine detail because of the multitude of tiny light sensitive molecules. Video, on the other hand, is limited to the number of scan lines and pixels which, by comparison, constitutes a far coarser way to reproduce an image. Therefore, film looks better than video because it has a greater capacity to resolve detail. That is also why film projects well on a large screen. The resolution is so fine that the image holds up well when enlarged. Video, on the other hand, struggles to maintain clarity as it is projected onto a large screen.

**Resolution Principle #2: Film and video equipment can be evaluated according to their abilities to handle and resolve a high contrast ratio.**

How well can the camera handle high contrast? A cheaper camera will have a hard time exposing for both very bright and very dark portions of the picture.

(5.3) In this high contrast scene, the lens aperture is closed down to expose properly for the bright outdoor scene in the background, leaving the subject underexposed.

(5.4) In this high contrast scene, the lens aperture is opened up to expose properly for the subject, leaving the background overexposed and washed out.

(5.5) In this medium contrast scene, the overall contrast range is within the camera's ability to resolve both foreground and background.

Imagine a scene that has dark forest and bright sky with a few clouds. The human eye can see the detail in both the bright and dark parts of the picture. But the camera has exposure limitations. Its range of ability to resolve both bright and dark is much narrower than the human eye.

Within the range of cameras on the market, some do a better job of handling contrast than others. When a poor resolution camera exposes for the dark or forest, the sky becomes washed out and the clouds are lost in a white wash. Or, when the camera exposes for the bright sky so that the clouds are visible, the trees lose all detail and look like a dark wash. A more expensive camera may get some detail in both. But the human eye is better than any camera.

The trick is to use the best camera possible and look for scenes that do not present high contrast. There are many ways to reduce contrast that will be discussed later in this book.

**Resolution Principle #3: The optics of the camera lens will affect the quality of resolution.**

A more expensive lens will have finer glass and optical construction which will contribute to resolution. A more expensive lens typically allows a wider iris opening, hence better exposure in low light.

High end cameras are often sold without lenses because the vendor knows that the customer may want to choose a more expensive or less expensive lens to go with the camera.

**Resolution Principle #4: Film and video can be evaluated by the camera's requirement for light level.**

A cheaper camera will require more light to produce a good resolution. A very expensive camera may be able to shoot in darker conditions and maintain good resolution.

In both film and video, lower light levels mean a grainier picture. A better camera will minimize the grain. In film, low light conditions require a faster film, which also translates to a grainier picture.

In video, the quality of the camera's internal electronic signal processing will also determine low light capacity. A cheaper camera with inferior electronics will reproduce a grainy image in low light. An expensive camera's picture will look less grainy.

## COPYING THE TAPE

Copying an analog tape reduces the resolution of the copy. Analog tape formats cannot be copied without an inherent *generation loss*. The resolution gets worse with every subsequent copy. The better the tape format and the method of copying, the better the copy will look. A copy made from a BetaCam SP tape using a component connection will suffer far less generation loss than a copy made from a consumer-grade VHS tape. Also, copies made from component output systems, described in chapter 3, will look better than copies made from composite output systems.

Digital tapes can be copied many times before showing any generation loss. Digital technology preserves resolution by the inherent means by which it operates. Since the digital process is comprised of strings of binary code numbers, as long as the numbers get passed back and forth accurately, the computer can reconstruct a new image with the same resolution as the original. Since copying back and forth is such an integral part of the video editing process, digital technology has had a huge positive impact on the industry by allowing copies of tapes and graphics files to be made without generation loss.

## CONCLUSION

Video technology improves each year and so does resolution. But the 525 scan line system has always been a major limitation. Better resolution TV systems could have been introduced to the marketplace years ago, but they would have been incompatible. Every home and TV station in America has already made an investment in the traditional system. That's why the advent of *high definition television (HDTV)* is so significant. It represents a method of getting past both the compatibility issue and the scan line limitation by doubling the number of scan lines and broadcasting that signal separately for those who have HDTV receivers. TV stations are now broadcasting two separate signals, one traditional signal for 525-line systems, and another signal for those who have high definition TV sets.

---

**A REAL WORLD APPLICATION, CONTINUED:**

The director at the lumber mill is considering the issue of resolution as he plans the production. He knows that shooting the production using the film medium would yield a high resolution. However, this budget does not allow for a film shoot (film processing and transfer to video would add too much cost to the production), so that's an issue out of his control. His job, then, is to make the video image look as good as possible.

The director knows that high contrast is something to avoid. Contrasty images will look particularly bad on video. As he tours the factory, he notes areas that are particularly dark and areas that are extremely bright from sun pouring in the windows. He figures out ways to avoid shooting in these areas and plans with his crew how to use lighting to diminish shadows and very dark areas.

The director also knows that choosing the right camera is essential. A good camera will handle contrast well and will provide better resolution all around.

---

A good lens is just as important. He goes to a TV equipment rental company and chooses a rather expensive camera and makes plans to rent it for the three days of shooting.

Finally, he chooses a high quality tape format, in this case the BetaCam SP format. He knows that the better the tape format, the better the resolution and the better the copies made for distribution.

Production elements will also affect resolution: the quality of the lighting, the amount of contrast, and the clothes people wear. Busy patterns such as pin stripes and fine plaids may cause rainbow patterns on the video. Very dark clothing may look muddy. Bright white may wash out.

Having dealt with each of these issues, the director is confident that he will be able to create video images with good resolution. The images will look crisp and clean. The images will reflect the detail in the scene.

# 6

# The 3-D Challenge

It's easy to get caught up in the technology and not pay enough attention to the art of picture composition. With the understanding that film and video are made up of individual frames, we can begin to appreciate that either medium is actually processing thousands of individual still pictures. Thus, we can talk about artistry and composition in the same way we would when evaluating a still photo or painting.

The job of the visual artist in any medium is to decide how best to compose a picture. Composition has to do with two main choices: what to put in the picture, and where to place the camera. It's smart for any motion picture director to have an understanding of composition. The principles that apply in painting or photography will carry over naturally to film or video. If you don't have any background in painting or photography, you may consider taking a class or doing some outside reading about picture composition.

In this chapter and the next, we'll deal with some basic compositional considerations that would typically occur in video production. Let's begin with one overall easy-to-remember concept: think of composition for video as the 3-D Challenge.

Here's what the 3-D Challenge is all about. Consider the broad category of visual art forms, of which TV is one. What kind of space does each require for presentation? For example, a dancer requires a big open space such as a theater stage with height, width, and depth. A sculptor also requires a three-dimensional space for a sculpture to stand. Painters, assuming they are painting on a canvas, don't use three dimensions. They require height and width, but no depth. Their medium is flat. But in their flat medium, they create the illusion of depth.

The same is true for film and TV. In the case of film, the presentation is made on a flat screen—a two-dimensional medium. TV, too, although the screen is sometimes slightly curved, is fundamentally a flat screen. Therefore, TV composition can be summed up as the pursuit of the illusion of three-dimensionality.

Flat pictures don't have to look flat. They can appear to be three dimensional. Thus, the 3-D challenge is to create the illusion of the actual three-dimensional world on a two-dimensional medium.

As a director you have the ability to accentuate or de-accentuate the 3-D look of your picture. It's up to you to assess your situation and decide what you can do to achieve a three-dimensional feeling in your composition.

First, you must know what tools you have at your disposal. Imagine that you preview a shot with your camera and decide that the picture looks too flat. You wish to know how to give the shot more feeling of depth. What are your options? What are your tools?

Some tools for meeting the 3-D challenge are:
• Lighting
• Depth of field
• Camera movement
• Subject placement

Let's explore these one at a time.

## LIGHTING

In TV production, we seldom rely on natural light—light as it happens to exist naturally in our scene. We usually add and manipulate light in order to achieve a more desirable effect. How we use light will affect the three-dimensional feeling of our subject.

Imagine that a camera shot is composed of a speaker standing at a podium addressing a group of people. We want to examine the brightness or darkness of various portions of the scene. If the light level on the speaker, the podium, and the wall behind him are all the same brightness level, then the picture will look flatter, less three-dimensional. However, if the light is carefully controlled so that the background is a bit darker than the foreground, that will help the foreground subject to stand out, emphasizing the depth in the picture. The depth is actually there already, but that depth can easily get lost in the translation to a two-dimensional medium. Controlling the various light levels simply draws more attention to the depth that exists naturally. Vary the light levels between foreground—enough for a pleasant sense of depth and separation.

Let's consider another lighting issue for the same scene. Imagine that all lights are hung over the audience, aimed at the speaker, and lighting him much like you would expect to see in a theater. If all lights come from the front, only the front side of his body is lit. This one-sided lighting will contribute to a flat look. Once the scene gets

(6.1) The subject is too close to the background. The light levels are the same. The look is flat.

(6.2) The subject has been positioned further forward, creating separation, brighter foreground than background, and a nice feeling of depth.

translated to a two-dimensional medium, the speaker will appear as a flat cut-out pasted directly onto the curtain or wall behind him.

To change this, let's hang a light above and behind him—a *back light*. The back light will aim toward the audience, but will be pointed down at the speaker so the light lands on the back of his head and shoulders. The light is hung high enough so it is out of the camera's field of view. The effect of this back light

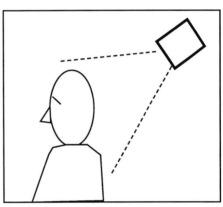

(6.3) Backlight placement.

(6.4) The speaker is not backlit. He looks flat against the background. He lacks 3-dimensionality.

(6.5) Backlight on the hair and shoulders helps him stand out from the background.

should be to create a subtle rim of brightness on the borders of his upper body. The light will also brighten his hair from behind. We have drawn subtle attention to the natural depth of his body through these highlights. The result is that we have helped separate the speaker from his background and made the scene look more three-dimensional.

## DEPTH OF FIELD

Another tool for meeting the 3-D challenge is **depth of field**—the amount of area that is in focus in front of and behind the focal point. The focal point in space out in front of the camera on which the lens is focused—the subject. If everything is in focus three feet behind the point and three feet in front of the focal point, then the depth of field is six feet.

Imagine that the camera lens is focused on the face of the speaker at the podium. The face is the focal point. A shallow depth of field means that very little is in focus before him and behind him, maybe only a few inches in front and behind.

You choose whether you prefer a shallow or deep depth of field. A shallow depth of field helps the subject stand out from the background. If the depth of field is three feet before and after the speaker, and the curtain is four or five feet behind the speaker, then the curtain will be just outside the depth of field and will be a bit soft. The speaker looks crisp and sharp. This effect draws attention to the two layers of depth: the speaker (sharp), and the wall behind him (soft).

On the other hand, there may be situations where a large depth of field is useful to show three-dimensionality. If the foreground and background are, in actuality, sepa-

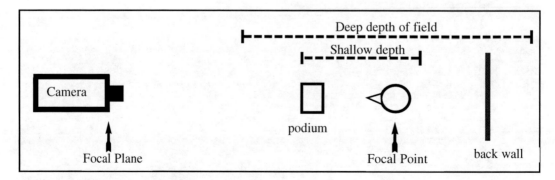

(6.6) Depth of field: the distance in front of and behind the focal point that remains in focus. The shallow depth of field does not include the curtain behind the speaker. The curtain will look slightly soft.

(6.7) The background is in focus. The depth of field is deep enough to include the background picture and wall. The look is somewhat flat.

(6.8) The background is slightly out of focus—a technique that helps separate the subject from the background.

rated by great distance, then a large depth of field may be preferable, keeping both near and distant subjects in focus. For example, imagine a shot of two gun fighters in an old western facing off in the street, separated by fifty feet or more. In this case, we don't want the background out of focus. We'd like to see both fighters clearly. The perspective in the picture is the vehicle for a feeling of depth. In other words, the placement of the camera and the way the two men appear in the screen creates a sense of depth.

## CONTROLLING DEPTH OF FIELD

Shallow depth of field is achieved by opening the lens iris and/or by placing the camera nearer to the subject while placing the subject further from the background. Read more on depth of field in chapter 11.

## CAMERA MOVEMENT

Another tool or technique for achieving a three-dimensional feeling is camera movement. Before the invention of the zoom lens, a camera had to be physically moved closer to an object to produce the feeling of "zooming in." This camera move is called a *dolly*. The camera dollies in or out on wheels or tracks as it gets closer to or further from the subject.

The advent of the *zoom lens* gave us the option to isolate a faraway subject without having to change location. The zoom lens also allows for a smooth transition from a *wide angle* to a *telephoto* (close-up) without having to change lenses. The question is: does it matter whether we zoom or dolly? Is there any substantial difference?

(6.9) Dolly shot. The camera operator runs the camera while the dolly pusher moves the dolly.

Imagine what, if anything, would look different if you zoomed in on the subject versus dollying in—a physical camera move.

When a lens zooms in, the camera stays in one place. The glass inside the lens changes and subsequently the framing changes—the field of view diminishes. However, as long as the camera stays in place, the relationship of objects to each other remains the same.

On the other hand, when the camera physically moves toward the object, the perspective shifts. Objects change in relationship to each other as the camera moves through space. Imagine yourself walking through a thicket of trees. As you walk, the trees appear to move in relationship to each other. If you stand in one place with a camera and zoom in, no relative change among the trees occurs.

Therefore, this experience of actually moving through the scene is more like what we do every day as we navigate through our three-dimensional environment. The dolly, then, provides a more three-dimensional realistic feeling compared to the zoom.

Zooming is convenient. It means you don't have to move the camera. But notice how any well-funded production such as a feature film almost never uses the zoom. A good director knows that the physical movement of the camera is aesthetically preferable. It enhances the three-dimensional feeling in the scene.

**SUBJECT PLACEMENT**

Another tool is subject placement. How do you place your subject in the frame? How do you arrange a group of subjects? Which direction does a person or object face? Where do you set up your camera to get the most three-dimensional view of something? These are all considerations that affect picture composition.

Let's line up a group of friends for a photo. If we stand them all on the same platform, shoulder to shoulder, then we have only emphasized width and a little bit of height. But if we place the group on a set of steps so that some people are a few inch-

(6.10) The fence looks flat against the background. The picture feels two-dimensional. Depth is not emphasized.

(6.11) The fence appears at an oblique angle, suggesting depth or three-dimensionality.

es higher than others and some are in front of others, then we have taken advantage of all three dimensions.

Let's take a picture of a train going by. We could take the photo from 90 degrees out to the side. The train would be running left to right through the frame. This composition takes advantage of width but not much height and no depth.

If we take the photo from an oblique angle, perhaps about 40 degrees off the train track, looking up the track as the train comes toward us, we get a much different feeling. Now the train cuts diagonally through the frame, apparently breaking through a flat medium as it comes toward us.

## SUMMARY

Whenever you set up a shot, ask yourself if you are making best use of your four tools to achieve three dimensionality

1) Is the lighting contributing to a separation of foreground and background?
2) Is the depth of field appropriate for the effect you wish to achieve?
3) Will there be camera movement or a zoom?
4) What have you done to compose the shot to emphasize three dimensions?

With these ideas in mind about three-dimensionality, you should be able to take a critical look at other people's composition. Start with photographs, pictures in magazines, posters, etc., and evaluate them for ways in which the photographer worked with the components that affect three-dimensional illusions. Then look at video programs and films with the same criteria in mind.

## A REAL WORLD APPLICATION, CONTINUED:

As the director tours the factory, he imagines ways to accentuate three-dimensionality in picture composition. He considers lighting as one of his tools. Using back lights on actors and interview subjects to highlight their heads and shoulders will help "pop" them out from the background. Lighting the subjects so that they are 20-40% brighter than their backgrounds will also help.

The director will talk to his camera operator about creating a slightly shallow depth of field during the interviews so that the background is ever so slightly out of focus. This will help focus attention on the subject. They will achieve the shallow depth by placing the subject a few extra feet forward from the background and placing the camera close to the subject. This ensures that when the subject is in focus, the background will likely be outside the depth of field. For added insurance, the camera operator will lower the light level enough to increase the aperture. The more open the iris, the smaller the depth of field.

As the director considers camera moves, he looks for smooth stretches of floor space to lay track for dolly moves. A moving camera will create a better sense of a three dimensional world. He knows that camera moves must be well-executed and take time to set up and rehearse. He hires a good dolly pusher to work with the camera operator to ensure smooth moves. He may use a crane for large up and down moves. He schedules extra time for grips to come in before the shoot to lay track for the dolly.

Finally, the director considers subject placement. He looks for ways to position the subjects in their environment with lots of depth in the background. He will avoid putting them in constrained areas which would feel flat and uninteresting such as against a wall. Anytime an interview can be shot with rows of machines in the background, the scene will have lots of depth and will feel more three-dimensional.

# 7

# Composition

With the 3-D challenge in mind, let's continue to explore composition. What makes a picture look good?

Everyone who has ever used a camera—from a tourist clicking a Kodak disposable camera to a Hollywood director using a 70 mm movie camera—is a composer of pictures. In each case, someone is framing a shot of a selected subject from a selected place of a selected field of view. In each case, the director and the camera operator can give thought to how the picture will be composed.

Ultimately, the director is responsible for the composition of each scene. Some directors give very specific framing instructions to their camera operators—they might ask to look through the viewfinder to preview each shot. Other directors stay less involved in the camera operator's job. They turn their attention to the actors in the scene and trust the camera operator to compose good shots. Either way, the director assumes overall responsibility for the aesthetic look and feel of the program.

Textbook principles of composition can only give you a point of reference from which to evaluate your pictures. Personal taste and experience apply. Some like to be avante garde. Some like to be conservative. The artistry cherished by some may be scorned by others. And the magic that occurs when the whole world rallies around a great piece of art cannot be explained by the artist simply having learned the rules of composition. Sometimes the great works are by those who broke the rules in a fashion that captured the imagination.

As subjective as composition is, it helps to have some guidelines. Think about some of these ideas as you compose pictures:

Every subject has four compositional qualities: *shape*, *form*, *texture*, and *color*. It's your job to consider which of these qualities you'd like to emphasize.

**Shape** - Imagine the subject as a silhouette. What is its shape? Is the subject square, round, triangular, or other? As you decide where to place your camera and how to frame your shot, you'll want to consider which angle best reveals the subject's shape.

Consider the *aspect ratio* of the shape. How well does the shape fit on a TV screen? Remember that TV is wider than it is tall. Traditional U.S. television has a 4:3 aspect ratio, four units wide by three units tall. The newer high definition format uses a 16:9 ratio screen, or 16 units wide by nine units tall. Therefore tall objects cannot fill the frame in the way that wide objects can. You can't frame a close-up of a tall building without cutting off a lot. But you can fill the frame with an automobile since it tends to resemble the aspect ratio of the TV screen. Consider framing people. The shape of a person is tall and slim. Thus, a full-figure shot forces the camera to zoom out and leave lots of margin on either side of the subject. However, a close-up of someone's head fills the frame quite well.

**Form** - The form simply adds a dimension to shape. A subject's form is its three-dimensional presence. Again, how you frame your shot will either enhance the sense of three-dimensionality or not. You must decide which angle looks best, which view is most pleasing or interesting.

**Texture** - Some subjects have wonderful texture—the bark on a tree, gravel, grass. Texture elements can look wonderful on the screen. However, because of television's poor resolution, some finely detailed textures will not resolve well. You may see fuzziness or a rainbow pattern on the screen as the TV processing circuitry struggles to resolve a fine texture. Notice how pinstripe suits or busy plaid patterns do not look good on TV. One solution when shooting fine texture is to zoom in and make the images bigger. This helps the TV camera latch onto the fine detail. Another solution is to avoid certain fine detail. Ask your human subjects—actors and spokespeople—to avoid busy patterns, plaids, and pinstripes.

**Color** - What color is your subject? Any color can be described by its *hue*, what color it is, by its *luminance*, how bright it is, and by its *saturation*, how deep the color is. You'll notice that some colors look better on TV than others, especially when copied onto a low-grade tape format such as VHS. For example, a bright red color tends to bloom or look fuzzy. The color blue tends to look very crisp and clean. Therefore, it's good to avoid such things as on-camera spokespeople wearing bright red blazers.

With these four qualities in mind, let's move on to placing and grouping subjects within a scene. Several principles apply when deciding how one or more subjects will appear in your frame.

**Principle #1** - *A picture should contain a center of interest*. What is the dominant feature of your picture? What stands out? What draws attention? The purpose of the

(7.1) The center of interest is not obvious. It may be the tree, the lake, the people, the geese, or the meadow, or the sky.

(7.2) The center of interest is more obvious.

center of interest is to draw the eye to the most important subject in the frame. There is no exact spot on the screen to place the center of interest. But, once you have identified it, you can think about the way all other items in the picture play off the center of interest. The center of interest may be by virtue of size, placement, brightness, and uniqueness. For example, a bright subject in a dark room may not need to be very large in order to be the center of interest. The center of interest does not have to be a solitary object. In figure 7.2 the center of interest is a pair of geese.

**Principle #2** - *A picture should have balance*. How do the elements in the picture appear in relation to each other? How do they fill the screen? Is there a sense of even distribution throughout the frame? Is there a feeling of balance? Is all the picture information loaded on the right side of the screen, making the viewer feel as if the TV set were about to lean? Is there unnecessary blank space in the frame?

(7.3) The subject matter is unbalanced. The two people are off to one side with too much dead space above and screen left.

(7.4) The subject matter feels balanced. The two people fill the space in a more pleasing manner.

**63**

(7.5) This proportion favors the sky and clouds.

(7.6) Changing proportion, this same basic angle favors the road.

Achieving balance does not mean giving all objects equal placement. Instead, it means deciding what elements of the picture have value and distributing that value around the screen. For example, the sky may have value along with the mountains. Together, they fill the screen, whether the sky is dominant or whether the mountains dominate the screen. The sum total feels balanced. On the other hand, elements that really have no value may contribute to a lack of balance. In figure 7.3, the extra space around the two subjects does not feel useful or relevant, thus the picture feels unbalanced compared with figure 7.4.

**Principle #3** - *The artist should consider proportion*. The word proportion implies a ratio. How much do you show of Object A compared with Object B. If you shoot a panorama of land and sky, where do you put the horizon? Do you place it in the upper third of the frame such that you have one-third sky and two thirds land? Or do you place the horizon lower such that you have two-thirds sky and one-third land?

**Principle #4** - *The artist should take advantage of perspective*. The camera sees the world the same way our eyes do: things closer are bigger and things further appear smaller. You can look at objects in relationship to each other from many different vantage points and achieve many different perspectives. Each has a different feeling and places different importance on the objects and their relationship to one another. Perspective is established when you decide where to place the camera. Your choice of camera placement will determine the way a subject is presented to the viewer, as something close and dominant, as something far away, as something powerful, as something weak, as something above, as something below.

(7.7) Notice the perspective in each figure. By showing both near and far, 3-dimensionality is emphasized.

(7.8) Another example of perspective.

Choosing perspective is also a great opportunity to enhance 3-dimensionality. By looking down the railroad track, the feeling of trailing off into the distance is far more 3-dimensional than looking at the tracks from the side.

**Principle #5** - *A picture can have rhythm*. A series of objects creates a visual rhythm within a static picture. A row of trees, the pattern of a picket fence, the ripples in water, the peaks of a mountain range, the leaves on a tree branch. The eye goes from object to object according to the rhythm inherent in the composition of the picture. Rhythm, as with music, may be pleasing or displeasing. One grouping of objects may seem intuitively more pleasing than another. When you compose a shot, think of visual rhythm and what pleases you the most.

(7.9) Notice the rhythm created by the composition of objects in each figure. The lamp posts and window frames create a regular beat.

(7.10) The dandelions create an irregular or syncopated beat.

**Principle #6** - *Simplicity can be a virtue.* This principle pertains especially to the TV medium. The TV screen is relatively small compared to a large painting or a movie projection. TV's resolution is inferior. Therefore, a lot of tiny detail in the picture never looks as clear as it would in another medium. TV's best images are simple ones that feature fairly large dominant subjects which, because of their relatively large size, resolve well on the screen. Therefore, a close-up of a face will be more pleasing than a distant shot of the same person. On a large movie screen, a wide shot may look very clear. But on a TV screen, the tiny detail in the wide shot won't be as crisp and clear. That's why TV has often been referred to as a "close-up medium." Close-ups are simple and easy for the TV medium to resolve. They look good both technically and aesthetically.

You may notice the simplicity concept at work when you compare expensively produced commercials with low-budget commercials. The expensive commercials, with more money spent on creativity and design, typically emphasize very simple and bold images. The perfume bottle fills the screen. The truck or the car fills the screen. On the other hand, a less sophisticated commercial that may not have as much expertise behind it often shows a busy cluttered scene: a warehouse full of stuff, or a showroom full of furniture. Too many things to look at. Consider how pleasing it is to see a simple framing of a few bold objects on a TV screen versus a cluttered array.

If the objects in your picture have small but essential detail on them such as wording engraved on a statue, it will be absolutely necessary to zoom in very close and allow this detail to show up large enough in the frame to resolve well. Otherwise, if your shot is too wide and the detail is too small, the information in your picture may not resolve adequately to be recognizable on the screen.

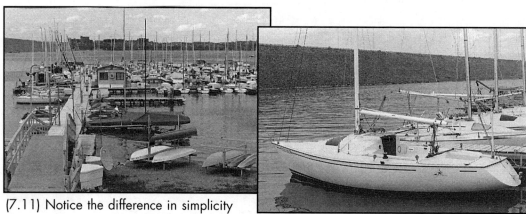

(7.11) Notice the difference in simplicity in each figure. This one looks busy and cluttered.

(7.12) This figure is simple in its composition.

(7.13) A shot showing the entire body is called a full-figure shot (FF).

(7.14) A shot framed at the knees is called a knee shot (KS).

(7.15) A shot framed at the waist is a waist shot (WS).

(7.16) Tighter still is a head and shoulders shot (H/S).

(7.17) Tighter still is a close-up (CU).

(7.18) Tighter still is an extreme close-up (ECU).

## COMPOSING FACES

Next, let's consider the human face. Faces will probably be your most commonly used subject matter. News shows, documentaries, training programs, sports and entertainment programs all feature medium shots and close-ups of human faces addressing the camera or addressing each other. So, let's look at ways to compose a single face and ways to compose two people talking to each other.

First, think about your field of view. How much of the subject will you see in your framing? If you want to see the entire body, use a *full-figure* or *FF* shot. A shot cropped at the knees is called a ***knee shot*** or ***KS***. A shot cropped at the waist is a ***waist shot*** or ***WS***. A nice framing for a portrait is a ***head and shoulders shot*** or ***H/S***. A ***close-up***, ***CU***, eliminates most of the shoulders, and an ***extreme close-up***, ***ECU***, makes the face fill the screen.

It isn't enough to pick a field of view. You still have to fine-tune the location of the head within the frame. You could place the head further up the screen, further down, further left, or further right. The head could be angled in any number of directions. How do you decide? Here are a few rules of thumb:

(7.19) Eyes are at about one-third of the way down the screen

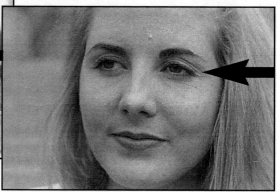

(7.20) As the framing gets extremely tight, it's necessary to cut off the top of the head.

## THE ONE THIRD RULE FOR EYES

The subject's eyes should appear at about one-third of the way down the screen. In figure 7.19 and 7.20, you see examples of the one-third rule for a head and shoulders shot and an extreme close up. If the eyes are too high in the screen, too much of the subject's head is cut off. If the eyes are too low, the mouth is cut off on an ECU. In a H/S, there's probably too much head room.

## HEAD ROOM

Another consideration is the relationship between the subject and the edges of the frame. Have you left some space between the top of the subject's head and the top of the frame? We call this space **head room**. Some head room is preferable to no head room or too much head room. If you follow the one-third rule for eyes, the head room should be adequate.

Head room applies to wide and medium framings—anything from a full figure to a head and shoulders shot. Once you zoom in closer than that, head room must give way in order to keep the eyes at one-third. If you maintain head room on an extreme close-up, the eyes will be too low in the frame. Notice figure 7.16. On a H/S shot, some headroom feels appropriate.Now, consider the ECU in figure 7.18. In this framing, the camera is zoomed in so far that the top of the head is cut off. But the eyes are at the proper one-third level. Head room isn't required. Here's another way to think about it: The area from the eyes down to the mouth and chin—the lower half of the face—is the most visually important part of the face. The eyes and mouth do all the communicating. So they should always have a prominent spot in the frame. Better to cut off the top of the head than to cut off part of the chin.

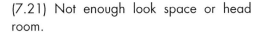

(7.21) Not enough look space or head room.

(7.22) Good look space and head room.

## LOOK SPACE

*Look space* is extra room on the side of the frame which the subject is facing. If the subject is facing the camera, look space is not an issue, but if the subject looks even a little bit screen right or left, then they should be given some look space—extra room in front of the face.

Consider figure 7.21. The subject has no head room and her face feels uncomfortably close to the side of the frame to which she is looking. In figure 7.22 on the other hand, head room feels comfortable and so does look space. Some directors like to exaggerate look space and frame the shot with large amounts of excess room by placing the back of the subjects head far to one side of the screen.

## HEAD ON, PROFILE, 3/4 PROFILE

Which way is the person looking? Are they facing the camera? If so, that may be termed a *head-on* shot. If they are facing 90 degrees to the camera, then you see a *profile*. And if they are looking somewhere between a profile and a head on shot, and if you can see both eyes, then the shot is considered to be a *3/4 profile*.

Does it matter which head direction you use? Usually the type of production will determine head direction. For example, when you watch the nightly news, you expect the newscaster to face the camera, hence a head-on shot. It would look pretty silly to see the news anchor in a profile. On the other hand, if you see someone answering a question being asked by a reporter off camera, then the likely view is a profile or three-quarter profile.

(7.23) Head-On

(7.24) Profile

(7.25) 3/4 Profile

*Is there any advantage to using the three-quarter profile versus the profile*?

The main advantage of the three-quarter profile is that it gives the viewer a better sense of the three-dimensionality of the face. It offers a partial side view and a partial front view.

Did you ever see someone for the first time in a profile? Until they turned their head toward you, you really didn't know what they looked like from the front. You could only imagine. Then they turned to face you and you couldn't help feeling surprised at how close together their eyes were! You had imagined a different appearance.

Similarly, did you ever see someone at first from the front—head-on? Then, they turned to a profile and you couldn't help feeling surprised at how big their nose was! The 3/4 profile alleviates these surprises by giving the viewer a three-dimensional sense of the subject's head.

## FRAMING TWO PEOPLE VIS-A-VIS

The most prevalent framing on TV consists of two people in conversation. Interviews, for example, are seen in most TV programs. Dramatic scenarios are also full of two-person conversations. So, what are your options for framing two people in a dialogue?

**Option 1) Two profiles**
The people face each other and the camera is perpendicular to them, catching both faces in the same frame, but both faces are in profile.

**Option 2) Over-the-shoulder shot**
Again, both people are facing each other. But in this case, the camera gets partially behind one person in order to see the back of that person's shoulder and a 3/4 profile of the second person. Keeping person #1's back of head and shoulder in the pic-

(7.26) Two profiles. Not the preferable way to watch two people talking.

(7.27) Over-the-shoulder shot (OS)

(7.28) The reverse angle tries to match the angle and field of view of the previous OS.

ture ensures that the viewer recognizes the relationship between the two people. The angle allows for an optimum view of person #2.

The problem is that only person #2 gets a favorable view. The solution is to switch angles and get an equal and opposite angle from behind the other person and alternate between the two shots. This is called a *reverse angle*.

In a multi-camera production, reverse angles are quick and easy because you have two cameras set up, one for each angle. Using the switcher, you simply select back and forth. But in single camera production, you must shoot one angle at a time and piece the back-and-forth sequence together in the editing room.

(7.29) Two Faces East, the only two-person conversation framing that reveals two 3/4 profiles.

### Option 3) Two Faces East

Have you ever watched a soap opera and noticed both people look in the same direction while talking to each other? Perhaps the woman, in disgust, goes to the window and stares past the camera. Then the comforting boyfriend comes up behind her, also looking out the window. It seems a bit contrived, because we probably don't usually position ourselves that way in real life. But in the soaps or the movies it works nicely because it allow for something that the other two options cannot provide. You guessed it—two three-quarter profiles.

## A REAL WORLD APPLICATION, CONTINUED:

The director knows that he must give his camera operator specific instructions about framing. He uses standard terminology:

"Give me a wide shot" or "establishing shot" when he wants an overall look at the scene.

"Give me a medium shot," when he wants a closer look at something. "How about a close-up on this shot," when it's time for something up close and personal. "On this next scene, we need a pan left from the host to the equipment."

Scene by scene, the director communicates clearly what kind of shots are needed. Watching a field TV monitor, the director corrects the shot with commands such as:

"Zoom out a little bit more and pan left." The camera operator responds.

"Hold that," the director says. The camera operator holds the shot.

The director asks the camera operator for all kinds of frames and moves: zoom in, tilt up, pan right, dolly out, truck left, arc right. When it comes to shooting people, the director is specific about framing. He asks for a 2-shot, or a single, or a full-figure, waist-shot, chest shot, head-and-shoulders, CU, ECU, etc.

The director plans shots with a sequence in mind. He knows that it's too abrupt to go from a wide establishing shot immediately to an extreme close-up. So he asks for shots that move in gradually, beginning with a wide shot, progressing to a medium shot, to a close-up, and perhaps to an extreme close-up if needed.

The director pays attention to framing. If he notices that someone's head is being chopped off on a head-and-shoulders framing, he says to the camera operator, "Give me more head room," or "tilt up a bit." If the face is too close to the side of the frame, he says, "Give me more look space." He is always trying to correct a shot before it is too late—before the tape rolls and records. If he wants a tighter shot, he says "Zoom in to a head-and-shoulders shot," or just, "Zoom in a bit, please."

When the director calls for a zoom he makes clear the difference between a "hot" zoom, which is a zoom executed during the actual recording, and a preliminary zoom used ahead of time to adjust framing. In this case, the director wants a static shot, but the framing is too wide, so he says, "Zoom in a little tighter," prior to recording until he is satisfied with the framing. Once the framing is set, the director calls, "Roll tape!"

In some instances, the camera will move by being pushed on a dolly that rides along a track. This move looks more three-dimensional than a zoom in. The director prefers to use the dolly move wherever possible. Sometimes it is not possible or practical to do a dolly, truck, or arc. Then the director may call for a zoom in as an actual "hot" move to be recorded and used.

The director is constantly evaluating the composition of the scenes that make up the production. He is careful to refrain from annoying his camera operator by constantly correcting his every move. In fact, the camera operator and the director get along quite well. They trust each other. They've worked together many times. The camera operator expects to be told what to do. After all, the director is the one who has spent quite a bit of time thinking through all these shots. At the same time, the director relies on the camera operator's good judgment and artistry.

# Section III

$S$ection I covered the definition of a TV director and an overview of technological developments. Section II covered some fundamental building blocks of the TV medium: composition, resolution, and frames. Now, we're ready to begin the practical steps in planning and executing a single-camera television production. We call these steps *pre-production*. They include:

- beginning with a concept
- writing a proposal, treatment, and budget
- writing a script
- creating a shot list
- conducting a site survey
- arranging for equipment acquisition
- hiring crew
- auditioning and hiring talent

# 8

# Concept and Script

Communication theorist Marshall McLuhan made popular a notion that the "medium is the message"—meaning the TV medium's form supercedes content as it impacts the viewer. Television's very existence is its power to influence.

Although television may often seem like "form over content," this view downplays the importance of crafting a message based on an idea, which is the director's responsibility. In this book about directing, a more useful perspective is that any message begins with the formation and development of an idea. The ultimate goal is to reach the listener/viewer with that idea. To pick up a video camera with no concept in mind would be like picking up the phone with nothing to say. The director's job is to adapt the content to the form in the most compelling way possible.

So, to get started with content development for your program, ask yourself the following questions:

## 1) *Whose idea is it?*

As director, you may or may not be the originator of a story idea. The idea may have come from other people and then handed to you. In many cases, the client determines the message. Or there may be a hired scriptwriter on the project. In any case, the director should stay in close touch with the content originator to make sure the message is clear and accurate.

## 2) *Is this your own personal project, or are you doing it for someone else?*

If the video program is simply your own creation, then you can do whatever you want. It doesn't have to please anyone other than you.

Perhaps your idea is for a production to fulfill a class assignment. In that case, you have to consider the parameters of the assignment.

If you are working for a company or for a TV station, then you also have to consider the guidelines of your assignment. Does the boss have specific requirements for the production? Or are you given freedom to pursue whatever you like?

### 3) *Who is responsible for developing the concept?*

It's one thing to have the idea. It's another thing to actually research the idea and write the script. Who will do all that work?

For example, you may be working for a corporate client who wants a training video made and knows exactly what information needs to be conveyed but has no means to write a script. You, as director, may help locate a writer, or act as writer yourself.

### 4) *What program format?*

Radio and TV stations like to categorize shows according to certain common styles. The stations may refer to these as program ***categories*** or program ***formats***. (*Don't confuse a program format with a videotape format*). Identifying a program format helps you position your concept and helps others quickly zero in on your idea. Your production may fit into one of the following typical formats:

**• *hard news***
Hard news is a timely news event, suitable for a daily newscast. A robbery that happens in the morning should be reported as soon as possible that same day.

**• *soft news / feature***
A soft news feature program suggests a news story that is informational but not immediate. Whereas a robbery is considered hard news and should be covered the same day, a feature might cover the building of a new airport—something that is of general ongoing interest. The story could be broadcast tomorrow, or next week.

**• *documentary***
A documentary is an in-depth feature. As the word implies, this type of program seeks to document some process or historical event.

**• *interview / talk***
An interview program depicts one or more individuals having a discussion. These programs are minimally scripted. Perhaps the only word-for-word scripting is in the opening and closing of the show. The rest is spontaneous discussion. An interview program may feature the host or reporter, or the program may be produced in such a way that minimizes the presence of the host and mainly shows the interviewee answering questions and making statements. In any case, almost all programs have some interview component.

• *commercial / infomercial*
Commercials are paid advertisements used to sell products, services, or create images and impressions about a company. Some commercials are short—five seconds to a minute. Some are very long and involved. The infomercial format is designed to look like a full length informational program, but it is actually a paid advertisement and designed to sell a product.

• *sales / marketing*
A non-broadcast form of a commercial may be called a sales/marketing program, used by companies to promote products or services. The program may look like an extended commercial and may be played at trade shows, shown at sales presentations, or mass-mailed to potential customers.

• *training / informational*
A training or informational program may be broadcast or used privately by companies to train employees, to inform clients or customers, or to communicate ideas for general community awareness. This could include anything from a Jane Fonda workout video to a patient orientation video in a doctor's office.

• *entertainment*
Entertainment is a broad category that includes performing arts, dramatic programs, and game shows.

• *sports*
Sports programs can include live action sports, sports features, and sports documentaries.

• *experimental*
All the above formats are familiar to us. An experimental program attempts to try new and unfamiliar styles, to play with atypical structures or no structure at all. When a technique is new, it may be considered experimental. Then, if the audience accepts the experiment and the technique gets repeated, with the passage of time, it may become regarded as conventional. The music video, for example, was once a novel form. Today, it is commonplace.

For those working in TV news, the categories can get even more specific. Here's a list of categories for an Emmy Award competition by one of the National Association of Television Arts and Sciences' regional chapters:

| | |
|---|---|
| Extended News Coverage | Documentary: Historic |
| Spot News | Target Audience Program |
| General News | Public Affairs Program |
| Live News | Informational/Instructional |
| News Feature | Interview/Discussion |
| News Series | Entertainment |
| Non-News Feature | Entertainment Short |
| Investigative Reporting | Youth/Children's Program |
| Special Event Coverage | Editorial Commentary |
| Sports Reporting | Public Service Announcement (PSA) |
| Sports Program | PSA Campaign |
| Documentary: Current Issue | Promotional |
| Documentary: Artistic or Cultural | |

### 5) *What kind of locations are needed?*

Will all the shooting locations be around campus? Around town? Will you require a studio? Will you need to travel across the country? Or overseas? Or is the whole idea to create locations and characters through graphics and animation?

### 6) *What kind of personnel are needed?*

In front of the camera, will you need actors? Hosts? Narrators? Will you need to call on real people to provide you with interviews? Does the president of a company need to address the camera in a sales/marketing program to represent his or her company? What if he or she performs terribly in front of the camera? Do you need to get a talent coach? Or convince the president to let someone else do the talking?

Behind the camera, how many crew members do you need? Is it a simple 2-person crew or a complex crew? Camera operator? Audio engineer? Lighting grip? Dolly pusher?

### 7) *Who is writing the script?*

Do the clients already have a script written and ready to be produced? Do they intend to have one written? Are they relying on you to write the script?

### 8) *What is the time frame?*

Is it a quick turnaround project? Or do you have lots of time? A concept may be wonderful, but may require more time than you have available. Is it realistic to proceed if you don't have the time to do the job well?

**9) *Do you have the budget to cover your desired concept, format, locations, and personnel?***

Though the details of your production can be worked out later, it's helpful to first know if you can afford the production. When you come up with an idea, what might it take to execute that idea? Is the idea realistic? Or too difficult to carry out?

What if your client wants to shoot in Italy, but doesn't have enough money for the production to leave town? Something has to give. Either the client has to come up with more money, or the concept may have to change.

It's typical for a client to ask, "How much will it cost to do this production?" But until the above questions have been answered, it's hard to know.

## THE PROPOSAL

One of the ironies in TV production is that the script is often written after the parties agree to undertake a project. Yet the script dictates so much about the scope of the project that the time and materials won't be fully determined until the script is finished. It's a chicken and egg puzzle: How can you determine what you want until you write a script? But how can you write a script until you determine what you want?

For this reason, a ***proposal*** is written first. The proposal embodies three elements:
1) a reason for being—an argument why this is a worthy project and why it would be a commercial success,
2) a short synopsis of the story idea called a ***treatment,*** and
3) a ***budget*** to show the funders know how much they are being asked to spend.

A treatment may be a couple of paragraphs or a couple of pages. It summarizes the ideas in the show and the technical considerations. It serves to paint a mental picture of what the show will be like and directly or indirectly answers many of the basic questions stated above. For example, this is the proposal submitted by the producer for the lumber mill safety program. It leads off with the argument of worthiness, followed by the treatment, followed by a budget.

# PROPOSAL
# FOR VIDEO PRODUCTION
# TO THE REGIS LUMBER COMPANY

WORKING TITLE: It Couldn't Happen To Me!

This proposal is to produce a half-hour training and educational video for the Regis Lumber Company.

In the last ten years, since the installation of new high-speed processing equipment, the accident rate has increased. According to the company policy, the only acceptable accident rate is: "none at all." It is clear that current training methods are not working. One of the problems cited has been a lack of cohesive training at locations throughout the world.

Video offers the best way to provide uniform training and information. The proposed program will teach and demonstrate a unified safety practice to all of the company's 4500 employees. This video will be especially useful as part of the orientation process for new employees. Company consultants have estimated that a uniform instruction to all employees could cut the accident rate by more than eighty percent.

CONTENT

The proposed program will have three sections:

1) An orientation to the new technology. Viewers will get an overview of the type of equipment being used today and the inherent dangers. The viewer will see actual shots of the equipment in use as well as animated scenes to show inner workings not easily shot with a camera on location.

2) Testimonials. The company president will make a statement in the program, expressing the company concern for safety and reviewing company policy. Various company employees will be interviewed, some to explain their role in safety procedures and others to explain how safe practice kept them out of harm's way.

4) Dramatic vignettes. Actors will be used to show safety practices. Each vignette will pose a possible dangerous situation. The actors will be faced with deciding on the best solution to a problem. In training situations, the facilitator can stop the tape and use these vignettes as jump-off points for discussion.

The content for this video will be developed in cooperation with the vice-president of operations for the company, using the latest safety guidelines as a base from which to develop the items to be covered. Department managers will review the script drafts to add any items that they deem important. The finished program will be packaged and distributed on cassette and DVD to all departments at all locations. A memo from the executive office will accompany the video, explaining its intent and suggested methods for incorporating it into the company training schedule.

**BUDGET**

| | |
|---|---|
| Pre-production | |
| Planning and scripting | $5,000.00 |
| | |
| Production | |
| Location shooting, 3 days @ $2500 | $7,500.00 |
| | |
| Post Production | |
| Rough cut editing 4 days @ $750/day | $3,000.00 |
| Online editing 2 days @ $1200/day | $2,400.00 |
| Narration | $  500.00 |
| Animation | $2,000.00 |
| VHS duplication | $3,000.00 |
| DVD authoring and replication | $6,000.00 |
| | |
| Personnel | |
| Writer | $2,500.00 |
| Producer | $4,000.00 |
| Director | $4,000.00 |
| Editor | $2,500.00 |
| Actors | $4,000.00 |
| | |
| TOTAL | $46,400.00 |

By reading this proposal, those who need to approve the production of this program get a quick but thorough idea of what this show is about. They know the basic who, what, when, and where. They can estimate cost and personnel commitment. And they have some idea of audience appeal.

In a TV newsroom, a proposal process occurs, though less formal. In this case, proposals and treatments are handled verbally in daily news team meetings where reporters and producers lobby the news director to pursue certain stories. The news team considers story relevance, time, and budget. There may be seven good stories to cover on a given day and only five ENG crews available. The news producers and the news director must decide which stories come first and which, if any, will be dropped.

## THE SCRIPT

The script is the fully written version of the proposed show. It spells out all necessary information for both sound and picture. Anyone writing a script is not just writing for the spoken word, but is also writing a description of all other sounds—music and sound effects—as well as a description of all visual information. Sometimes, the script is submitted prior to program approval. But often, the program has been approved based on the proposal. Then, scriptwriting occurs under contract.

Typically, a writer is hired to research and write the script. Or, the writer adapts material already supplied by the client. In some cases, the producer is also the writer. In other cases, the client does much of the writing and the writer or producer simply helps shape the script into a TV format.

Some programs can be fully scripted ahead of time, such as dramas and training programs. Other formats do not lend themselves to full scripting prior to shooting. For example, if you are on a news team covering a fire, you may need to shoot first and write later. But even so, a professional news crew will have a good idea of the structure to a story from having done it hundreds of times, and will gather shots, interviews, opinions, and information necessary to put the story together.

Even if the story cannot be fully scripted, it should be scripted as much as possible, even to the point of imagining what might happen. For example, a documentary program cannot always be scripted ahead of time. The director may not know all the events that will unfold before the camera. At the same time, the director should go into the situation with as much structure in mind as possible. Just as a courtroom lawyer should know the answers to the witness' questions even before they are uttered, similarly, a director should know as much as possible about a story before going into a situation with camera and crew.

Your best bet is to write a script that anticipates as much as possible, even making up interview dialogue that you might expect to get from your interviews. Then go into the production with a script draft, knowing that it may change.

Why bother writing first? Like the treatment, a script not only expresses the ideas in your show, but it serves as an organizing tool. Writing as much as possible ahead of time helps you consider all the details. It helps you collect your thoughts and consider what your show is about. It gives you a direction. It's easy to change direction once you have one. It's much harder to know where to go or when to change direction when you never really worked out where you were going to begin with.

## SCRIPT FORMATS

A script can be formatted on the printed page in various ways. In the TV and film industry you will see certain commonly-used formats.

Let's look at four typical formats:
• Two-column format
• Single-column format
• Corporate teleplay format
• Storyboard format

Notice how each format incorporates both sound and picture information:

## THE TWO COLUMN FORMAT

In the *two-column format*, all the visual information is listed in one column and all the audio information is listed in a second column. Why? This provides an easy way to distinguish between different parts of the script. The narrator can read his or her part easily in the audio column. The director can look for shot descriptions easily in the video column.

Spoken words are capitalized to make them jump off the page, which helps actors and narrators read their lines.

Scene and shot numbers are added as an organizational aid. In the following tongue-in-cheek script, we're looking at Scene 1, Shots 1 through 8 of a drama called, "Mutiny on the High Seas."

SCRIPT: MUTINY ON THE HIGH SEAS
(*Two-column format*)

| AUDIO | VIDEO |
|---|---|
| (Scene 1, Shot 1)<br>Theme music<br><br>Narrator:<br>AFTER WEEKS OF BAD WEATHER, PIRATE ATTACKS AND DWINDLING PROVISIONS, THE CAPTAIN PACED WORRIEDLY. HE DIDN'T KNOW IF HIS CREW COULD TAKE MUCH MORE. | Fade up to wide shot on deck of ship in storm. Captain pacing. |
| (Scene 1, Shot 2)<br>Sound of waves crashing over deck. | Wide shot of ship. |
| (Scene 1, Shot 3)<br>Narrator:<br>JUST THEN, THE FIRST MATE CAME RUNNING. | Medium shot. First Mate enters. |
| (Scene 1, Shot 4)<br>First Mate:<br>CAPTAIN. I'VE GOT SOME GOOD NEWS AND I'VE GOT SOME BAD NEWS. | Over the shoulder: First Mate |
| (Scene 1, Shot 5)<br>Captain:<br>WHAT'S THE GOOD NEWS? | Over the shoulder: Captain |

| AUDIO | VIDEO |
|---|---|
| (Scene 1, Shot 6)<br>Mate:<br>THE CREW CAME UP WITH<br>A GREAT IDEA. THEY THINK<br>A BIT OF ENTERTAINMENT<br>MIGHT LIFT THEIR SPIRITS. | CU: Mate |
| (Scene 1, Shot 7)<br>Captain:<br>THAT'S WONDERFUL!<br>WHAT'S THE BAD NEWS? | CU: Captain |
| (Scene 1, Shot 8)<br>Mate:<br>THEY THOUGHT IT WOULD<br>FUN TO SEE IF YOU CAN<br>SWIM FASTER THAN THE SHIP. | CU: Mate |

## THE SINGLE COLUMN FORMAT

The *single-column format* puts the same information in one column. Why? Typically because the director desires one entire side of the page to be blank for notes or directing commands and cues. Those who direct live television or live-to-tape studio productions often prefer this format for cue notations.

Note that in order to differentiate between visual and audio information, the script uses upper case and upper/lower case. Again, the capitalized spoken words are easy to read.

| | |
|---|---|
| SCRIPT: MUTINY ON THE HIGH SEAS <br> (*Single-column format*) <br><br><br> Theme Music <br><br> Fade up to wide shot <br> on deck of ship in storm. <br> Captain is pacing. <br><br> Narrator: <br> AFTER WEEKS OF BAD WEATHER, PIRATE ATTACKS, AND DWINDLING PROVISIONS, THE CAPTAIN PACED WORRIEDLY. HE DIDN'T KNOW IF HIS CREW COULD TAKE MUCH MORE. <br><br> Wide shot of ship. <br> Sound of waves crashing <br> over deck. | |

Medium shot.
First Mate enters.

Narrator:
JUST THEN, THE FIRST MATE
CAME RUNNING.

OS of First Mate

First Mate:
CAPTAIN, I'VE GOT SOME
GOOD NEWS AND I'VE
GOT SOME BAD NEWS.

Over the shoulder of Captain

Captain:
WHAT'S THE GOOD NEWS?

CU: MATE

Mate:
THE CREW CAME UP WITH
A GREAT IDEA. THEY THINK
A BIT OF ENTERTAINMENT
MIGHT LIFT THEIR SPIRITS.

CU of Captain

Captain:
THAT'S WONDERFUL!
WHAT'S THE BAD NEWS?

CU of First Mate:

First Mate:
THEY THOUGHT IT WOULD BE
FUN TO SEE IF YOU CAN SWIM
FASTER THAN THE SHIP.

## THE CORPORATE TELEPLAY FORMAT

The **corporate teleplay format** is a variation of Hollywood's screenplay format. It assigns music, narration/dialogue, and visual information to different tab or indent settings.

The far left column describes
the scene.

> The first indent is for dialogue,
> music, and sound effects.

> > The second indent is for
> > narration.

This format offers the advantage of being able to easily scan down any given indent column. A narrator, while reading, can easily scan the narration column.

---

SCRIPT: MUTINY ON THE HIGH SEAS
(*Corporate teleplay format*)

1. Fade up to wide shot on deck of ship in storm.
Medium shot: Captain is pacing.

> Theme music

> > Narrator:
> > AFTER WEEKS OF BAD
> > WEATHER, PIRATE
> > ATTACKS AND DWINDLING
> > PROVISIONS, THE CAPTAIN
> > PACED WORRIEDLY. HE
> > DIDN'T KNOW IF HIS CREW
> > COULD TAKE MUCH MORE.

---

2. Wide shot of ship

> Sound of waves crashing
> over deck.

3. Medium shot. First mate enters.

> Narrator:
> JUST THEN, THE FIRST
> MATE CAME RUNNING.

4. Over the shoulder: first mate.

> First Mate:
> CAPTAIN, I'VE GOT SOME
> GOOD NEWS AND I'VE
> GOT SOME BAD NEWS.

5. Over the shoulder: captain.

> Captain:
> WHAT'S THE GOOD NEWS?

6. Close up: first mate.

> First Mate:
> THE CREW CAME UP WITH
> A GREAT IDEA. THEY THINK
> A BIT OF ENTERTAINMENT
> MIGHT LIFT THEIR SPIRITS.

7. Close up: captain.

> Captain:
> THAT'S WONDERFUL!
> WHAT'S THE BAD NEWS?

8. Close up: first mate

> First Mate:
> THEY DECIDED TO SEE IF
> YOU CAN SWIM FASTER
> THAN THE SHIP.

## THE STORYBOARD FORMAT

The *storyboard* format uses a series of sketches, illustrations, or photos to depict the look of each scene.

As you can imagine, a lengthy program might be impractical to storyboard. But a short piece such as a commercial that is heavily dependent on precise shot composition can benefit from a storyboard. This allows the director to show the client exactly what he or she has in mind before going through all the trouble of shooting.

---

SCRIPT: MUTINY ON THE HIGH SEAS.
(*Storyboard format*)

Narrator:
AFTER WEEKS OF BAD
WEATHER, PIRATE
ATTACKS, AND DWINDLING
PROVISIONS, THE CAPTAIN
PACED WORRIEDLY. HE DIDN'T
KNOW IF HIS CREW COULD TAKE
MUCH MORE.

Scene 1, shot 1.

Sound of waves crashing
over deck.

Scene 1, shot 2.

Narrator:
JUST THEN, THE FIRST MATE
CAME RUNNING.

Scene 1, shot 3.

---

First Mate:
CAPTAIN, I'VE GOT SOME
GOOD NEWS AND I'VE
GOT SOME BAD NEWS.

Scene 1, shot 4.

Captain:
WHAT'S THE GOOD NEWS?

Scene 1, shot 5.

Mate:
THE CREW CAME UP WITH
A GREAT IDEA.  THEY THINK
A BIT OF ENTERTAINMENT
MIGHT LIFT THEIR SPIRITS.

Scene 1, shot 6.

Captain:
THAT'S WONDERFUL!
WHAT'S THE BAD NEWS?

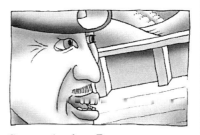

Scene 1, shot 7.

Mate:
THEY THOUGHT IT WOULD BE FUN
TO SEE IF YOU CAN SWIM FASTER
THAN THE SHIP.

Scene 1, shot 8.

Formats may be used in combination. For example, a program may have one brief animated sequence to be created by a computer graphics artist. That particular section of the program requiring animation may need to be storyboarded so that the artist has an exact series of sketches to follow. However, the rest of the script may not require storyboarding, and a two-column script may be used.

## THE SHOT SHEET

When the script is finished and approved, a summary of all the scenes and shots can be helpful. This is called a *shot sheet* or *shot list*. It is an organizing tool—a checklist. It alleviates the need to constantly thumb through the entire script to see if everything has been shot.

To create a shot sheet, go through the script and itemize each shot and scene in one summary list such as the following:

---

**SHOT LIST**

| Scene | Shot | Description |
|-------|------|-------------|
| 1 | 1 | Wide shot deck of ship, captain pacing |
| 1 | 2 | Wide shot of ship |
| 1 | 3 | Medium shot. First Mate enters. |
| 1 | 4 | Over the shoulder: First Mate |
| 1 | 5 | Over the shoulder: Captain |
| 1 | 6 | CU: Mate |
| 1 | 7 | CU: Captain |
| 1 | 8 | CU: Mate |

---

## SUMMARY

Any program begins with a concept. Then the concept needs to be developed. Early on, someone must decide whether the concept is practical for an actual production. Is it feasible? Can it be accomplished within a given budget and timeline?

The treatment aids the decision-making process by describing the idea and reasons to believe in its success. The script fleshes out that idea and adds all the audio and visual details. The shot sheet helps the production crew keep track of all the shots that need to be completed. As a director, you should be satisfied that the script and shot sheet are in good order before any shooting takes place.

---

### A REAL WORLD APPLICATION, CONTINUED:

After the lumber mill executives approved the proposal and signed a contract with the producer, a writer was hired to research and write the script. The writer, having written for TV before, knew the importance of checking in with the director early on in the process. The two spent time going over ideas, formats, how much information to convey, and how to make it all interesting.

The writer spent hours with company executives and employees going over the proper safety information. It was the director's idea to use actors in vignettes. The writer liked the idea.

The writer immediately began imagining both words and pictures that the script would have to describe. The script would need to include all dialogue, narration, music, sound effects, and visual descriptions.

The writer then continued fleshing out the treatment into a full script. The writer used the two-column format. Storyboards will be used only for an opening and closing animated logo treatment.

The producer and director looked over each draft and made helpful comments and notations. As the director got a clear idea of the content in the script, he was better able to look over the locations in the mill and imagine ways to shoot the required scenes.

---

When the script was finished and approved, the director took a copy and referred to it as he made a shot sheet. There would be a total of 125 shots in 15 scenes. The director began organizing the shots by location and day of shooting. Since it takes so much time to set up and take down each location, the director chooses to shoot out of sequence and get all shots done in each location before moving on. It will be much more efficient to shoot out of sequence. The shot sheet will become invaluable for keeping track of shots, especially since the scenes will likely be shot out of sequence according to location.

# 9

# The Site Survey

The following is a true story:

A few years ago, a major news network funded an independent writer/director who had written a documentary with global environmental themes. Shooting took place in exotic locations around the world. Two small production crews spent four months traveling to numerous countries, up and down mountains and into remote areas.

Onc of the locations was Cubatao, an industrial town near Rio de Janeiro. The director chose Cubatao because he wanted to show a place completely burned out by industrialization. Not only was the town supposed to be dirty and filthy, it was supposed to be a place devoid of life, so polluted that the streams and river banks were dead—no plant life, a quagmire of chemical poison.

Shipping TV equipment around the world was no small task. Cases and cases of equipment, customs declarations, insurance binders, and finding suitable rental vehicles made the entire process tedious.

The camera crew arrived in Cubatao before the director. Upon arrival, the crew members looked around and scratched their heads. Cubatao looked pretty normal. Third World, yes, but rather pleasant. Bull rushes, egrets, and herons flourished by the river. Plants grew everywhere. The town looked much like any other industrial town. This site did not fit the image of sterility and toxicity that the director had described.

The crew got on the phone. "This place isn't dead at all. It's quite alive and well," they reported. The writer/director answered back, "Well, that's not what Jacques Cousteau wrote in his book!"

After hours on airplanes, and the constant hassles of loading and unloading countless cases of TV production equipment, the production incurred quite an expense before learning that the location really wasn't what the director had hoped for.

The same writer/director on the same project had another surprise, this time in France. The crew arrived at the location of a famous French chateau, again, one that had been read about. Upon arrival, there was no chateau to be found. "Oh," exclaimed the villagers. "That chateau burned to the ground several years ago."

In each case, the writer/director took a risk by choosing a location based largely on something he had read or heard about. Unfortunately, a lot of time and money was wasted.

The solution to problems like this is called the *site survey*. Somebody needed to survey the site ahead of time. That might have meant flying someone to Cubatao or to the French countryside—certainly cheaper than sending all the crew and equipment. Or a still cheaper method would have been asking a local person to report back and send photos.

A more common situation for the news or corporate production is to survey an office where an interview will be taped. Don't be surprised if the office space that someone reserved for you is much too small to accommodate the lights and camera. Or the air conditioner is too loud and nobody knows how to turn it off. These roadblocks occur all the time.

Feature films and major television productions, in particular, have to conduct site surveys because so much money is on the line. Some people make a living doing nothing but scouting locations for large-scale TV and film productions. They'll look for locations that meet the director's wishes for given scenes. They'll take Polaroids to bring back and show the director. And they'll make recommendations as to whether the location presents any technical difficulties.

For smaller budget ENG/EFP shooting, you may not always have the luxury of doing a site survey. Or it may be impractical. A news team may not be able to go evaluate the location in which a robbery is about to take place. However, when possible, a site survey should be done. You can spare yourself a lot of wasted time and ensure a more successful shoot by surveying the sites first and asking:

- Is the location inside or outside?
- Does the location look and feel appropriate for the purpose at hand?
- Is there enough room to work?
- Does the location provide adequate electrical power?
- How much lighting is needed?
- Is it quiet enough to record audio?
- Are there any major distractions that would make shooting difficult?
- Do you have any control over the environment?

Go through your script and note the types of locations you need. Visit as many of them as possible. Consider whether there is any flexibility in the location. Does a certain scene absolutely have to be shot in a particular location? Or if you decide that the location has some serious disadvantages, can you go elsewhere?

Consider the aesthetics of the location: How well-suited is this environment for the intended scene? Does it look pleasing and appropriate?

Consider the logistics. Do you need permission to shoot at this location? Is it public property? Will it impede the flow of traffic? Do you need cooperation from local authorities such as a state film commission or city police department?

Let's outline some of the important things to look for when evaluating both an interior and exterior location.

## INTERIOR LOCATION

### 1) Evaluate the sound environment.

It is usually easier to control noise inside. The goal is to weed out as many unwanted sounds as possible—to create a pristine sound environment so that the only sound you hear is the sound you *want* to hear.

Once you are inside, typical outside noise such as traffic and wind should be out of hearing range. Noisier culprits such as airplanes and motorcycles may not be audible. Hopefully, you won't hear the irksome beep-beep-beep of a backing truck.

However, the indoor environment may present some noises to deal with: air conditioners, flickering fluorescent lights, and people talking on phones in neighboring rooms or offices. Despite the problems that might occur, in general it is easier to control noise once you are inside. You may want to shoot at night or on the weekend to avoid noise. For example, an episode of a popular police drama required use of an actual underground subway platform that was in normal operation every day. So the producers had to negotiate with the train authority to shoot during off hours. The crew shot several nights in a row from late at night until dawn while the subway system was closed for business.

### 2) Evaluate the amount of usable space in the room.

To do an interview, you need enough room for two people to sit face-to-face with ample space around them for the camera to get reverse angles. Avoid having either host or guest backed up against a wall. You want enough space between the back of the person and the wall to allow for adequate depth and to allow shadows from lights to fall off on the floor instead of on the wall.

### 3) Evaluate the aesthetic quality of the scene.

Does the background look acceptable from each angle? Keep in mind that you'll only see a small portion of the room in your field of view, so the whole room does not need to look good—just the section that you will see. A table may be a mess, but that table may be out of the picture. More importantly, is the background of the framed shot a mess? Is the background drab? Is it too contrasty? Too white? Too black? Can you make changes to the furniture and decor?

### 4) Evaluate lighting needs.

Just as with audio, it's easier to control lighting inside. Outside, the weather is hard to control. The day may be perfect at one moment, but it may also snow or rain, or be too bright or too dark. Large budget productions can employ huge lights and diffusion screens to compensate for conditions, but only to a point. Sometimes you are just plain out of luck. Working inside usually offers a better chance of controlling lighting.

One of the basic goals in lighting is to raise the level of light in the room to suit the camera's need. Cameras need plenty of light—more than the human eye needs. So if the room is huge and dark, you may need to bring in lots of lighting equipment. If it's small and bright or if you are only using a small area, you may not require much additional lighting.

Along with evaluating lighting needs is an evaluation of the color temperatures in the room. (The subject of color temperature, covered briefly here, will be covered again in the chapters on camera operations and lighting.)

Different light sources emphasize different colors in the spectrum. The camera sees these differences more readily than the human eye. For example sunlight has a lot of blue. Fluorescent light bulbs have a lot of green. Incandescent light bulbs look red.

The TV production crew can use filters and gels to make the various light sources as uniform as possible. Knowing that the room has a big window with lots of daylight pouring in is useful in the planning process. Or knowing that the room is lit chiefly by rows of fluorescent lights is good planning information as well.

If various light sources are present in the location, the crew will want to plan a way to homogenize them. (See "color temperature" discussions in chapters 11 and 12.)

**5) Evaluate electrical power sources.**

Lights and equipment need electricity. The question is: Does the location offer sufficient power? Or does an additional power source need to be brought in?

What amperage capacity are the circuits on location? The video camera and VTR draw very little power. But portable TV lights may draw anywhere from five to twenty-five amps, depending on how many you use and the wattage of your bulbs. Most newer homes have fifteen to twenty amp circuits. Two lights each drawing six amps could work off of one circuit without tripping the breaker.

But what if you need three or four lights? If you have too much wattage for one circuit, are there more circuits in the room? Or can you run an extension cord to a nearby room that's on another circuit?

If you happen to trip the breaker and all the power shuts off, do you know where to find the circuit breaker box to turn things on again? How would you reroute the wires to keep the problem from happening again?

The lights will most likely have three-prong plugs which include a ground wire. Does your room have three-prong grounded plugs? If not, you'll need adapter plugs. If there isn't sufficient electrical power, you may need to bring in a generator.

## EXTERIOR

Interiors may have some advantages for environmental control, but many shots will need to be shot outside. So next, let's consider an exterior location.

**1) Evaluate the sound environment.**

Stand in the space and listen. Is there too much traffic noise? Are there any other distracting sounds in the environment? If so, would moving somewhere nearby minimize the noise?

**2) Evaluate the space.**

Is it a reasonable place in which to do your shoot? Can you keep each subject at least several feet away from a wall or other background in order to create more depth?

### 3) Evaluate the aesthetic quality of the location.

What is the environment like? Is it an appropriate setting for the type of show you are directing? Does the setting look pleasing for your purposes?

### 4) Evaluate the lighting.

When you're outside, the overwhelming source of light is the sun. Portable TV lights are like dim candles compared to the brightness of the sun. So, your best bet is to work with the natural sunlight. A bright sunny blue-sky day is great for going to the beach. But it's not so great for shooting film or video because the bright sun creates high contrast ratios. A slight cloud cover diffuses the light nicely.

• Will the position of the sun at a particular time of day work well for you?
• Are you under trees or other objects that might throw unwanted shadows?
• Is the background too bright compared with your subject?
• Can you wait for a slight cloud cover to diffuse the sun and reduce contrast?
• Or can you shoot in early morning or late afternoon before the sun is throwing direct light so as to avoid harsh direct sunlight?
• If you need to shoot in harsh direct sun, can you get scrims or reflectors to help even out the shadows and bright spots?
• You may require large lights that are color balanced for sunlight.

### 5) Evaluate power sources.

Is there AC electrical power available? If not, can you bring enough battery power to complete your shooting? Do you need a generator for additional power?

## SUMMARY

When things get busy, it can seem like a bother to take the time for site surveys. If you skip the survey, the consequences may not be as severe as flying a crew to Cubatao. But even on small budget productions, the site survey is good for both practical and artistic reasons. You not only want to avoid wasting time and money, you also want a location that looks just right for your production.

## A REAL WORLD APPLICATION, CONTINUED:

As the director tours the lumber mill, he realizes that his production has some limitations when choosing locations. The director cannot simply choose any site in which to work. This production must take place in the mill. So whether the mill is a good place to shoot or not, he must work there. So, he will carefully evaluate the locations and do the best he can with what he is given.

The director tours the facility with company managers who can answer a lot of his logistical questions. They determine that shooting during the normal working day will be perfect for showing the mill in action. However, the noise during this period of time would be terrible for trying to conduct interviews. So they decide to schedule all interviews for a weekend when the heavy equipment is shut down.

The noise also presents a problem for shooting the vignettes with actors. They decide that a weekend would be best for the dramatic scenes as well.

The producer budgeted for a three-day shoot. The director proposes a three-day shooting plan:
Day 1 - Friday - All shots of equipment in action and people working.
Day 2 - Saturday - All interviews in the morning. Rehearse and begin to shoot dramatic vignettes in the afternoon.
Day 3 - Sunday - Shoot all dramatic vignettes.

During the facility tour, the director keeps an eye out for lighting needs. Many areas of the mill are dark or full of shadows. Lights will be brought in. The mill uses big equipment, so there is plenty of electricity to run the lights. The director asks the company electrician about the circuits around the mill. Most are at least 20 amp circuits. Since most of the lights to be brought in use 600 watt bulbs, they should be able to plug in about two lights per circuit. The 1000 watt bulbs may need to each have their own circuit. The director and the electrician locate the main breaker boxes so they know where to go in case a fuse blows.

Some areas of the mill are particularly displeasing to the eye. The director does anything to avoid shooting in these spots. Other areas are newer and cleaner. He notes which areas these are and tries to use them for the interviews and dramatic vignettes. He realizes that a mill is not necessarily a pretty place. His main concern is that there be no unnecessary distractions such as clutter, or an ugly or dingy background. During the site survey, the director refers to his copy of the script in progress. He notes which locations would best suit each scene.

# 10

# Equipment and Crew

**D**uring the production phase, the director relies on a crew of technical support staff, performers, and a supply of equipment. In this chapter, we'll consider what and whom to choose for the shoot.

From a planning standpoint, people and equipment naturally go together. For example, you need a camera and someone to operate it. You need lights and someone to set and focus them. Audio equipment and someone who knows how to use it. On smaller productions, one person may wear several hats—the camera operator may also do lighting, or the director may run the camera. The larger the shoot, the more specialized the crew positions become.

News crews—ENG teams—consist of only one to three people. The smallest crew is a one-person configuration—a camera person goes solo to capture footage for a news story. He or she carries a camera, tripod, and audio gear to record sound and pictures. A two-person crew may include a reporter to do a stand-up report in front of the camera. In this case, lighting may be needed for the reporter's on-camera *stand-ups*. Now one person acts as director, camera, audio, and lighting. In a three-person news crew, the additional crew member may help with audio and lighting.

Figure 10.1 shows a basic field production equipment package including camera, tripod, headphones, video monitor, batteries or plug-in power source, and lighting. Although a news crew may pack only the minimum gear for quick mobility, the following pages will list additional equipment that any ENG or EFP crew might use.

(10.1) Basic EFP equipment:

- Lights and stands
- Camera/VTR with tripod
- Microphone (on camera)
- Headphones
- Videotape cassette
- Video monitor
- AC power supply or battery

(10.2) 1-person ENG crew—director/camera.

(10.3) Add reporter.

(10.4) Add audio engineer.

## CAMERA EQUIPMENT

**Camera** - You're probably familiar with the consumer video camcorder in which the *camera* and the ***videotape recorder (VTR)*** are combined in one unit. But in the world of industrial and broadcast video equipment, the camera and the VTR are regarded as two separate pieces of equipment, whether or not they are physically attached.

In some cases, the camera stands alone and is linked to the videotape recorder by a video cable. In other cases, the VTR is mounted on the back of the camera. It may be detachable and interchangeable with other VTRs. One might put a BetaCam VTR on the back of a camera. Someone else might detach that VTR and replace it with a different format VTR such as Hi-8 or DVCam.

Cameras come in many levels of quality. The cheaper cameras have only one chip or tube instead of three, produce mediocre resolution and more video noise, and they don't handle contrast or poorly lit situations very well.

Higher quality cameras have a set of three light sensitive chips or tubes, one for each of three primary colors. Higher quality cameras make crisper and cleaner pictures, handle higher contrast ratios, and do well in poorly lit scenes. TV news crews, in particular, depend on high-quality cameras to perform better in less-than-perfect conditions. News crews don't always have time to light a scene evenly to reduce contrast. They must be ready to roll in nighttime situations, dark alleys, basements, and any number of other dark or contrasty situations.

Cameras, like VTRs, originally processed the video signal in an analog method. Throughout the late 1990s, digital processing cameras appeared on the market. Sony Corporation, for example, has both digital and analog cameras in its high-end broadcast offering. VTRs also come in analog or digital formats. Although digital cameras do not necessarily produce better looking pictures than analog cameras, they offer many more menu settings for special features that can be stored and recalled such as: hue settings, black levels, and color temperature settings.

**Lens** - On broadcast and industrial grade cameras, the *lens* can be chosen separately from the camera. You might choose a lens that's a wider angle or one that's more telephoto. Consumer grade lenses often have automatic focus features. However, a professional camera operator will want to control his or her own focusing rather than relying on the sometimes unpredictable nature of an auto focus feature. Similarly, the iris may have an automatic setting feature. Again, the operator will want other means to confirm a proper exposure such as a waveform monitor or a light meter. (These will be discussed in chapter 11.)

**Filters** - *Filters* are pieces of glass or plastic placed in the path of the lens, either behind it or in front of it. Filters alter the light, either by adding color or by adding a special effect such as a "soft" look for romantic scenes.

**Monitor** - Since the picture in the camera's viewfinder is small and black and white, a separate TV *monitor* on location allows you to see right away how your shot looks in color. By definition, a monitor does not pick up TV stations on the air. It has no tuner. It only accepts a video signal from the camera or tape player.

**VTR** - VTR stands for *video tape recorder.* Are you shooting VHS? 3/4-inch? Hi-8? Digital BetaCam? It's not the camera that determines the format, it's the VTR. The format is determined by the type of tape or disc that records the signal. Most VTRs can be rented separately from the camera. Put together the lens, camera, and VTR package that suits you.

**Tripod -** The *tripod* allows the camera operator to mount the camera on a stable base to make steady shots and smooth moves. Unless you have some other way of steadying the camera, without a tripod you run the risk of shaky camera shots. Hand-held or shoulder held shots are only for special occasions—the necessity of running after a news story, or the desire to achieve a purposely shaky effect. Typically, though, the stability that comes with tripod-based shots is necessary for a professional look.

The tripod creates a stationary base from which to execute camera moves: pans, tilts, and zooms. In order to do moving shots, you need wheels for the tripod. Wheels allow you to perform *dollies* (forward and backward), *trucks* (side to side), and *arcs* (moves that maintain a constant radius around a subject).

Tripods consist of two parts: the **head** and the **legs**. (Legs are also referred to as "sticks.") The legs are the three telescoping extensions that extend and spread out to form a base of support. Some legs are lightweight aluminum for ease in transport. Some are made of wood. Others are heavy metal, providing a solid unmovable base of support for a camera.

The tripod head attaches to the legs and supports the camera. The head offers the pan and tilt mechanisms. The mark of a good tripod head is the smoothness with which it allows the operator to perform pans and tilts. Smooth moves require some resistance from the head as the operator pushes the control arm left, right, up, or down to execute a move. This resistance is called **drag**. As you push the tripod handle one way or the other, the drag creates a steady smooth move. Cheaper heads have spring loaded mechanisms to offer such resistance. The best heads use a viscous oil-like fluid inside them which offers a smooth resistance as moves are executed.

It's important to choose a tripod that is strong enough for your camera. A heavy broadcast camcorder needs a heavy-duty tripod or $50,000 worth of camera may topple.

**4) Power source -** The VTR and camera need power. If you want to move around, then batteries are the way to go. The main drawback is that batteries have a limited use before requiring a recharge. Make sure you have enough batteries. Also, make sure that your batteries are fully charged before going out.

Plugging into the wall socket that supplies **AC power** has one big advantage—you won't run out of electricity. However, there's one big disadvantage—you're tethered to the wall. Consider which is better for your shoot: batteries or AC power.

## AUDIO EQUIPMENT

**Audio** is processed simultaneously but independently of the video. Audio has its own circuitry within the VTR and is recorded on its own tracks on the videotape.

The audio process begins with the **microphone**, or "mic" for short. It's a good idea to have at least one mic available at all times. Even if you are just shooting outdoor scenic shots and the sound doesn't seem very important, record the natural outdoor sounds anyway. They will make the picture seem more realistic, more alive. Shots of trees, for example, come across better with the accompanying sound of wind in the leaves.

Many cameras have built-in microphones. These are extremely limiting since they cannot be placed close to the subject. If you're interviewing people, for example, you will want to get a remote mic on a cable in order to place it closer to the subject. Choose the type of mic, the number of mics, and the necessary cable length to run from the camera/VTR to the subject.

**Mixer** - If you use more than one mic, you may need an ***audio mixer*** to funnel the various mics into one input on the VTR. A mixer will accept several audio inputs, allow the user to set individual volume levels for each source, and mix them into one output.

**Headphones** - Don't forget headphones. Without them, you have no way to monitor your audio. You can buy hundred-dollar headphones, or just use the ones from your Walkman.

**Lavaliere mic** - A *lavaliere* is a tie-tack or clip-on mic.

**Shotgun mic** - A ***shotgun mic*** is a highly directional mic in a long tubular casing.

**Fishpole** - A *fishpole* is a telescoping pole with an attachment on one end for a microphone. The fishpole is used to reach a mic out over a scene, close to the subject, but out of the camera's view.

**Mic cables** - Microphone cables connect to the mic on one end and to the VTR on the other. When a mic is wired to the the VTR, it is called a ***hard wire*** mic.

**Wireless mic** - When the mic uses a transmitter and receiver instead of cables, it is called a ***wireless*** mic.

**Windscreen** - A ***windscreen*** protects the mic from wind noise.
(Read more on audio in chapter 13.)

## LIGHTING EQUIPMENT

If you're shooting inside, you'll want lights wherever possible. A room looks better on camera when the illumination is raised above the normal level.

Also, the TV lights are balanced for your camera's tungsten setting to produce a more realistic color than the variety of lights you'd find in natural settings which may include: incandescent, tungsten, fluorescent, mercury vapor, etc. TV lights provide consistency and brightness, both of which help the camera produce good pictures. Your light kit should include: lighting instruments, bulbs, stands, clamps, gels, scrims, sandbags, flags, and gels.

**Lighting instrument** - The actual unit that houses the bulb is called the *lighting instrument*.

**Bulbs** - *Bulbs* go in the instruments. They are categorized by wattage and color temperature. Bulbs break. Bring extras.

**Stands** - Lighting instruments may be mounted on tripod-based *stands* that are easily portable. For added safety, a *C-stand* is a commonly used heavy-duty all-purpose stand with three legs that fold out to form a wide, stable base.

**Clamps** - *Clamps* are used to hang lighting instruments or to hold pieces of hardware together.

**Gels** - *Gels* are placed over lights to alter color or create effects.

**Scrims** - *Scrims* are placed over lights to diffuse them.

**Sandbags** - *Sandbags* are for safety, placed on the bases of top-heavy light stands.

**Flags** - *Flags* are flat opaque cards made of cloth or metal, placed near lighting instruments to block the throw of light to unwanted areas such as background walls. (See more on lighting chapter 12.)

## ELECTRICAL EQUIPMENT

**Generator** - A *generator* is a gasoline-powered machine brought to the location to create additional electricity. It may be needed when many high-wattage lights are being used that surpass the capacity of the regular wall sockets at the location. Generators are also needed out in the countryside or at the beach where there may be no power source.

**Wiring** - Almost all TV equipment needs to be plugged into power. Batteries may help alleviate this need. Nonetheless, bring extension cables. You may need hundreds of feet of power cords just to plug in your lights to various separate circuits around the vicinity of your shoot.

**Batteries** - *Batteries* allow for portability. Almost any TV equipment—even lights—can be run off batteries. Get to know your type of battery. Some have specific requirements for charging and recharging.

## GRIP SUPPLIES

**Grip truck** - A *grip* is a person who handles hardware which includes lighting, electrical supplies, and dolly equipment. A grip often provides a *grip truck* which is fully outfitted with lighting hardware and electrical supplies.

**Dolly and track** - A camera move toward or away from a subject is called a dolly. So is the piece of equipment used to create the move. A *dolly* is a cart on wheels that rolls along a smooth floor or along a track. The dolly allows the operator to create a smooth moving shot such as a truck left or right or a dolly in or out.

**Mounts** - Sometimes a tripod is not practical. Special camera mounts may be used for cars, planes, boats, and helicopters. These often employ gyroscopic mechanisms to help smooth out the movement of the vehicle.

**SteadiCam** - A *SteadiCam* is a trademark of Cinema Products company for a shoulder-mounted spring-loaded mechanism that smooths out the shaky camera motion caused by running with a camera in hand. SteadiCams do not offer the same steadiness of a tripod or dolly. They are best used for fast-paced action when the movement in the scene distracts from the slight movement by the operator.

## TAPE STOCK

**Field tapes** - You might forget your American Express, but don't forget to bring along *videotape* to put in the VTR. Nothing is more embarrassing than arriving on location without sufficient tape supply. The videotape shot in the field is commonly referred to by any of the following: *field tape*, *source tape*, *original footage*, or *raw footage*.

**Mastering tapes** - The mastering tape or *edit master* is the new videotape on which the show will be constructed in the editing phase. Shots from the field tapes are transferred to the master tape during the editing process.

Many students shoot on the VHS, S-VHS, or Hi-8 formats which come in long or short lengths. Consider the advantage of buying several short tapes rather than a single long tape. Doing so saves you a lot of time shuttling through many scenes to find the shots you want. You might put all of location number one on Tape 1 and all of interview number one on Tape 2.

This completes the basic equipment list for a single-camera field production. You won't necessarily need everything on the list, but you can use it for planning. Any of these items can be rented by the day. Cities across the country have companies that rent and sell TV and film equipment. Expensive specialty gear may not be worth owning. It depends on how often you use it. Items such as a helicopter camera mount or a fog machine are best rented if used rarely. Whether you rent or own, part of the pre-production process is to plan and schedule equipment.

## PERSONNEL

Now that we have examined equipment needs, let us consider the range of crew and performers that could be required on the shoot. Any of these people may be hired on a freelance basis by the day or per project.

## CREW

**Producer** - *Producers* perform both creative and administrative functions. They oversee productions and hold ultimate authority.

**Director** - A *director* is responsible for the creative and technical execution of the production.

**Assistant director** - An *assistant director* does as much footwork and logistical preparation as possible in order to allow the director to concentrate on the content of the production.

**Production assistant** - A *production assistant* takes care of errands and details for the producer or director.

**Writer** - The *writer* writes the script. The writer may be the creative visionary who actually originates the idea. Or the writer may simply perform a function—fleshing out someone else's idea or adapting existing material for the TV medium.

**Camera operator** - The *camera operator* runs the camera. In more complex shoots, a *director of photography (DP)*, may be separate from the actual camera operator. The DP is in charge of camera operations, but spends a lot of time planning and strategizing. The operator actually shoots the footage.

**Audio engineer** - The *audio engineer* is in charge of selecting and placing mics, and monitoring audio during production to ensure good quality.

**Lighting director** - A *lighting director* is in charge of designing the lighting. In a smaller production, he or she may actually hang and focus the lights. In a larger production, grips and gaffers will do the work instead.

**Grip** - A *grip* handles hardware—light stands, set pieces, dolly and track, etc.

**Gaffer** - A *gaffer* handles electrical needs: lights, wiring, generators.

**Make-up** - The *make-up person* applies make-up to the on-camera talent.

**Editor** - The *editor* pieces the show together after the scenes are shot. In some cases, the editor has a lot of artistic leeway with the selection of shots. In other cases, the director plays a strong role in the editing process and gives direct instruction to the editor. In such cases, the editor is primarily performing a technical service for the director.

**Composer** - Original music may be scored for the production. The *composer* may both write and arrange music specifically for the program.

**Graphic artist** - If special graphics or animation are required, a *graphic artist* may be employed to produce graphics or animation using a computer and program that creates art in the video environment.

So, how does a director find and hire these crew people? Some of them may work on the staff of production companies and TV stations. But many crew people are freelancers. They hire on for particular productions and then move on to new projects afterward. They get paid by the day or by the project, and they may or may not come with their own equipment.

For example, an audio person may come with an equipment package including a selection of microphones, fishpoles, and headsets. A camera operator may come with his or her own camera. But in many other cases, the person comes armed only with skills and the production team provides the equipment.

Next, let's look at the various classifications of performing talent, the people who speak, act, or in appear in your production. These people are referred to as *talent*, *actors*, or *performers*.

## PERFORMERS / TALENT

**Spokesperson** - A *spokesperson* is one of several performing classifications. The spokesperson is an on-camera host.

**Actor** - Another performance classification is *actor*, also called *day-player*. This person learns and delivers lines as a dramatic character.

**Model** - A *model* does not speak but simply appears on camera.

**Extra** - *Extras* are actors who fill in the background but have no significant role: audience, crowd, soldiers marching, customers shopping. Extras are further classified into those who have speaking parts and those who do not speak.

**Narrator** - A *narrator* provides a voice for the sound track. The narrator is only heard. Once he or she is seen on camera, they become a spokesperson.

## TALENT AUDITIONING AND HIRING

If a director is already familiar with a performer, he may choose that person immediately and bypass the audition process. However, it is typical for a director to hold auditions in which a variety of interested people show up at scheduled appointments to show themselves and recite samples of the script. This allows the director to decide which people will work best in the show. Based on the auditions, performers are hired.

Performers may choose to be represented by talent agencies or personal agents. An agency or agent will handle all the business details on behalf of the performer, from arranging the audition to negotiating the employment contract. For this service, the agent takes a percentage of the performer's wage, usually 10-15%. That means the director is more likely to deal with the agent than the performer for all business matters. The director deals with the performer only on matters of the performance itself. Thus, when a director first wants to find performers, he or she can contact talent agencies. This is very convenient for the director because the agency provides a selection of people to choose from, a meeting place to hold auditions if desired, and an efficient manner in which to handle all the contractual details.

Other ways to find performers include:
• Family members
• Friends

• Fellow students
• Local theater groups

Performers may belong to talent unions—The Screen Actors Guild (SAG) or the American Federation of Television and Radio Artists (AFTRA). Producers should expect to pay additional percentages when using union talent. AFTRA, for example, adds a 13.5% fee for its pension fund.

Talent may also include those who must appear in the program because of their connection to the subject matter. Perhaps the company president must address the employees in a video. Perhaps employees will be featured in on-camera interviews or discussions.

It's very common to work with non-TV-professionals when doing any kind of training, educational program for a business, or any news or documentary program. These people are not trained actors or performers, yet they must come off well in the video. It is a challenge for the director to make sure these non-TV-professionals look as good as possible on camera. They may require coaching and rehearsing. Your job is not to change them into actors, but to assess their abilities and establish realistic performance expectations in your own mind. Give the rookie performer some helpful tips, but not so much as to overwhelm them. (See more on directing talent in chapter 16.)

---

**A REAL WORLD APPLICATION, CONTINUED:**

Meanwhile, back at the director's office, plans are being made. The director has drawn up an equipment list. His assistant director checks the TV production company inventory to see which items are available and which need to be rented from a local rental company:

• Camera: Sony 400A camera with a BETA SP back. This Sony camera has a "clear scan" feature which allows the operator to dial in the frequency of any computer monitor, thus avoiding flicker or picture roll.
• Lens: Canon 8X6 zoom lens
• Tripod head: Sachtler Video 18
• Sticks: Sachtler

- Dolly: Doorway dolly with 20 feet of track, 2 curves, 4 straight sections
- Lighting: 2 Lowell DP light kits with 1000 watt bulbs, stands, barn doors
- 1 Lowell Omni light kit with 600 watt bulbs, stands, barn doors
- Color correction blue gels # 85A
- Diffusion sheets, flags, gels, and scrims
- 2 IDX "Endura" Lithium-Ion batteries for camera/VTR
- Battery charger
- 50 foot lengths of AC power cable
- Audio: 1 shotgun mic and fishpole
- 2 lavaliere mics
- Headphones
- Grip supplies: sand bags
- 13" color monitor
- Utility cart

Next the director puts together a crew list. He chooses people he has worked with before:

- Camera operator
- Lighting assistant
- Audio assistant
- Grip
- Gaffer
- Production assistant
- Make-up artist

Finally, the director puts together a talent list:

- Host
- Company president
- Miscellaneous interviews with company employees
- Actors: 3 female, 3 male

The director has no choice but to use the company president. He doesn't know yet how well the man will come across on camera. The director is a little bit nervous about that but prepared to coach him.

However, the director does participate in the selection of employees to interview. He looks for those who speak well and look comfortable and pleasant on camera. He also looks for ethnic and gender diversity to appeal to a potentially diverse audience.

When it's time to choose actors, the director calls up an agent with a  local talent agency. He describes the characters of the three male and three female actors needed. He wants to have ethnic diversity among the actors. The agent schedules an audition and calls a variety of actors to come in for an appearance. One by one, the actors introduce themselves and read lines from the script.

When the director is finished watching all the actors, he makes some notes and gives his preferences to the agent. The agent contacts the actors, checks their availability for the shooting dates, and confirms with the director. A contract is drawn up between the TV company and the talent agency.

# Section IV

Chapters 11 through 17 cover the steps in the production process. We'll cover the hardware required for production—cameras, microphones, lights, etc.—and principles to guide the use of this equipment. More importantly, the following chapters will offer you, the director, an understanding of the production process.

# 11

# The Video Camera And Recorder

The *camera* and the *videotape recorder (VTR)* are two separate pieces of equipment that function together to record images. The camera produces the image and sends it to the VTR for recording. A camera and VTR may be found in various configurations. A camera/VTR permanently molded into a single unit is called a ***one-piece*** configuration. Attached but separable is called ***dockable***. And physically separate and linked by cables is called a ***two-piece*** configuration.

Let's explore the technical make-up and operation of the camera and VTR. Later in this chapter, we'll look at types of shots and camera moves.

People often use the terms "film" and "video" interchangeably. It's true that the two media have some major similarities: they both create motion pictures through the process of recording individual frames. But the two types of cameras differ technically in the way they operate, record, and store images. Let's compare the two.

Starting at the front of each camera, the lens is the only piece of hardware common to both film and video. Past the lens, the processes are completely different. Video is an electronic process that records electronic signals onto magnetic tape. Film uses a photographic process that records light variations onto a chemical film.

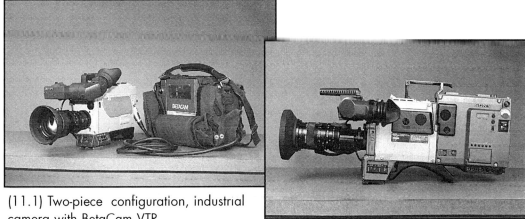

(11.1) Two-piece configuration, industrial camera with BetaCam VTR.

(11.2) One-piece detachable camcorder, broadcast camera with BetaCam VTR.

(11.3) Cutaway view of video camera shows rows of circuit boards.

(11.4) Cutaway view of film camera shows a reel of film passing behind the lens.

Opening the side of a motion picture film camera reveals a reel of film, a take-up reel, and a motor to drive them. Film passes behind the lens where a shutter opens and closes twenty-four times a second to expose photographic frames. On the other hand, opening the side of a video camera reveals rows of electronic circuit boards. An image is focused on the surfaces of light-sensitive tubes or chips and converted to electronic impulses. The rest of the process is electronic. Some cameras process the signal using analog technology. Many newer cameras process the signal using digital technology.

## CAMERA OPERATING POWER

Since the video camera is electronic, it needs electricity to create a picture. Camera and VTR equipment runs on *direct current (DC)*. Batteries produce DC.

Instead of running on batteries, camera/VTR equipment can be plugged into the household wall socket which delivers *alternating current (AC)*. In fact, the camera is still running on DC even when plugged into the wall because AC power from the wall socket is converted to DC in the camera's *power supply unit*, located either within the camera or on the power cord.

Batteries are preferable over AC power because they allow for mobility. But attention is required. Be aware of how much battery life you have. It's very disappointing to drive miles and miles to a location, only to find that your batteries won't provide enough running time to complete shooting.

Camera batteries are designed to be recharged. Rechargeable batteries often have requirements in order to preserve their life span. For example, some need to be drained all the way before being recharged. Be aware of any special characteristics of the type of batteries and charging system that you are using. Improper use can quickly reduce the life of the battery. A battery designed to last for an hour may only last for 10 minutes if improperly used. Consider turning off the camera between scenes. Some cameras have a "standby" power setting that preserves battery life by shutting down the spinning tape heads while leaving all menu settings intact.

## THE LENS

The lens focuses an image on the camera's focal plane. In the eye, the focal plane is the retina. In the film camera, the focal plane is the film. In the video camera, it's a prism which in turn splits the image into three primary colors and directs each of the three color-separated images to three light sensitive pick-up tubes or three light sensitive computer chips called charge coupled devices (CCDs). (See figure 3.3.)

(11.5) Parts of the lens:
1) Focus ring
2) Aperture/f-stop ring
3) Motorized zoom control

The *lens* with a zoom feature allows you to adjust three parameters:
1) focus,
2) aperture, and
3) field of view.

The focus ring on the lens has a distance scale printed on it. Determine focus either with your eye, or by dialing the proper number on the scale printed on the focus ring. If you dial in 13 feet, then when your subject is thirteen feet away, the subject should be in focus. Most of the time, you will use your eye to verify focus, but occasionally, you may need to anticipate where to focus, which will require you to measure the distance from focal plane to focal point.

Many cameras have an *auto focus* feature. It's best to manually override both auto features because they may react and change at inopportune moments.

## FOCUSING

When zooming in, depth of field diminishes. Focus becomes more critical. Your image may have appeared to be in focus when the field of view was wide, but now that you zoom in, you discover, to your dismay, that the focal point was behind or in front of your subject. Your subject goes soft as you zoom in and something behind your subject comes into focus.

To avoid this problem, you must pre-focus before recording. In other words, every shot requires a moment of preparation. Zoom all the way in to your subject. Set focus. Zoom back out to whatever field of view you desire. Now, you can be sure where your focal point is. As long as you and your subject remain the same distance apart, you can zoom without fear of losing focus.

## IRIS / APERTURE

The terms *iris* and *aperture* are synonymous. They refer to the variable size hole in the lens through which light must pass. The iris can be opened and closed manually by using a dial on the lens. The camera's iris is similar to the iris in the human eye. In darker conditions, it should open to let in more light; in brighter conditions, it should close to reduce the brightness. Closing the iris does not affect the image size. It only affects the light level. A properly set iris should yield a properly exposed image—not too dark and not too bright.

Most cameras have an *auto iris* feature. It works via a light meter in the camera that averages the brightness of the scene and tells the iris what size hole will let in the right amount of light to create a good exposure. An auto iris opens and closes the aperture automatically. With the auto feature turned off, the operator must select an aperture setting by hand. This is often the preferred method since the auto feature may fluctuate abruptly while shooting. Most professionals use the auto iris to aid in establishing a good *exposure* while setting up the shot, then turn off the feature and stay in manual mode while shooting.

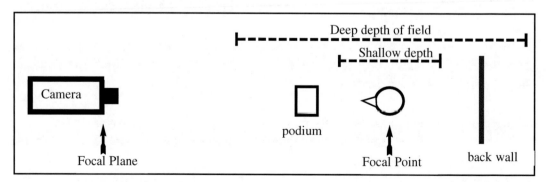

(11.6) Depth of field—the distance in front of and behind the focal point that remains in focus. The shallow depth of field does not include the podium or the curtain behind the speaker. These will look slightly soft.

A bad exposure means that parts of your picture are too dark or too bright and details in the picture are lost to **over exposure** or **under exposure**. Unfortunately, it's hard to see a good exposure just by looking in the viewfinder. You need an objective form of measure such as a light meter. The auto iris in the camera can help. But remember, the auto iris is only an average of bright and dark parts of the scene. You may have to manually override and compensate for parts of the picture that are bright or dark. Open the iris to add more detail to a dark scene. Close the iris a little to bring out detail in bright scenes.

The iris also has an impact on **depth of field**. As you close the iris, the depth of field increases. As you open up, the depth diminishes. This defies intuition, but you'll see the truth of it readily when you play with the camera.

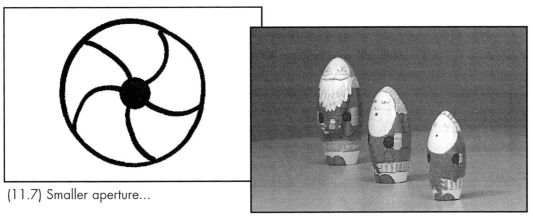

(11.7) Smaller aperture...

(11.8) ...greater depth of field.

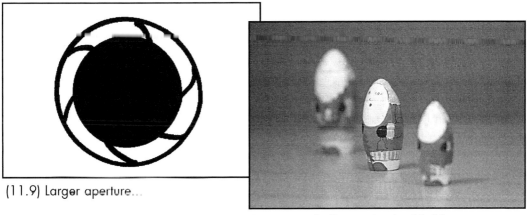

(11.9) Larger aperture...

(11.10) ...shallower depth of field.

If you are near-sighted, you can easily experience the aperture's power. Simply remove your glasses and create a tiny hole by touching three or four fingertips together. Look through the hole. The world looks clearer. You've created a greater depth of field and better focus for your eyes by passing the light through a small aperture.

Aperture settings are measured using the term *f-stop*. The smaller the f-stop number, the larger the aperture. The f-stop number scale varies a bit from lens to lens, but the general range is f-2 for wide open to f-16 for closed down to the smallest opening. Figures 11.7 and 11.8 show a high f-stop, small aperture, and a deep depth of field. Figures 11.9 and 11.10 show a low f-stop, a large aperture, and a shallower depth of field.

## COLOR TEMPERATURE AND WHITE BALANCE

Our brains always know what color things should be. But a video camera must be adjusted for proper color reproduction. Film cameras have a similar need. You must select the proper film stock for the proper color temperature. Or you can place color correction filters over the lens. Otherwise the image will look too red or too blue.

A video camera must be calibrated for the type of light used. Daylight, for example, has a different color temperature than light bulbs. The camera isn't smart enough to adjust on its own. (Also see chapter 12.)

White light is made up of all the colors of the visible light spectrum. One might expect each light source to emit a perfect white light. But none do. Each light source has its own unique mix of colors, such that light from the sun has more blue in it, incandescent light bulbs have more red, and fluorescent lights have more green.

The human brain does a remarkable job of compensating for these color variations. When you look at a piece of white paper under the sunlight, your brain reads it as white, even though it is tinted blue. And when you hold that same paper under indoor incandescent light bulbs, your brain still tells you it's white, even though it's tinted red. If you stand near the window and flip the paper back and forth under each light source, you should notice the difference—the hue on the paper changes slightly. To the camera, the change is much more pronounced. If you don't cater to the camera's needs, you may get strange coloring.

## KELVIN TEMPERATURE

Light sources are categorized according to their respective *color temperatures*. An Irish physicist named William Thompson Kelvin devised a temperature scale used for scientific applications. We don't see this scale used much today, but it is still used in fields such as theater, film, and photography to refer to the color temperatures of light sources.

We use the Kelvin scale to rate the differences in color among light sources. In these cases, we don't consider the actual hot or cold sensation of the light. Instead, the temperature rating refers to the color of the light waves emitted by the light source. Any light source can be associated with a number of *degrees Kelvin*. For example, sunlight is about 5600 degrees Kelvin. *Tungsten* light bulbs are typically rated at 3200 degrees Kelvin. *Incandescent* household light bulbs are about 2800 degrees Kelvin.

The video camera needs to be corrected for each new color temperature. As you move from location to location, you must recalibrate the camera for the new lighting conditions. Uncorrected, moving from indoor light to sunlight will produce a blue cast over the image. Moving from sunlight to indoor light will produce a red cast. There are a few ways to calibrate a camera for proper color balance:

1) Put color correction filters over the front of the lens to adjust the color of the incoming light.

2) The camera may have a filter wheel placed just behind the lens offering a convenient selection of internal filters for indoor and outdoor light.

3) The camera may have a *white balance* button for ease in calibration. Simply aim the camera at a piece of white paper under the light source you will be using. Fill the screen with this white image. Then engage the white balance switch. In a moment or two, the camera will calibrate for white under these lighting conditions. Remember to recalibrate if you change light sources.

4) Some newer cameras have auto white balance features that sense whether the camera is in the bluer sunlight or the redder indoor light and compensate accordingly. It may take a few seconds for the camera to sense and adjust to each new setting

(11.11) Camera operator monitors through viewfinder. He sees a black & white image.

(11.12) Camera operator uses external monitor, allowing him to see color and verify good color temperature calibration.

## MONITORING VIDEO

The easiest way to monitor your shot is by looking through the camera's viewfinder. But most viewfinders are black and white and tiny. So, in addition to the viewfinder, you can monitor your scene on a larger screen. If your camera has a *video out* port, a video cable may be used to link the camera to a color TV monitor. You can verify that your color temperature balance is proper simply by viewing the monitor. If you don't have the ability to monitor video, or if it is impractical because you are on location or moving around a lot, then you must rely on the black and white image in your viewfinder and trust that your color balance is proper.

Be aware that what you see in your viewfinder is not necessarily proof that the signal is being properly recorded on tape. The picture created by the camera goes off in two different directions. One signal goes to the tape and the other goes to the viewfinder. It's possible for the viewfinder to see a clear image while the signal going to the tape gets distorted due to problems with the recording mechanism. Therefore, the only way you know for sure whether you are recording a good image is to play back the tape after you have finished recording.

It's a great idea to do a quick test record and playback to confirm that the equipment works before taking it out in the field for your actual shoot.

## VIDEOTAPE RECORDERS

*Videotape recorders* (*VTRs*) record the images that cameras create. At the professional level, cameras and VTRs are often separate units. You can choose which camera to link with which VTR. In some cases, the VTR is linked by a cable. In other cases, the VTR is directly docked to the back of the camera. The VTR determines the format you are shooting. BetaCam, Hi-8, VHS, and DV are all tape formats, regardless of the type of camera to which they are linked. Some VTRs record analog signals onto the tape, others record digitally. Remember, a camera may produce a digital signal, but it may be recorded using an analog VTR and is, then, no longer digital.

## VTR RECORD SWITCH

When ready to record, the operator starts the tape deck by pressing a VTR switch. The switch or button is found on the VTR. An alternate remote switch is often found on the camera near the lens controls. The camera's viewfinder displays a light indicating that the VTR has been activated and tape is rolling. VTR decks are made to run very quietly so as not to disturb audio recording. Sometimes they are so quiet, you can forget whether or not you turned them on. It is not uncommon for a camera operator to shoot an entire scene and then realize that the tape was not rolling.

## VTR PRE-ROLL

After shooting, the footage goes to the editing room. At that point you will discover that videotape editing machines in the editing room need at least five seconds of *pre-roll* time prior to any edit. In other words, the tape machine will roll back five seconds prior to the desired beginning point. Then, the machine rolls forward in order to get a running start at the projected edit location. In order for the pre-roll to work, there must be a continuous video signal on tape for the machine to stabilize the playback signal. So, when shooting, it's smart to start recording for five to ten seconds before the actual scene begins. For example, if the actor is about to walk in the door, roll tape, count slowly to five, then call for action.

## CONTROL TRACK

Whenever a VTR records a signal, it automatically creates an electronic pulse called *control track*. This pulse serves to regulate the precision speed of the VTR. You may have experienced inconsistency in tape speed when you play audio tapes in various machines. The voice on the tape is noticeably higher or lower, faster or slower from

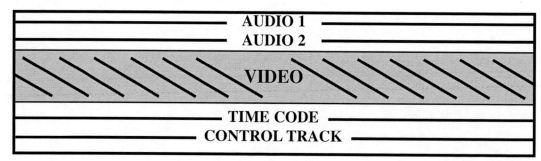

(11.13) A section of videotape showing separate tracks. Notice the diagonal lines on the video track. This "helical" method of scanning is used on both analog and digital videotape formats. The diagonal scan is achieved by orienting the tape path diagonally to the spinning drum containing the video heads. Helical scanning increases relative head-to-tape speed, hence more information per inch of tape.

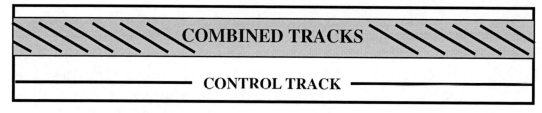

(11.14) Some video formats combine video, audio, and time code in one track.

machine to machine. In VTRs this variance is unacceptable. The control track assures consistent speed.

When control track is present, the digital timer display on the VTR advances the clock time as the tape plays or records. In other words, the computer displays a running clock time. If the numbers do not appear when playing a tape, that may mean there is no control track on the tape. Editing systems rely on consistent control track.

**TIME CODE**

Time code is an optional feature on VTRs. Most professional models use *time code*. It is an encoded clock time that occupies another track on the tape. Both control track and time code advance a clock time read out. However, control track displays numbers which are arbitrary and can be reset like a stopwatch. Thus, they are imprecise for logging scene locations on tape. Time code, on the other hand, offers a precise time reference encoded on the tape. A location that is noted as 02:30:23:04 will always be at that position on the tape for future reference.

Since time code locations are accurate right down to the frame, computer controllers use time code as a means to communicate with equipment. A computer editor, for example, marks in-points, out-points, dissolve rates, etc., by means of time code numbers. These numbers are the only way to log precise editing decisions.

In summary, control track must be present with any video signal and indicates its presence by a stable picture and an advancing clock time readout. Time code is an optional feature that offers an embedded clock time signal on another track for use in referencing locations throughout the tape. For more information on time code, see chapter 4.

## NEW VIDEOTAPE

A new videotape cassette, just out of the wrapper, has no recorded signal on it. There is no control track and no image. The absence of a video signal will be seen on the monitor as electronic snow. The digital clock time numbers will not advance when the new unrecorded tape plays. Once the VTR starts recording a video signal, control track and video information get generated simultaneously onto the videotape. The numbers advance on the display and an image appears on the screen.

## TAPE FORMATS

Videotapes come in various sizes and quality specifications. With the older analog tape formats, it used to be simple to evaluate tape quality—the larger the tape, the better the quality. Today that rule does not apply. Technological advances including digital recording allow newer smaller tape formats to meet or exceed the technical specifications of older, larger formats.

Since size is not an indicator, the only way to know which tape format to choose is to compare technical specifications. How is the tape format rated in terms of *signal-to-noise ratio* and resolution? The signal-to-noise ratio is a technical specification of how much unwanted electronic fuzzliness appears on the screen as part of the picture.

Look twice at a cassette or you may confuse formats. Many cassette formats look similar. A BetaCam cassette may look similar to a 3/4-inch cassette. A Hi-8 may look like a mini DV cassette. (See figure 3.9 for a list of video formats.)

## AUDIO INPUTS

Next to the video track are the *audio tracks*. Typically, professional VTRs have at least two channels designated for audio. Two separate audio sources such as microphones can be plugged into these channels. You might plug microphones directly into these inputs. Or, you might plug the output of an audio mixer which combines several microphones. Or, you may plug in the output of a piece of audio equipment such as a tape player, CD player, etc.

## LINE LEVEL, MIC LEVEL

Microphones have little or no internal amplification. Thus, they produce a very weak signal called *mic level* that must be amplified. Other audio equipment such as tape players and CD players may already be amplified to some degree. They produce a *line level* signal. When plugging in a mic or other external audio source into a VTR, make sure you select either mic level or line level, whichever is appropriate. The line level setting assumes a stronger signal coming in from an amplified source. The mic level input assumes a weaker signal coming from a mic or other unamplified source. If you plug a line level source into a mic level input, the signal will be overpowering and sound terribly distorted.

Familiarize yourself with how the microphone attachments work on your camera/ VTR. Also, look for ways to monitor the audio signal, to confirm that the microphone is working. Is there a meter on your deck to confirm audio levels? Do you have headphones you can wear to listen to your audio signal as it is being recorded? (Audio techniques are covered in chapter 13.)

## TECHNICAL TIPS

Here are a few things to keep in mind when using cameras and VTRs:

1) Camera lenses get dirty. Wipe the front of your lens. Use a clean cotton cloth or special lens cleaning tissue.

2) Watch for flares and glares. Any light shining at the lens can cause a glare in the lens. Use a flag to block the light or change angles.

3) Confirm proper filters and white balance. Use a monitor to confirm proper color.

4) Periodically clean the video heads. Video heads are found on a silver spinning drum in the VTR. Use rubbing alcohol or special head cleaning fluid to clean heads every few weeks or months depending on amount of use. Tape manufacturers also make head-cleaning cassettes that can be played for a few seconds to clean heads.

# Part 2 - Creating Shots

It's not enough for the director to say, "Give me a shot of that man." The director must be more specific. Is it a close-up? A wide shot? From what angle?

(11.15) CS of bicycle.

(11.16) MS of bicycle.

(11.17) CU of bicycle.

(11.18) ECU of bicycle.

Camera shots are categorized by:
• how wide the *field of view* is relative to the subject
• the camera's *angle* to the subject

Here are some typical shot types:

**Cover Shot (CS)** - A *cover shot* is a wide shot used for introducing the scene so that the viewer can see the entire context. The bicycle is small. We see the surroundings. When shooting, a CS like this is good to capture first, showing the overall scene. However, in editing, the CS should not last too long since it is a busy shot with small detail. The viewer naturally wants to move closer.

**Medium Shot (MS)** - The *medium shot* uses a longer focal length lens, a closer zoom position, or a closer camera placement. A good sequence of shots will take the viewer step by step into the scene. Once the surrounding has been shown, the shots can get closer and feature the main subject(s).

**Close-up (CU)** - The *close up* uses an even greater focal length, closer zoom, or a closer placement of the camera. Now the bicycle fills the frame. Since a television screen is small, a close-up always looks pleasing. Give the viewer lots of close-ups.

**Extreme Close-up (ECU)** - A close-up may not be close enough. The closest possible framing is called the *extreme close-u*p. Extreme close-ups are exciting and make the viewer feel up close to the action. It's too abrupt to cut to ECUs from wide shots. Work your way in close and out wide through sequences of shots.

There is no absolute rule of measurement to say where a cover shot ends and a medium shot begins. These are approximations. As director, you and your camera operator can decide what constitutes wide and medium, close, and extreme close.

Angles can be low, straight on, or high. As director, you must specify what angle you desire.

### Why choose high, low, or eye level?

Your choice of angle may be purely creative or purely practical. On the creative side, you may choose a high angle because it is visually interesting, stimulating, or unique. On the practical side, you must consider which angle best shows your subject matter. If a piece of machinery is best understood by looking at its operation from above, then your best choice as director is to frame a high angle.

(11.19) Low Angle            (11.20) Eye Level            (11.21) High Angle

## FRAMING A PERSON

People are such common subjects in any television production, learning to frame a person or people is essential. You can review the options for framing one person and two people in chapter 5, which covers:

- The head-on shot
- The profile
- The 3/4 profile
- Two profiles
- Over the shoulder shot (OS)
- Two Faces East
- Look space
- Head room

## CAMERA MOVES

All camera moves are best performed with the tripod. Tripods are the only guarantee of smooth motion and steady shots. Hand-held camera shots invariably look shaky. Even subtle movement is noticeable on screen, so a tripod or other means of steadying the camera is always preferred.

Tripod heads rotate sideways and up and down. They have controls that allow the operator to adjust the amount of resistance when moving the head up, down, or sideways. This resistance keeps the tripod head from moving too freely, thus eliminating any jerky moves and promoting smooth moves. Before shooting, adjust the resistance to your satisfaction.

## PAN

A *pan* is a side-to-side pivoting movement of the camera. The tripod stays put while the head pivots. The camera pans right or pans left.

## TILT

A *tilt* is an up or down pivoting move. Again, the tripod stays put. The camera tilts up or tilts down.

## ZOOM

A *zoom* is a convenient way to change the focal length of the lens without changing lenses. Before the zoom lens existed, if you wanted to change from a wide angle lens to a telephoto, you would physically change lenses. The zoom lens allows a single lens to change focal lengths on demand.

You can use a zoom lens in two ways:
1) As a quick way to change framing. In this case, the zoom action is not seen on tape. It is simply a fast way to alter the field of view between takes.

2) As a way to do "hot" moves. A hot move means that it is actually seen in the final product. You may zoom for effect, to show the framing change as the scene unfolds.

The following moves require the use of wheels on the tripod or a platform that moves. In these moves, the camera actually moves across the floor.

## DOLLY

A *dolly* is a move toward the subject or away from it. The camera dollies in or dollies out. At first glance a dolly seems similar to a zoom. In some ways it is—the framing changes. But there is a big difference.

The zoom only changes the focal length. It does not change the spatial relationship between objects in the environment because the camera does not move past anything in the scene. It stays in one place. However, when the camera physically moves toward something, other objects in the foreground appear to change in their relationship to one another as the camera moves past them.

Consider the difference between the zoom and the dolly in terms of achieving a sense of three dimensionality in the scene.

## TRUCK

A *truck* is a side-to-side movement of the camera, perpendicular to the dolly. Again, tripod wheels on a smooth surface or on some kind of track are important for allowing a smooth move, free of bumps and shakes. The camera trucks left or trucks right. Like the dolly, the truck gives a three-dimensional feeling as the camera moves through space and the environment changes accordingly.

## ARC

An *arc* is similar to a truck, except that the camera makes a partial circle around the subject while maintaining a constant radius.

## STATIC or LOCK DOWN

A *static shot* (sometimes referred to as a "lock down" shot) is a camera shot with no movement at all. The camera framing remains motionless for the duration of the scene. A good director will make use of static shots. You do not want a program composed entirely of camera moves. The viewer will get dizzy after constant pans, tilts, and zooms. Instead, consider the static shot to be the norm. Then use camera moves as they seem appropriate.

## PAD ALL SHOTS

Every move—zoom, pan, tilt, dolly, truck, arc—should have *pad* on either end. Pad means a few seconds of a static shot on either end of the move. This gives the editor the time needed to initiate a cut, dissolve, or wipe to the shot before the move begins and a transition away from the shot once the move is over. Without pad, you force the editor to transition in the middle of a move which seems abrupt. So, to add pad to every camera move:

1) Frame the shot.
2) Practice the move a few times.
3) Start recording.
4) Hold a static shot for a few seconds.
5) Initiate the move.
6) Finish the move by coming to a smooth halt.
7) Hold steady for a few more seconds.
8) Then stop recording.

The shot is now ideally suited for the editing room.

## HAND-HELD

A hand-held shot is one that is done with the camera in hand or on the shoulder instead of mounted on a tripod.

Typically, professional productions use tripods in every possible situation to ensure smoothness and steadiness. Nothing looks less professional than shaky footage unless done purposely for effect.

But when a tripod is not available or is impractical, any of the above moves can be done hand-held. The challenge is to keep the shot as steady as possible. So, if you do any hand-held shooting, you must devise ways of steadying yourself as much as possible. This may involve tricks such as:

• Holding your breath during a shot.
• Leaning against a solid object to steady yourself.
• Using wide shots instead of extreme close-ups to minimize noticeable shaking.
• Experimenting with your own body positioning and placement to create the steadiest foundation for your camera.

Hand-held shots work well when there is lots of movement in the scene. A sporting event, for example, with people running every which way, is perfect for hand held camera work because the intense movement in the scene distracts from lesser movement by the camera operator.

Hand-held shots do not work well in static situations. A sit-down interview, for example, would be a bad choice for a hand-held shot. Any little movement by the camera operator as he breathes, wiggles, and shifts from foot to foot, will show up very noticeably on the screen. Even the heartbeat can cause noticeable movement. Therefore, use a tripod whenever possible.

## THE DIRECTOR'S ROLE

The director must be familiar with all camera move options in order to choose the right move for a given scene.

The director must decide whether a pan or a truck is to be used, whether a zoom or a dolly is best, or whether the camera should be static with no movement at all.

As director, your job is to know what you want to achieve, and communicate that to the camera operator. You may choose when to be specific about shot types and when to let the camera operator make his or her own choices.

Give clear direction. Here are some examples of director's communication to the camera operator:

"Pan from left to right on a medium shot."

"Zoom in slowly from a cover shot to a close-up."

"Tilt up slowly from the desk to the person's face."

"Give me a static cover shot of the mountains. Hold that shot for about 15 seconds."

"Arc left from a medium shot of the drummer to a medium shot of the guitarist."

"Truck right from the man to the woman."

"Start with a close-up of the birthday girl. Wait about ten seconds and then dolly out to include the whole group."

"Go hand held and follow the man walking down the sidewalk."

In some cases, these moves may already have been specified in the script. But most of the time, the script will only describe a scene. The director will decide what kind of framing and what kind of movement the camera will make.

## DIRECTORIAL TIPS

1) Static shots are nice in their simplicity. Too many pans, tilts, and zooms can make the viewer dizzy. Consider using static shots wherever possible.

2) Dolly shots look better than zooms. But only if there is plenty of foreground interest that will change when the camera moves in or out. If there isn't much foreground interest, then a zoom looks similar and is much easier to accomplish.

3) Good camera moves—trucks, arcs, and dollies—require smooth surfaces and good wheels. If you don't have these, you might be smart to forego the move. Shaky moves are not worth doing.

4) It's easy to forget the "pad" rule. Be sure to pad the beginning and end of every move with a few seconds of static shot. You want each move to have a clear beginning and end.

5) You don't always know the ideal duration of a camera move. In the editing room, you may have a 10-second zoom-in and find yourself wishing it was only a five second zoom. So, when shooting, try a variation of moves, each a different rate.

6) Shoot a variety of framings: wide, medium, and close.

## PRACTICE COMMANDS

Look at each of the shots on the next page. What command would you give your camera operator to correct each shot?

(11.22) Correction?
a) pan right
b) pan left
c) tilt up
d) tilt down

(11.23) Correction?
a) zoom in & tilt down
b) pan left & tilt up
c) zoom out & pan right
d) zoom in & pan right

(11.24) Correction?
a) pan right & tilt up
b) zoom in & tilt up
c) tilt down & pan right
d) zoom in & pan left

(11.25) Correction?
a) pan right just a little
b) pan left just a little
c) tilt up just a little
d) tilt down just a little

## A REAL WORLD APPLICATION, CONTINUED:

The director has chosen a high-end broadcast camera for this production. The camera has a BetaCam SP VTR on the back—a dockable configuration. BetaCam SP means that the tape is metal and records an image with less video noise in the picture, hence better resolution than regular Beta tape. The camera is a Sony 400a which retailed new for about $50,000. The TV production company does not own the camera since it is so expensive.

If they were using it every week, it might be worthwhile. But since they spend much of their time in pre-production and post-production, weeks go by with no shooting going on. Therefore, it makes most economic sense for them to rent the camera from a local film/video rental company. The camera rents for $450/day.

The director makes sure that plenty of tape stock will be on hand for the days of taping. He orders twenty 30-minute Beta SP cassettes.

The director meets with the camera operator ahead of time. They have looked at the sites together and the director has given some instruction about the types of shots he is looking for. He does not want camera movement in the interviews or the shots around the facility. However, during the dramatic vignettes, he would like to use a dolly and track to do arcs, trucks, and dollies. The camera operator suggests a good dolly pusher to add to the crew. They also figure on an extra half hour per scene to lay track for the dolly.

The director and camera operator have worked together on many productions. The director knows the camera operator's sense of framing very well. He knows that he will not need to make lots of corrective commands about framing. In fact, he often trusts the camera operator without having to check framing in the viewfinder or on a monitor. However, since this is an important shoot, and since the client will want to see a color monitor, the director makes sure that a monitor is set up so that all can see what the camera operator has framed before rolling tape.

Before taping each scene, the camera operator will frame the shot, and the director will check it. Then the director calls, "Roll tape." The camera operator activates the VTR switch on the front of the camera. The Beta SP tape begins to roll and record. A red light in the viewfinder tells the camera operator that the VTR is recording. "Speed," calls the camera operator, confirming that the tape is rolling. The director waits at least five seconds for ample pre-roll time and then calls "Action."

# 12

# Lighting

**I**t's common to hear a newcomer to a TV production set exclaim, "These lights are so bright!" People are not used to the light levels required for TV production.

Sometimes scenes are shot with nothing more than regular available light. But in most cases, light is purposely added to the scene.

*Why is brightness needed? Why not just shoot with natural light all the time?*

1) Because cameras require more light than our eyes do.
2) Because cameras can't handle contrast as well as our eyes can.
3) Because cameras can't compensate for color temperature variations as well as our eyes can.
4) And because we want to control lighting effects.

Let's explore these ideas in detail.

## 1) CAMERAS REQUIRE MORE LIGHT THAN OUR EYES DO.

The camera and our eyes work on similar principles. Both need light to see. Light is the medium by which we see and by which the camera senses an image. Light bounces off the subject, enters our eyes, and stimulates nerve endings. Light enters a film camera and stimulates light-sensitive chemical particles. Light enters the video camera and stimulates either the light-sensitive face of a glass pick-up tube or an electronic chip.

*(12.1) Portable TV lighting:*

- *Instruments*
- *Bulbs*
- *Barn doors*
- *Stands*
- *Scrims and gels*
- *Power cables*

Although the camera and the eye work similarly, the eye can see much better under low light than a camera can. Where the human eye may recognize detail in a dimly lit situation, the camera will only see darkness.

A common example of insufficient lighting is found in the use of the home camcorder in settings such as weddings or family events in the home. The camcorder is a low-grade piece of equipment that does a poor job in dark situations.

However, the same inexpensive camera placed outside in bright light creates very good pictures. Why? Because light is a camera's best friend. The camera needs plenty of light to effectively resolve all the detail in the picture.

A simple solution for the recreational camera person shooting at home in the living room is to use some additional lighting. This will greatly enhance the quality of the image. The camera will be able to resolve a much better picture. Any scene can be made brighter and better for the camera with use of lighting.

On the professional level, video cameras have made tremendous progress in light sensitivity. Years ago, cameras required enormous amounts of light to create good pictures. Every year, new models of professional cameras are designed to work well under lower light conditions. But they still don't rival the human eye. The rule of thumb lives on—dark situations will always tax the camera's ability to make the picture look good.

Familiarize yourself with your camera's abilities. Evaluate how low the light can be before you consider the picture quality to be unacceptable. At what point does the picture start looking muddy, grainy, and the detail gets lost?

Learn to evaluate a scene, not by what looks bright enough to the eye, but by what looks bright enough to the camera.

## 2) CAMERAS CAN'T HANDLE CONTRAST AS WELL AS OUR EYES DO.

The word *contrast* implies a ratio of brightness to darkness within a given scene. As the spectrum from the darkest dark to the brightest bright in the scene increases, the contrast ratio increases.

(12.2) Medium contrast. The light levels in the scene are well within the camera's ability to resolve detail.

(12.3) High contrast. The range from dark to light is too much for the camera to handle.

Imagine a police interrogation room with the stereotypical light bulb hanging over the accused as the detectives lean over and rifle questions. The surrounding room is dark. The light in the middle is very bright. Hence, a high contrast ratio exists in the overall scene—very bright and very dark.

Now, put a lamp shade over the bulb and turn on the other room lights. The brightest bright and the darkest dark are not so distant from each other anymore. The contrast ratio is reduced. The light levels in the room evened out.

Video cameras are notoriously bad at handling contrast. Film cameras do much better. For this reason, many high-end productions such as movies and commercials are shot on film and then transferred to video. The film medium does an overall better job of producing good resolution in contrasty situations.

But, again, the human eye outshines either camera. The eye can accommodate a higher *contrast ratio* than either film or video. For example, you can look at that high contrast interrogation room and see all the detail in both the bright and dark portions of the scene. The camera has a harder time adjusting to both extremes. It prefers to expose for one or the other, but not both. If you close the iris to expose for the bright light, then the dark portion of the scene gets too dark to see. If you open the iris to expose for the detail in the dark portion of the room, then the bright light gets washed out and takes all the detail with it.

The video camera requires a lower contrast ratio than the eye. A high-contrast ratio that is acceptable to the eye may not be good for the camera. If you shoot a contrasty situation, you are likely to lose detail in either the bright or dark portions of the picture, depending on which end of the contrast spectrum you are favoring with the iris

**145**

exposure on your lens. So keep in mind that the camera does not see as well as you do. Your job is to make it easier for the camera to resolve images by increasing light in exceedingly dark areas, dimming overly bright areas, thus lowering contrast.

## 3) CAMERAS CAN'T COMPENSATE FOR COLOR TEMPERATURE VARIATIONS AS WELL AS OUR EYES DO.

We've already mentioned the concept of color temperatures, measured in *degrees Kelvin*. Color is a product of selected light waves. Why is an apple red? Because other colors in the light spectrum are absorbed into the apple, but the red wavelength bounces back to our eyes.

The color white is the sum of all colors in the visible light spectrum. If all light sources emitted a uniformly white light, then that apple would appear the same shade of red whether the light shining on it came from the sun, a reading light, or a fluorescent light.

But light sources are not uniformly white. Each light source emits a different combination of light waves, thus each is a different color. The sun's light has more blue waves than red ones, hence the sun's light is bluer. Indoor room lights are redder. They have more red waves in their emissions.

Thus, colors fluctuate under different light sources. An object's color looks a little redder under indoor light and bluer in sunlight because of the different amounts of blue or red light waves hitting it. Although our eyes and brain compensate for differences, the camera readily sees these color fluctuations.

Try this: Hold a white piece of paper under the sunlight. It's bluer than it looked inside. Now hold the paper under indoor lights. It's redder. This difference may be hard to notice because the brain, knowing that the paper is supposed to be white, says, "It's white." But if you shift back and forth between the light sources, you should see the change. The camera, however, will show a pronounced difference.

When using a video camera, you must compensate for every light source. To make life simpler, try to use one uniform light source when you shoot a scene. That way, when you calibrate the camera for a particular light, such as *tungsten* TV lights, your scene will have a consistent look throughout.

As mentioned earlier, sunlight has a lot of blue in it and is rated at about 5600 degrees Kelvin. Tungsten light bulbs are cooler on the light spectrum. They have much more red than blue and are rated at about 3200 degrees Kelvin. Incandescent household light bulbs are cooler still–about 2800 degrees Kelvin.

In TV, film, and photography, we are concerned about the relative color that is associated with a Kelvin rating. For example, we want to know that, at 5600 degrees Kelvin, we can expect more blue in the light waves, and that at 3200 degrees Kelvin, we can expect more red. We need this information to balance our light sources and filters in our cameras so that colors come out looking right. Our brains make automatic compensations for changes in color temperature as they affect our vision, but the camera cannot make such accommodations. We must help the camera by choosing appropriate filters, and by white balancing the camera.

Today's consumer cameras, such as the mini-DV camera, make life easy with auto white balancing and color viewfinders for quick confirmation. However, many professional cameras have black and white viewfinders which will not reveal color temperature problems. Thus, the only way to visually confirm the right color balance in your scene is to attach a separate color monitor.

So how do we help the camera accommodate the variations in light sources?

1) *Color correction filters* can be placed in front of the lens.

2) The camera may have a *filter wheel* just behind the lens that allows the operator to dial in a filter for indoor or outdoor light.

3) A *white balance* function may be performed. Most industrial and broadcast video cameras have a white balance button. You simply aim the camera at a piece of white paper under the light source you will be using. Fill the viewfinder with this white

(12.4) White balance switch.

(12.5) Filter wheel.

image. Then engage the white balance switch. In a moment or two, the camera will calibrate for white under that lighting condition, thus compensating for any excess blue or red light waves. Remember to change filters and white balance again anytime you change to another light source.

4) Some cameras have nothing more than an indoor/outdoor selection switch. This is a coarse adjustment, but adequate in most cases.

The TV and film industries have attempted to standardize certain light sources so that we don't have to dial in many Kelvin temperature settings for different light sources.

The two basic settings you'll find are:
1) 5600 K - outdoor sunlight
2) 3200 K - tungsten light bulbs found in TV lighting supplies

Although there are many other light sources with color temperatures other than the two listed, these can be accommodated through the white balance feature or by placing selected color correction gels over the lens.

## COLOR TEMPERATURE MISMATCHES

The camera can only deal with one color temperature at a time. Every time you move to a new location with a different light source, you must re-establish proper color correction by white balancing again or changing filters.

So, the challenge is to avoid mixing light sources of significantly different Kelvin temperatures. When looking at a room with two or more light sources, the eye won't notice a color discrepancy. But the camera will see part of the room as redder, part bluer, part greener depending on the variation of light sources present. The goal is to find a common color temperature for the whole room.

When shooting indoors, try to use a light source that has a known Kelvin rating. Tungsten lights with a 3200 degree Kelvin rating are the lights of choice. You can rely on any of the TV light kits that your school owns or that you might rent or purchase from a TV equipment dealer to have the same 3200 degree rating. Any professional camera will have a filter or setting to accommodate tungsten light.

Try to maintain uniform Kelvin temperatures in your scene. Then balance for that temperature by selecting the proper filter or by white balancing.

Windows present color mismatch problems. Indoor light and sunlight are both present, but the camera can only accommodate one or the other. If you balance for the window, the indoor light looks too red. If you balance for the indoor light, the window looks too blue.

What do you do if you find a situation with mixed temperatures? Try to alter light sources in the scene to make them match each other as closely as possible. Choose a primary source and make the others match by choosing which lights to keep on and by using color correction gels on appropriate lights and windows.

Here's a sample scenario. Imagine that you need to shoot an interview in an office. The office has fluorescent lights on the ceiling, a desk lamp of unknown Kelvin rating, a big window that lets in the daylight, and you have a TV light kit that has 3200 Kelvin lights. What are your options? You must select among the light sources and filters at your disposal. Let's outline three possible approaches.

### Option #1 - Block out other light sources
1) Pick tungsten lighting as your uniform light source
2) Pull drapes or blinds over the windows to block out the sunlight
3) Turn off the fluorescent lights
4) Turn off the desk light
5) Light entirely by using your tungsten TV lights
6) Select the tungsten filter setting on your camera–3200 degrees Kelvin
7) White balance your camera if possible for an extra measure of accuracy

### Option 2 - Use the daylight
1) Pick daylight as the uniform source
2) Use the window light
3) Turn off the fluorescent lights and the desk light
4) Use your TV lights and put blue gels over each instrument so that the light balances for the daylight
5) Select your daylight filter setting on the camera–5600 Kelvin
6) White balance your camera if possible for extra accuracy

### Option 3 - Carefully mix two sources
1) The fluorescent lights are filling the room very nicely
2) Cover the window to block sunlight, eliminating that source
3) Use the fluorescent lighting in the room.
4) Evenly mix in your tungsten TV lights along with the fluorescent lights.
5) White balance the camera and see if the camera was able to find a happy medium between the two light sources.

**149**

Color can be manipulated for special effect. For example, a color may be added to a scene for artistic purposes. Bluer light suggests nighttime. Redder light looks warmer and cozier. You may intentionally alter the light or add certain colors in the scene to create a desired look.

People's colors naturally change as they go from place to place. On a dance floor, a person may have various colors in the face that they would not have in a dimly lit room. A face at sunset on the beach looks a different color than a face on a snowy winter day. A face indoors looks different than a face outdoors. Once you white balance or choose the proper filters and gels, you can choose to accentuate color difference by using additional gels on your lights. A warm colored gel on one of the lights, for example, may bring an added degree of warmth to the face.

## LIGHTING HARDWARE

Lighting hardware comes in all shapes and sizes. Large scenes may call for dozens of huge 2000-5000 watt lighting instruments that require large trucks for transportation and gasoline generators to supply power. Portable TV light kits usually contain instruments of 300-1000 watt capacities.

Lighting instruments can be hung from above or placed on stands. When shooting in a studio, there is often a grid of bars on the ceiling from which to hang lights. However, on location, you're moving from place to place. You can't assume that good lighting is available. Therefore, a light kit with stands is good to have along.

Here's the anatomy of a portable TV light kit:

- Lighting instruments
- Power cords
- Sandbags
- Bulbs
- Flags
- Gels
- Barn doors
- Scrims
- Stands

Let's examine the anatomy piece by piece.

**Instrument** - The encasement for the light bulb is called a *lighting instrument*. Some instruments have a lens to focus the light. Some have a knob that moves the bulb back and forth within its casing to create a more flooded or more spotted light.

**Bulb** - The light *bulb* is what's mounted in the instrument and produces light. The bulb is rated by *color temperature* and by *wattage*. The wattage, or watts, is a measurement of how much power the bulb consumes and how bright the bulb shines. A higher wattage bulb is brighter.

You need to know whether the circuit you plug into can handle the wattage of a given light bulb. You don't want to blow the breaker. Here's a formula to help:

**Watts = Volts** x **Amps**. (*Volts* and *Amps* are measures of the force of electrical current.) We know the voltage. In the US, normal household plugs are standardized at 110 volts. We know the wattage of the bulb. It's either printed on the bulb or on the box. Let's say it is a 600 watt bulb. Now we want to know whether our circuit can handle one or two of the bulbs. Let's say the circuit is rated at 15 amps—a common rating for most households and commercial buildings.

Plug the numbers into the formula: 600 Watts = 110 Volts X ? Amps.

The answer is: 5.45 amps. That's just a little more than one-third the capacity of a 15 amp circuit. In other words, a 15 amp circuit using 110 volts can handle at least two 600 watt bulbs without blowing a fuse or tripping a circuit breaker.

**Barn door** - *Barn doors* are metal flaps on the instrument that act as blinders to block light from spilling into other parts of the room.

**Diffusion** - A semi-translucent material such as a fireproof cloth or mylar covering the light source. When light is harsh, the subject is hit with strong shadows. Some shadows are natural. But strong shadows are contrasty and unpleasant. Diffusion helps soften the light to reduce or eliminate shadows.

**Flag** - A *flag* is a piece of opaque material that is used like a barn door to block unwanted rays of light. The flag may be any shape, but typically is a square or rectangular piece of lightweight metal such as foil. The flag is positioned near the lighting instrument to control light spillage into unwanted areas. Or, a flag is placed near a camera lens to prevent glare from lights or the sun.

**Scrim** - A *scrim* is a partially translucent material—usually a metal screen—that cuts down on the light's intensity.

**Gel** - A *gel* is a colored piece of acetate—a clear plastic paper. The gel colors the light source. Gels can be broken down into two main categories: colorizing gels and color correction gels. Colorizing gels simply add the color of choice to the scene. If you want to make the scene feel warmer and create more of a fireplace look, you might add a gold color to your lighting. If you want a dark scene to look more like

(12.6) Barn door.

(12.7) Flag.

nighttime, you might add a blue gel. Color correction gels are used specifically to balance for color temperatures. A blue gel balanced for sunlight may be placed over a tungsten light to adapt it for outside use.

What if you want to colorize the sun to balance for tungsten? You can't very well place a gel right over the sun. But you can place a large roll of gel over a window to balance the light coming in to match the tungsten lights being used inside.

Another form of gel is a *neutral density gel* which only acts to cut down the light level. It has no influence on color. You might use large sheets of neutral density gel to cover a bright window to reduce contrast with the interior of a room.

**Stand** - The *stand* is a portable pole and base on which to mount a lighting instrument. It's more convenient than climbing ladders to hang lights from ceiling grids.

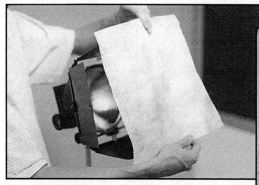

(12.8) Scrim.

(12.9) Gel.

Stands have one major drawback: since they are on floor level, they can get in the way of shots. Therefore they must be placed discreetly.

**Power cord** - The lighting instrument needs to be plugged into a power source. Small light kits use standard 110 volt plugs. Larger watt instruments may use 220 volt push and twist plugs.

**Sandbag** - The higher the stands are stretched, the more top heavy and more prone to tipping over they become. *Sandbags* provide a measure of safety by adding weight to the base of a light stand.

These are some of the basic components that make up a typical portable TV light kit. Next, we'll look at how to put it all to use.

## LIGHT MEASUREMENT AND PROPER EXPOSURE

*How do you know how bright the light is or should be?*

A light's intensity is measured by a scale called *foot candles*. Each camera requires a minimum number of foot candles to create an acceptable picture. Newer cameras can function reasonably well with fewer foot candles—dimmer light.

Even if a camera can get by with dimmer light, your picture may not appear well-lit. You must take control and use lighting to achieve the levels of foreground and background brightness that you desire. You need tools with which to measure.

One tool is the *light meter*, a hand-held instrument that measures light intensity. With this instrument, you not only get an objective measure of how much light is in your scene, but you can also measure contrast. Here's how. Imagine a scene in which bright sunlight passes through a window in the room. Meanwhile, a far corner of the room is extremely dark. By measuring each area with the light meter, you get a foot candle reading for each and a sense of the overall contrast range. The contrast range is probably very great. Next, gel the window to reduce the sunlight intensity, then add some light to the dark part of the room. The contrast range still exists, but it is minimized. Notice the new light meter readings. The numbers are not as far apart. You can keep notes about what range seems to work best for your camera. In general, the camera will produce a better picture if the contrast range is not extreme.

Another tool for measuring light is the **waveform monitor**, an electronic oscillo-scope which looks like a small TV screen. It measures the video signal coming out of the camera and shows the light levels within the scene. On its screen, an electronic scan of high and low peaks represents the bright and dark portions of the picture. The waveform's reference grid shows a scale of unit numbers from 1 to 100. The brightest part of the picture should not exceed 100 units, the top of the scale. The darkest part of the picture should not dip below 7.5 units. The 7.5 number was established by TV engineers as the legal definition of TV black, the darkest part of a broadcast video signal. Thus, the contrast range of a TV picture should fall between 7.5 and 100 units.

### *How do I make corrections if the signal goes over 100 or under 7.5?*

The iris on the lens controls the brightness. If a signal's peaks hit 105 on the wave-form, close the iris a little and the video level will decrease. **Black level** is adjusted on the camera using a switch that automatically calibrates the darkest part of the picture at 7.5 units. This adjustment may also be called **pedestal** or **setup.**

In reality, ENG crews chasing hard news stories do not have the time or manpower to carry waveform monitors in the field, to set them up, and to make adjustments. Fortunately, automation helps the camera operator with proper light levels.

The **auto iris** is a feature built into most professional and consumer cameras. It's a light meter within the lens that senses the range of light levels coming in the lens and finds a good average iris setting, also called **exposure**.

(12.10) Waveform monitor and corresponding image.

(12.11) On the left of the image is a white vertical stripe which reads on the waveform as the brightest part of the picture.

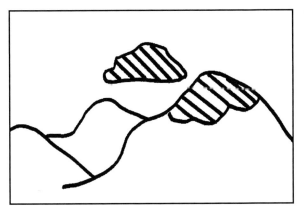

(12.12) Zebra bars appear in the viewfinder as little stripes on anything approaching 100 units. In this case, they appear first on clouds and snow.

There are two cautions about the auto iris feature:

1) The auto iris reading is just an average. You may want to override this setting to accommodate bright or dark areas of your picture. Open up your iris to see more detail in a dark area or close the iris to see more detail in a bright area.

2) The auto iris is reactive. If the light changes momentarily from someone walking by, the auto iris may open or close abruptly causing an unwanted fluctuation in the exposure. The best remedy is to use the auto iris at the outset of a scene to set the right exposure. Then turn the feature off and stay on a manual setting which will not fluctuate at will.

Another helpful tool for measuring light and proper exposure for the camera is called *zebra bars*. It provides information similar to the waveform monitor, indicating when the video signal exceeds 100 units. Zebra bars—seen in the viewfinder as little stripes—appear over a bright portion of the picture when it approaches 100 units. The camera operator sees the stripes and can close the iris slightly until the stripes disappear. Zebra bars can be adjusted to show up at desired exposures. Sometimes they are set for 100 units, or for 95 units. Check your camera against a waveform to see exactly where the zebra bars are showing up.

Normally, all these forms of measurement should confirm each other. If the auto iris exposes correctly, the zebra bars and the waveform monitor should both indicate when a scene is peaking at 100 units. Zebra bars are more convenient since they are internal to the camera. Waveform monitors are not always practical to lug around, however they are the most accurate form of measurement.

## LIGHTING TECHNIQUES

Now that you have an overview of the hardware, let's explore the use of lighting equipment and the art of lighting. First, consider some of the reasons to use lighting:

1) **Reduce contrast**. There will always be contrast in your scene. Your job is to avoid excess contrast. Look at your scene. Is there something too bright and shiny? Try to reduce the light on it. Is there a dark part of the scene that doesn't show any detail on camera? Try to brighten it up a little.

2) **Raise the overall light level**. Is the room dark and shadowy? If so, it will only look gloomier on camera. Use lights to raise the general level of illumination. With more light, the resolution will improve. The picture will look crisper and cleaner.

3) **Light to create depth**. Depth, or three-dimensionality, is accentuated when the foreground subject is brighter than the background. This makes the subject "pop out" in the picture. Use lighting to establish and control brightness levels between subject and background.

4) **Light for effect**. Light may be used purely to create colors, patterns, or dramatic effects. Colored gels may be used over the lights to create color effects. Lighting might be used to simulate fire burning or the flicker of a TV screen or movie projector. You can cut a pattern in aluminum foil and place it over the lighting instrument to create a shape or pattern with the light—for example, the suggestion of Venetian blind shadows on the wall or leaf patterns from a tree. (These foil cut-out patterns are called *gobos*.) Light may be used to suggest nighttime. A dark scene with blue highlights suggests moonlight.

## DIRECT, DIFFUSE, AND REFLECTED LIGHT

Any lighting instrument can be configured as a direct light, a diffused light, or a reflected light.

*Direct* - Direct light means that the instrument is pointed directly at the subject. It is the most harsh light and is quite contrasty because of the shadows it creates. Bright sunshine on a clear day is an example of direct light.

*Diffuse*- Diffuse light is a direct light with some sort of material over the front of the light to soften the intensity. That material may be a gel, or a scrim made of metal, cloth, or mylar. Sunlight from behind cloud cover is an example of diffuse light. Diffuse light is preferable to direct light because it is less contrasty and therefore less shadowy.

*Reflected* - Reflected light means that the lighting instrument is pointed away from the subject but the light reflects back to the subject. The light could be pointed at a

(12.13) The light on left light is reflected using an umbrella. The middle is diffuse, using a flame-proof scrim to soften the otherwise direct light. The right light is direct.

photographer's umbrella or a white board or the wall or ceiling. Reflected light is very soft, yielding a low contrast with little or no shadow. Sometimes, reflected light is so mild that it is insufficient for the camera.

Choosing between direct, diffuse, or reflected light depends on your desire for brighter, higher contrast or softer, less contrasty lighting.

With these principles in mind, let's pick some subjects to light and explore the techniques involved.

## LIGHTING THE HUMAN FACE

The most common subject to light is the human face. The techniques for lighting the face are simple and can also be applied to many other subjects as well.

A traditional method of lighting the face is called ***three-point lighting***. This requires three lights: a key light, a fill light, and a back light. The light designated as the key light is the primary light source. It is aimed at the subject from about 45 degrees above and 45 degrees to one side of the subject's face. The fill light is also 45 degrees up, and 45 degrees to the other side of the face.

The fill light is set at about half the intensity of the key light. The theory is that two lights of varying intensities aimed at the subject from two sides creates a more three-dimensional look by providing some subtle but natural shadowing on the subject's face. It assures that, as the subject looks slightly one way or another, he or she remains well lit.

The back light hits the subject from behind, also from about 45 degrees above. The light should fall on the head and shoulders. The back light serves to highlight parts of the body that would otherwise fade into the background and appear flat. Highlighting the head and shoulders makes the person stand out from the background, giving the picture more depth. (See figures 6.1 through 6.5)

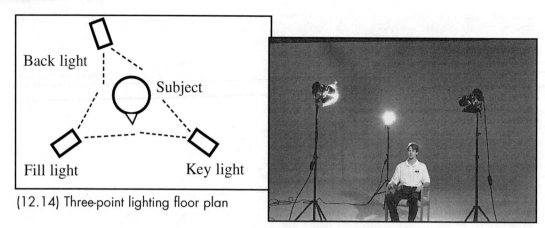

(12.14) Three-point lighting floor plan

(12.15) Three-point lighting

Three-point lighting is a basic formula that you can rely on and vary from. There may sometimes be reasons why three-point lighting is not practical. For example, you might not have three lighting instruments available, or there may not be enough AC power, or there may be no place to hang a back light without seeing it in the picture. But if you understand the theory, you can decide when to use the basic three-point lighting formula and when to vary from it.

Consider an alternative—using just one light head-on to the subject. This would tend to make the subject's face look flat and washed out. There may be times when a flat light is desired. In such a case the single front light should be diffuse. A reflected or diffuse light will insure that the face is not harshly lit.

You will often hear the terms: *dramatic lighting*, *flat lighting*, and *harsh lighting*. Dramatic lighting means creating shadows on the face for a realistic three-dimensional look, much the way one might appear under natural light. Flat lighting is a heavily scrimmed or diffuse lighting that yields almost no shadows on the face. And harsh lighting is the effect of one or more extremely bright lights on the face.

Have you seen news crews equipped with a single direct light on the front of the camera? The effect is never flattering. Normally, it's wise to avoid harsh lighting. The choice between flat lighting and dramatic lighting is up to you as director. Dramatic lighting takes more effort to create because attention must be paid to shadows on the face. Some shadows look pleasing, some look distracting or too intense. Flat lighting is not as interesting or artistic, but it's a practical and safe way to light. You don't have to worry about whether shadows look good or bad.

Let's take all the concepts that have been covered and apply them to some different situations.

(12.16) Dramatic lighting—shadows carefully controlled—a natural look.

(12.18) Harsh lighting—the sun or direct light creates bad shadows under the nose and eyes.

(12.19) Example #1 -Window light makes a good key light.

(12.17) Flat lighting—minimal shadow.

## LIGHTING EXAMPLE 1

In this example, (see figure 12.19) the director has seated the subject near a window to take advantage of natural light. It's a cloudy day and the daylight pouring in the window is not creating any harsh shadows on the subject's face because the sun is diffuse. The window light is considered the key light since it is a dominant light source. One lighting instrument from a TV lighting kit is placed in back for a back light. Another is placed in front opposite the window for a fill light. Both instruments are gelled with blue to balance the incoming daylight. The camera's filter wheel is selected for 5600 Kelvin and the camera is white balanced.

(12.20) Example #2 - Applying neutral-density gel to a widow. The brightness is cut down to better match the indoor light levels.

## LIGHTING EXAMPLE 2

Normally, daylight is so bright that a window looks too bright compared with the inside of the room. In this example, the director asked the grip to put neutral density gel, as well as color correction gel, on the window so that he could include the window in the framing. By using both types of gels, the light intensity was brought down to a reasonable contrast ratio and the daylight color now matches the tungsten lighting inside.

The director chose to place a table lamp near the subject for a natural fill light. The reading light is about 2800 degrees Kelvin, which means the light is a little red compared with the 3200 degree tungsten lights. But the director didn't mind that. In fact, the extra bit of redness coming from the table lamp looked good on the subject's face. The redness, in small dosage, translated aesthetically to a warm, homey look. A back light was used and gelled blue to avoid excessive redness in the scene.

(12.21) Example #3 - No back light is being used. However, lighting and subject placement create separation from the background.

## LIGHTING EXAMPLE 3

In this example, the production crew only had two lighting instruments. The director decided to use the two as key and fill lights. Knowing that the purpose of a back light is to enhance separation between the subject and the background, the director decided to find other ways to accentuate the depth.

The subject was placed several yards out from any wall or backdrop. The key and fill lights were aimed to fall off behind the subject so as not to light up the back wall too much, thus creating depth between subject and background. The subject appears brighter than the background, creating a 3-D look.

## LIGHTING EXAMPLE 4

In this example, the subject is out-side. The sun is bright, but there are clouds passing across the sky. The director waits for clouds to pass in front of the sun to diffuse the light. Since the light is diffuse and low contrast, no additional scrimming or lighting is necessary.

(12.22) Example #4 - On a slightly cloudy day, the subject's face is not too contrasty. A subtle shadow from a hidden sun is just enough to define the facial features.

If the clouds are heavy, the subject may look too dark or too flat. But with light cloud cover, the subject has some subtle facial shadows which look good. Light overcast, when shadows are slight, is an ideal opportunity to shoot outside.

## LIGHTING EXAMPLE 5

In this example, the subject is also outside. Today, no clouds, so the director is concerned about harsh light and shadows. The director realizes that the sun is a single light source and he wants to consider the sun a key light but add a fill. So rather than bringing a light outside, he has a production assistant (PA) hold a reflector that bounces light from the sun back toward the sub-

(12.23) Example #5 - On a sunny day, a reflector provides fill light to even out the shadows

ject from the other direction. Thus the harsh shadows are reduced.

Note: The production assistant is careful to hold the reflector as high as possible. If the PA held the reflector from below and pointed it up at the subject, the subject would have an up-lit jack-o-lantern look.

## LIGHTING EXAMPLE 6

In another outdoor example, the director is producing a commercial for national distribution. The lighting has to be perfect and very controllable. So the production team brings lighting instruments on location to ensure a consistent three-point lighting even though the sun may change.

They decide not to use tungsten lights from a TV kit for two reasons: 1) The small 600 watt TV kit lights are too weak to match the sun. 2) The Kelvin temperature mismatch. Tungsten lights are 3200 and the sun is 5600. Blue gels would work, but portable TV lights are weak compared to the intensity of the sun.

So the team uses a special series of high-wattage outdoor lighting instruments called *HMI*s. The "H" is part of Hg, the chemical symbol for Mercury. "MI" means medium source iodide. This chemistry creates a color temperature that is balanced for sunlight. And the wattage is strong enough in the presence of the bright sunlight to create a noticeable key or fill. HMIs are not practical to use for daily news and small-budget shoots because they require enough power that a generator must be brought on location or a power source must be established nearby.

## CONCLUSION

You can evaluate your lighting both aesthetically and technically. The aesthetic evaluation comes from looking carefully at the scene once it has been lit. Look with your naked eye, then look through the viewfinder. What do you notice? Any unwanted reflections? Any hot spots (too bright?) Any dark spots? How does the back light look on the subject's head and shoulders? Is the foreground/background contrast ratio to your liking? Does the subject seem to stand out nicely from the background?

For technical evaluation of the lighting, use a waveform monitor, zebra bars, or an auto iris. Keep the video from exceeding 100 units. Avoid excess contrast. Use your lights to correct problems: dim them, brighten them, or move them to reduce contrast and achieve both technical and aesthetic perfection.

## A REAL WORLD APPLICATION, CONTINUED:

The director considers the lighting needs for each of three types of shooting: interviews, action around the mill, and dramatic vignettes. For the interviews, he will use three-point lighting. The interviewer will not be seen or heard in the production so only the interviewees need to be lit. The director would like to have each interviewee appear in his or her work environment. This sometimes means interviewing them near windows where daylight pours in. In some cases, the director chooses to move the subject to avoid harsh sunlight. Closing the blinds or curtains can help, too. In other cases, the crew puts neutral density filter paper over the outside of the window so that the light level is cut down and the scenes outside the window are well-exposed. In each scene, the camera operator decides whether to set the filters for daylight and color correct the tungsten lights, or set the filters for tungsten and color correct the windows.

For the shots that require general mill activity, the director wants to maintain a natural look. He uses lights mainly to enhance the available light in the room. Lights from the portable TV kits are used to raise the light level a little bit in dark areas and reduce contrast.

For the dramatic vignettes, the crew has more control over the situation. Therefore, more time is taken to set lights. Actors in each scene will be moving from place to place. Three-point lighting must be broad enough to cover a wide area. Two sets of key lights, fill lights and back lights are positioned to cover the area. The director looks for spots where the actors will stop to talk. The crew marks these stopping points on the floor and the director works with the lighting person, making sure that these areas look especially well lit.

The mill has lots of heavy equipment and therefore plenty of electrical power available. The wall sockets are all ready and able to accommodate the high wattage TV lights. Just to be safe, the director inquires about the location of a breaker box in case someone should trip a breaker and cause a blackout.

As each scene is prepared, the director views the monitor to look for:
• undesirable shadows on the faces
• dark parts of the picture that will look muddy on camera
• bright parts of the picture that will look washed out

• hot spots, places where a bright reflection or glare off glass or metal causes an extreme waveform reading compared with the rest of the scene.

When all the corrections are made and the scene looks good, the shooting gets underway.

# 13

## Audio

There is a joke occasionally heard in the TV business that audio "gets no respect." The insinuation is that TV crews spend most of the time focusing on the visual component of the production and fail to allow ample time for the audio. They spend hours adjusting the lighting and the camera angles and then, in the last few minutes, say, "And what about audio?"

Of course, any good crew will pay a great deal of attention to the audio component of the shoot. The crew knows that the sound is just as important as the picture. It deserves the same level of craft and professionalism.

Audio reminds us of how complex a TV production really is. It's the integration of the entire visual component with the entire audio component—two separate technologies—that make a cohesive television production.

So, in this chapter, we'll add to your level of technological and artistic know-how by examining some of the tools for recording audio. Then, we will look at directorial considerations when using audio in the production process.

Let's begin by defining the following pieces of equipment and technology that are basic to the audio recording component of a video shoot.

- Microphones
- Microphone style
- Microphone pick-up pattern
- Microphone power source
- Booms
- Fishpoles
- Mixers
- Wind screens
- Headsets
- Filters

## MICROPHONES

Just as the video camera converts light waves into electrical signals, the microphone converts sound waves into electrical signals. Once the sound wave is in the form of an electrical pattern, it can either be recorded on tape or fed to an amplifier/speaker.

The process of converting sound waves to electrical signals is called **modulation**. Modulation means "to vary." The sound waves in the air cause a vibration of a small electronic sensor in the microphone called an **element**. The microphone element, once it has been modulated by the sound waves, in turn sets up a variation in the electrical signal passing through the wire. That variation acts like a code—sound-waves are coded as electronic signals. These electronic signal variations will be recorded magnetically on the videotape. The audio signal is recorded and processed separately from the video signal.

## MICROPHONE CLASSIFICATIONS

For a carpenter, there is no single screwdriver that does every job. Even though all screwdrivers have basically the same function, they come in different types, shapes, and sizes for different applications. Same with microphones. Microphones can be classified by: 1) style, 2) pick-up pattern, and 3) power source.

## MICROPHONE STYLE

The style refers to the physical construction and application of the microphone. Here are four common examples of style.

## HAND HELD

The hand-held style is held the way one would hold an ice cream cone. This mic can easily be held in one hand and raised to the mouth while talking. Hand-held mics are frequently used by reporters and talk show hosts.

*Advantage.* The hand-held mic gets placed very close to the subject for optimum sound presence—a short distance from mic to mouth.

*Disadvantage.* The mic is visible in the picture. However, in certain situations, visibility is not a problem. In news, for example, we expect to see a reporter holding a mic. Same with a talk show host. However, in a drama, we wouldn't want to see the actor holding a mic.

(13.1) Hand-held (13.2) lavaliere

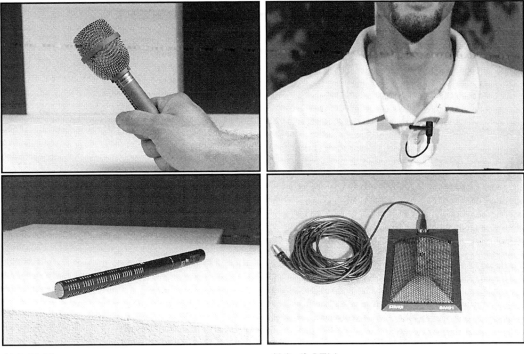

(13.3) Shotgun (13.4) PZM

## LAPEL / LAVALIERE

The lapel mic, also known as a **lavaliere** or **lav** for short, can be pinned onto the tie, collar, or lapel. It is usually visible, though quite small. The lav is frequently used in interviews.

*Advantage*. It's a hands-free configuration. It sits close to the mouth, offering close-up sound presence.

*Disadvantage*. The mic is visible in the picture, unless carefully hidden within cloth-ing. If hidden, the mic is subject to interference from clothes rubbing against it, so it's best to keep the lav visible. In a dramatic scene, it would be aesthetically strange to see a mic clipped to clothing. However, in a journalistic program such as an inter-view or news show, there's nothing wrong with a visible lav.

Also, the lav is subject to the wearer inadvertently touching the mic. It is remarkable how many people put their hands over their hearts at some point while they express themselves. Their hands not only bump the mic, but the sound gets muffled. This is a chance you take when using the lav.

Try to "dress" the lav—make it look neat and clean. Don't just clip to to someone's shirt and let it dangle. Instead, tuck the cord neatly inside the shirt or jacket. You may want to ask the talent to run the cable down their shirt rather than reaching into someone's clothing yourself! The goal is to make the lav look neat and inconspicuous. (See figure 13.2 for a good example of "dressing the mic.")

## SHOTGUN

The *shotgun* is a long cylindrical-shaped mic. The shotgun is the mic of choice when the actor or spokesperson must be hands-free to move about. The shotgun is positioned just out of the picture frame but as close to the talent as possible. It is typically mounted to a pole or boom to reach it out and over the subject and out of the camera's view.

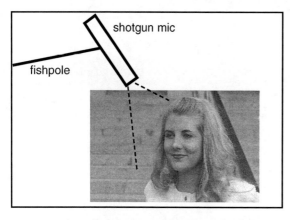

(13.5) The shotgun, mounted on a fishpole boom, is positioned just outside the frame and pointed toward the face for close or "near-field" presence.

*Advantage.* By using a boom, the shotgun can be both close to the talent for good sound quality, yet out of camera sight. The talent has hands-free movement.

*Disadvantage.* By keeping the shotgun out of the picture frame, you may not be able to get in as close to the mouth as you could with a hand-held or lav. Like any mic, when held further away, the presence (feeling of closeness to the subject) diminishes. Although the shotgun is designed to be extremely directional, the audio person still must be careful to keep the mic as close as possible, while remaining out of the view of the camera. A good shotgun operator will always pay attention to the camera framing and will take advantage of the opportunity to place the mic barely outside the frame and slightly in front of the speakers head, pointing back toward the mouth for maximum presence.

## PZM

The *PZM* is a small mic mounted a few millimeters off the surface of a flat plate which acts as a sound wave reflector. Sounds from around the room bounce off the plate and hit the mic element. This style is typically used in large-room situations

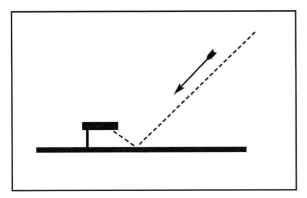

(13.6) A PZM mic consists of a small microphone element raised a few millimeters off of a plate. Sound waves around the room bounce off the plate and hit the mic element.

where sounds come from all over. An example is a round table discussion. The mic is placed in the middle of the table.

*Advantage.* The PZM offers an easy way to mic a large area. The mic may be visible in the scene, but its small flat size makes it hard to notice.

*Disadvantage.* Like the shotgun, in typical applications the PZM is usually at a distance from the subject, not nearly as close as a hand-held or lav. Again, care must be taken to place the mic as close as possible to the subject.

## PICK-UP PATTERNS

Microphones are designed with the ability to favor sounds in certain directions. This characteristic is called the mic's ***pick-up pattern***. Our ears have a pick-up pattern. They tend to hear everything around. With one ear on each side of our heads, we are sensitive to a sphere about our heads. Our ears' pick-up pattern is ***omnidirectional***. If we want to focus our pick-up pattern in one direction, we may cup our hands behind our ears. We block out sound coming from behind us and favor the sounds coming at us from in front. Microphone designs offer a range of choices. We can choose those that are designed to favor sound from all around. Or we can choose those that are designed to favor the sounds coming from certain directions.

For example, if a news reporter is doing a stand-up report in a construction zone, there is likely to be lots of extraneous noise in the area. You may want the mic to favor sounds coming straight from the reporter's mouth. Sounds off to the side would ideally be muted. Thus, you select a mic that has a more directional pick-up pattern that favors sounds directly ahead of it and mutes sounds to the sides.

1) ***Omnidirectional*** - spherical, favors all directions. Suggested use: ambient sound, large groups, large music events, any situation where important sounds come from all directions.

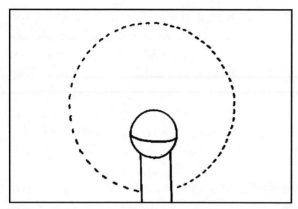

(13.7) Omnidirectional pick-up pattern. The dotted line represents the area most sensitive to the mic element.

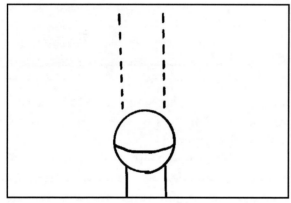

(13.8) Unidirectional pick-up pattern

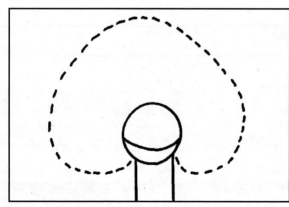

(13.9) Cardioid.

2) **Unidirectional** - cylindrical, favors an area directly in front of the mic. Suggested use: vocalists, stand-up news reporters, favoring the voice of the speaker and muting sounds from other directions.

3) **Cardioid** - heart-shaped, wider than unidirectional, picks up more sound from the sides than unidirectional. Suggested use: interview mic, the reporter can point the mic to a guest and it doesn't matter if the mic is not perfectly in line with the guest's mouth.

4) **Super-cardioid** - an elongated version of the cardioid—also called **hyper-cardioid**. This is the technical term for the "shotgun" mic. The pattern favors sounds out in front but mutes sounds to the sides. Suggested use: any situation in which attaching a mic to the subject is not appropriate; any directional coverage from a slight distance; nearby overhead coverage of actors or spokespeople. Shotguns are usually attached to the camera, held with a hand-grip called a **pistol-grip**, or at the end of a fishpole.

**POWER SOURCES**

A third classification of microphones is the **power source** required to run the mic. The elements in each microphone have something in common—they fluctuate when soundwaves hit them. But there are different kinds of elements. Some do not require any additional electrical power other than the cur-

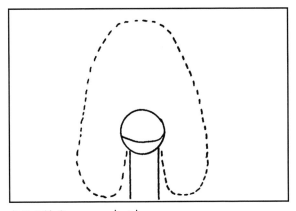

(13.10) Super-cardioid.

(13.11) This hand-held mic is a dynamic mic

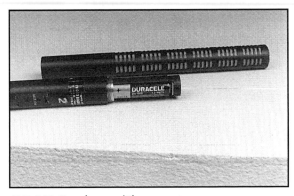

(13.12) Condenser/Electret mic.

rent that already flows through the mic cable from the VTR. But others need a boost from a power supply such as a small battery.

When selecting a mic, note the power requirements. Some mics require unusual batteries, ones that must be ordered and cannot simply be bought at the drug store. You wouldn't want to arrive on location in Faroffistan and find you are fresh out of a rare 6.9 Volt Mercury battery that must be shipped from Dallas and will take three days for delivery. Fortunately, many mics use standard batteries such as "AA" and A-6 calculator batteries that can be purchased at any convenience store. Let's look at two examples.

## 1) Dynamic mic

Our first example, the dynamic mic, needs no additional power at all. You simply plug the mic and cable into the record deck. The electricity within the camera/deck system powers the mic element through the microphone cable.

## 2) Condenser/Electret mic

This mic uses an electrical element called a condenser (also known as a capacitor) to store and release electrical charges as part of the process of converting sound into electricity. This little component, the condenser, requires additional power to operate. The power is either supplied by a battery or by an additional power supply in the VTR which sends a higher voltage charge down the wires.

The electret mic is a variation of the condenser mic. This mic's built-in condenser already has an electrical charge on it and therefore needs a much smaller auxiliary power source, usually a small calculator battery. An advantageous feature of these mics is that they are extremely small. Both the condenser and electret condenser mics are very sensitive, produce a better and brighter frequency response than the dynamic mic and therefore are often more pleasing to the ear. The only drawback is this: you must supply the necessary power. Have an extra battery along!

Some mics require a special 48 volt power source called *phantom power*. This can be supplied by a series of batteries or by special power supplies built into many cameras and audio mixers.

## MICROPHONE DELICACY

Microphones have always been delicate. An old style mic used a ribbon made of foil as an element. The ribbon mic provided high quality but was extremely fragile. Anyone from the golden days of radio still shudders when they hear someone blow into a microphone to test it. The old ribbon mics could be ruined by such practice. Although most modern mics are not as sensitive to blowing, it's a good practice to lightly tap the mic to test it. Microphone wires are delicate as well. Wrap them gently when storing.

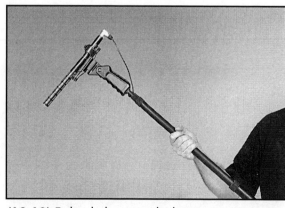

(13.13) Fishpole boom with shotgun.

## BOOMS AND FISHPOLES

A *boom* is a mechanical arm on the end of which the mic is attached. This allows the audio person to reach over the top of the picture, out of sight of the camera, and get the mic in close, over and in front of the talent's head. Booms are found in TV studios and sound stages. The operator rides the boom and watches an on-board TV monitor so he or she can keep the mic out of the shot.

A *fishpole* is a portable hand-held variation of the boom. Like the boom, it telescopes to a desired length. It allows the operator to get the mic in close but stay clear of the camera's field of view.

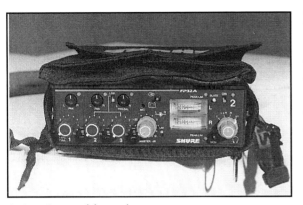

(13.14) Portable audio mixer

## MIXERS

A *mixer* combines two or more audio sources into one mixed source. A mixer is needed anytime the number of audio sources exceeds the number of audio channels on the record VTR. For example, a typical professional VTR has two audio channels. But you may be recording a panel discussion of four people, each wearing a lav. Plug each mic into the mixer inputs. The mixer will combine these into one output which can be fed into one of the audio channels in your VTR.

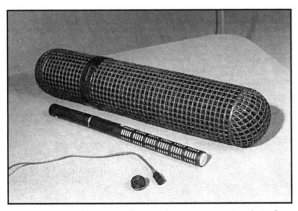

(13.15) Windscreen for a shotgun mic (right); for a lavaliere (left).

## WINDSCREENS

If you're shooting outside, it may be windy. Wind noise sounds terribly exaggerated on a mic. It can ruin the audio. A *windscreen* is a material that allows the sound waves to come through but blocks the wind. A windscreen can be made of foam or wire mesh and fit snugly around the mic. Windscreens are not miraculous solutions to the wind problem. Sometimes they work well. Other times, they can't block all the wind noise, in which case you either wait for the wind to die down or change locations.

## MICROPHONE PRESENCE

Should the mic be placed far away from the subject? Should it be close? Extremely close? Does it matter? It matters a great deal. The mic responds much like your ear. When you are far away from someone, they sound as if they are far away. When you are right next to them, they sound as if they are next to you. If you are too close, the sound may get distorted and hurt your ears.

*Microphone presence* refers to the feeling of distance from the listener. Someone yelling from far away should have a distant-sounding or *far-field* presence. Someone standing right next to you should have a close or *near-field* presence. Close presence is preferred. Narrators, reporters, and actors should all sound close. If they are close to the mic, they will sound close to the listener. When the person is close to the mic, background sounds diminish and the person sounds dominant and clear. When the mic is further away, the person's voice is in competition with all the other sounds in the environment and will sound far away. If the subject is close to the mic, the recording volume level doesn't have to be turned up as high. Thus the background sounds diminish by comparison. However, if the subject is far from the mic, the recording volume has to be turned up, thus allowing increased environmental noise.

Sometimes, the choice is purely artistic. Consider two ways to mic a piano recital. The mic can be placed right inside the piano for close presence. Or the mic can be placed out in the auditorium for a distance presence. The close mic (near-field) makes the piano sound as if it were in a recording studio. The sound is crisp, clean, and direct. There is no extraneous echo. However, with the mic out in the auditorium (far-field) the sound includes the presence of the entire room and the reverberations of music bouncing off the walls and ceilings of the concert hall. In other words, it sounds as if you are sitting in a concert hall.

A room sound that includes a lot of extraneous echo or reverberation is called *live sound*. A room sound with little or no echo is called *dead sound*. Sometimes people prefer a bit of live sound. A singer who goes into the bathroom to record a song is looking for reverberation—the liveness of soundwaves bouncing off tile walls. On the other hand, a narrator goes into a recording booth that is covered wall to wall with acoustic foam to absorb all the soundwaves and prevent echo, creating a dead sound.

In general, close presence and a fairly dead sound are preferable, a sound quality with a minimum of echos or extraneous background sounds. In reality, there are almost always extraneous sounds that are part of the world around us: traffic, wind in the trees, air conditioners, people talking in the background. The world is hardly ever a totally quiet place. Achieving a dead sound can be challenging.

In short, the further the microphone is from the subject, the more:
1) the subject sounds further away,
2) extraneous sounds get picked up.

Strive for close presence. A good audio person will look for creative ways to get a microphone as close to the subject as possible. That's why hand-held and lav mics are used so much. They put the mic inches from the mouth.

When recording narrators, find a quiet room or a recording studio. Listen for unwanted sounds such as air conditioners. Use a room that sounds reasonably dead rather than a room full of echos.

## HEADSET MONITORING

You only know the audio is good if you monitor the sound. Headsets are your best means to do so. The VTR or mixer will have a headset plug. It's embarrassing, having neglected monitoring audio, to get home and discover that there was a problem with the sound that could have been easily avoided. Someone should wear the headsets during all recordings, listen for audio disturbances, wind noise, and bad mic presence. It's the audio engineer's job to inform the director if a problem occurs. The answer is probably as simple as doing the shot over. Or it may require a change of equipment. When monitoring through the headset, listen for:

(13.16) Wearing headsets to monitor sound.

• **Interference**. Sometimes mic cables act as antennas and pick up nearby radio signals. Solution: Change the length of the cable or reposition it.

• **Bad mic presence**. The person sounds far away. Solution: Check on the mic placement. Can it be repositioned closer?

• **Popping "P"s.** Every time the person says a word that starts with the letter "P," the "P" sound creates a small burst of distortion in the mic. Solution: Hold the mic a little further away from the person, or slightly offline from the mouth.

## FILTERS and EQUALIZATION

*Audio filters* are used to root out certain frequencies. If there is a low rumble from nearby machinery, you might filter out low frequencies. If there is a high hiss, you might filter out high frequencies. Filter controls are found on audio mixers, on microphones, or as separate units.

Another name for this filtering process is *equalization* or *EQ* for short. EQ gets its meaning from the process of trying to equalize the frequency range of a given sound source. If the bass is too low, it can be boosted. If the treble is too loud, it can be turned down.

In practice, the term EQ doesn't just refer to equalization but to the selective boosting or cutting of certain frequencies in order to eliminate or accentuate certain sounds.

A high pitched whine might be filtered out by finding its frequency and using the EQ system to selectively turn down the volume of that frequency.

But be careful that you don't filter out frequencies that are part of your primary audio. For example, the human voice typically ranges from a frequency of 20,000 cycles per second to 50,000 cycles per second, known as Hertz (Hz). You would want to protect this range as much as possible. An engine noise occurring at 35,000 Hz would undoubtedly compete with important frequencies in the voice range. Filtering out the engine would also filter out parts of the voice.

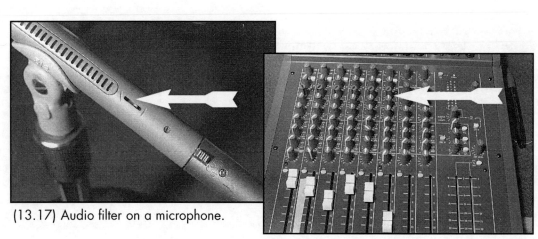

(13.17) Audio filter on a microphone.

(13.18) This audio mixer has some filtering capability through EQ controls.

Some microphones have filters built in. You can switch to high frequency roll-off or low frequency roll-off. These may eliminate certain sounds such as low rumbles from motors or high pitched whines from electrical equipment.

## SCENARIOS

Here are four scenarios. We'll describe each scenario and consider, as a director would, options for how to choose and place the microphones.

### SCENARIO #1 - Interview

In this scene, imagine two people facing each other in an interview.

We want them to be hands-free, so we won't choose a hand-held mic. If we placed one mic between the two people, the distance to the mic from each mouth might be two to four feet. That's getting pretty far away to maintain close presence. Always ask, "How can the distance be shortened? How can the presence be made closer?" Although we could place one mic between them, it would be better to put one mic on each person for closer presence.

The best way to shorten the distance and keep the people's hands free is to place a separate lav on each person. If your VTR has two audio inputs, simply plug one mic line into each input. If you only have one input, you can use a mixer to receive the two mics. The single output of the mixer goes into the audio input on your VTR.

If no mixer is available, you may have to sacrifice close presence and place a mic equidistant between the two subjects and seat them close to each other.

Another option is to use a shotgun with a fishpole operator. The operator can point it at whomever is talking. What kind of pick-up pattern would work? When a fishpole is used, the implication is that the mic is at least two feet away from the speakers. That's why the shotgun with its super-cardioid pattern is preferred. It does a good job of muting any sound from the side.

If the interview is shot in two stages—first the interviewee and then the reverse angle of the interviewer—the temptation may be to place the single lav on each person as they are being shot. That can work as long as there is absolutely no cross talk. As soon as the person off camera speaks, they will sound very far afield since they have no mic on. For that reason, whenever shooting multiple angles, it's best to maintain a consistency in the mic placement so that the sound presence stays the same from angle to angle. Otherwise when different angles are edited together, the sound quality may shift noticeably.  For consistency, either mic both people at all times, or keep one mic between them in the same place at all times.

## SCENARIO #2 - Host/spokesperson on camera

The aesthetic question is whether the spokesperson holds a mic or not? Viewers accept certain conventions: talk show hosts hold mics; news reporters hold mics. How about other kinds of hosts and spokespeople? You decide what is acceptable. If you don't mind that your spokesperson holds a mic, then choose a hand-held cardioid mic and rest assured that the sound will be good close presence.

If you don't want the mic to be hand-held, or if the host should be hands-free to walk and talk, then try a lav. The lav's wire cable will have to extend far enough to go from he host to the VTR. The lav will show up in the picture, but that's not a problem in this case. Better that the host sounds good and is hands-free. If you want no mic on the host, perhaps because he or she needs to move about, then try a wireless lav, or a shotgun on a fishpole just overhead and out of the frame.

## SCENARIO #3 - Dramatic scene

Actors generally do not wear or hold microphones in dramatic scenes. You want no visual indication of a mic in the picture. You are trying to create a fantasy world and therefore you want no reminder of reality.

Dramatic scenes usually employ fishpoles or booms with shotgun mics just overhead. Since the dialogue is often scripted, the operator can anticipate where to position the shotgun to pick up the actors' voices.

If scenes get complex with various people spread around the room, the director may call for more than one boom operator. It is not uncommon for two booms to be at work in the same scene. If that gets too complicated, the scene will have to be broken down into segments and shot a bit at a time.

For example, if the scene calls for someone across the room to make a remark, the director may call for a special close-up in which that person is both shot and miked for close presence. That scene will later be edited into the normal flow of the conversation.

## SCENARIO #4 - Music ensemble

If you have a five-piece jazz band, your choices are: 1) far-field single miking, 2) near-field single miking, or 3) individual miking and combining all the mics through an audio mixer.

1) Far-field miking gives you that large-room feeling. You can use a cardioid mic from a distance to pick up the whole band at once.

2) Near-field means placing the mic up close to the band. You may want an omnidirectional mic or a PZM that picks up a 180-degree hemisphere.

3) If you want total control over the sound level of each band member, then each musician gets miked separately and each mic line goes into your mixer. From the mixer, you can control individual levels and send the composite output to your VTR.

## CONCLUSION

Audio, like other aspects of TV production, is both science and art. Since every situation is different, you must combine technical knowledge with creative adaptation to get the best audio possible.

Consider the sound quality you desire: close? dead? far-field? live?

Any mic will record sound. But the wise selection of style and pick-up pattern, together with skillful mic placement, makes the difference between good and poor audio quality.

## A REAL WORLD APPLICATION, CONTINUED:

The director considers mic selection for the lumber mill shoot. For the interviews, he chooses lavaliere clip-on mics. Why? Because the lavs sit very close to the mouth for good presence. The interviewees will probably be stationary, so the mics can be wired directly to the VTR. No need for wireless mics which are more prone to static and interference. The director considered using a shotgun on a fishpole for the interviews. A closely placed shotgun just over and in front of the interviewee's head would produce good sound quality. But the director decided against the shotgun because it takes an additional crew member to hold the boom and there would be the added issue of boom shadow in the background to watch out for. So, the lavs seem like the simplest and best way to go.

For general mill activity, the director is concerned with picking up ambient sound of the various machines in operation. The shotgun, aimed in the general direction of the equipment, will work just fine. If the sounds of people's voices are important, the director will have an audio person hold a fishpole with the shotgun out over the people talking. As the shotgun gets closer to the voices, the voices become more prominent. Since the shotgun does a good job of muting other sounds in the area, the voices should register quite clearly.

For the dramatic vignettes, the shotgun/fishpole combo is definitely the way to go. Most dramatic scenes are taped or filmed this way. Why? Because actors need freedom of movement. The shotgun just overhead is the best way to allow the actors to move through their scenes without any concern for wires or mics. If there is a lot of movement, the fishpole operator has to be quick to follow. The mic must stay just in front of the actors' heads at all times. If several actors are in the scene, more than one shotgun/fishpole may be used, perhaps one for every two actors.

The director knows from experience that the key to professional sounding audio is close mic presence. Mics must be placed as close as possible to the subjects. When a shotgun is being used, the fishpole operator is constantly finding the fine line between keeping the mic close to the subject and staying out of the frame. He or she often watches a monitor to see whether or not they are dropping the mic in too close.

# 14

# The Jump Cut

We have all learned to expect a certain logical sequence of events in the world around us. We expect the sun to rise early in the east and set late in the west. We expect that when one turns off the water faucet, the water stops running. When the cue ball gets hit, it rolls across the table. In order for a person to walk out of a room, they first had to walk into the room. If a car moves from left to right, then moves right to left, it must have changed direction. The football team runs in the same direction in the course of four downs. And it takes time for certain things to happen. A person can't get dressed in two seconds. Likewise, if a man has shaved, when you see him the next day, he shouldn't have a beard yet. These are examples of the linear, logical flow that we expect from the time/space world we live in.

In most cases, we try to honor these same logical expectations when we produce TV shows—to acknowledge the same natural laws at work. But it's not always easy, because we're constantly dissecting and reconstructing the normal flow of action in the way we shoot and edit. Every time we shoot scenes out of sequence and from various angles, we leave ourselves open to making glaring mistakes in how we present reality. In the course of editing scenes, we may manipulate reality to some degree, but we have to be careful.

We often need to condense time. An interview lasts half an hour but there's only time to show two minutes. We don't want the interview to seem disjointed, so we try our best to dissect and reconstruct a series of edits that presents the pieces we like in a smooth linear flow of dialogue.

We also want to avoid portraying the tedium of life, so as not to bore the viewer with mundane details. Instead of showing the car drive all the way to a destination, we advance the car quickly through time and space, showing the viewers just enough to convince them that the trip took place.

## MANIPULATING REALITY

TV directors purposely manipulate reality, or at least extend a reasonable invitation for the viewer to suspend disbelief. The director wants the viewer to accept two main things: 1) that a scene shot repeatedly from several angles with a single camera can represent a live multi-camera shoot, and 2) that time can be condensed.

*Jump cuts* are an illogical or strange juxtaposition of shots—the consequence of distorting a realistic flow of events. When someone can point to a transition and say, "That couldn't have logically happened like that," you likely have a jump cut. Maybe things occurred out of sequence. Maybe the person appeared to "jump" locations. Maybe there was just a disconcerting shift in the scene. Maybe there was simply a displeasing juxtaposition of shots.

There may be times when you purposely want to distort reality. But for now, we'll assume that the goal is to portray a realistic linear flow of action.

Here are some examples of ways we manipulate reality when doing TV production that can lead to noticeable jump cuts:

## 1) Manipulation #1 - The suggestion of multiple cameras.

In single-camera production, our goal is to make the finished product look as if there were multiple cameras. So we shoot various angles and edit them together. As soon as we repeat action for subsequent takes, we run the risk of action that won't match up logically in the edit room.

In an interview, for example, it's preferable to cut back and forth so as to see each person talking. In other situations, you may want many different angles. In a demon-

(14.1) Over-the-shoulder shot (OS)

(14.2) The reverse angle simulates another camera.

stration, we want at least three angles: a wide shot to show the person demonstrating, a close-up to show the object being demonstrated, and a close-up of the host. In a dramatic scene, we want to show angles of each actor. The only way to achieve this angle variety with only one camera is to shoot the scene several times from different angles, then edit them together. We are suggesting to the viewer that the scene was captured by several cameras, that the cuts happened in a real-time flow of action.

Here is the problem: As soon as we start shooting things out of sequence or shooting multiple takes of the same scene in order to get angle variety, we leave ourselves open to errors in logic. If we're not careful, we may change the order of things. People speak out of sequence. The sun rises in the evening. The water keeps running after it's been turned off. The actor is dressed in two seconds. The freshly shaven face has hair a minute later, and the daytime scene all of a sudden is dark. Avoiding this kind of jump cut simply involves paying attention and anticipating. Keep track of the action. Which hand was that glass in? Which way was he looking? Good actors remember body positions and sequences and repeat them from take to take.

## 2) Manipulation #2 - The suggestion of condensed time.

In another example, the production team is shooting a political speech. The politician speaks for 10 minutes, but the production only has time to use 3 minutes from the speech. The director has picked two segments: a 1-minute segment from early in the 10-minute speech, and a 2-minute segment that occurred near the end of the speech. The director wants to edit these two pieces together.

(14.3) Shot from early in the speech.

(14.4) Shot from later in the speech. An edit from 14.3 to 14.4 would jump. A cutaway is needed to bridge the shots.

The edit point that occurs between the two excerpts is a jump cut. At the moment the edit occurs, you see a shift in the body of the politician. Why? Because you have distorted reality. You cut out a section of real time. Even though the politician stood in the same place looking the same direction, her body, through the course of talking, changed slightly. Even a subtle shift would be noticeable on the screen. Unless every cell in her body was in the same place and unless the camera had stayed absolutely still, the edit would reveal some sort of physical shift of the politician–hence, a jump cut.

Thus, our desire to simulate multiple cameras combined with our desire to condense time leaves us vulnerable to creating jump cuts.

Jump cuts can show up in three forms:

1) An illogical juxtaposition of shots.
2) A failure to match action.
3) A disconcerting or displeasing juxtaposition of shots.

Let's examine each.

**1) An illogical juxtaposition of shots.**

Imagine a scene in a restaurant. A dialogue is going on between two men at the bar, each with a drink in his hand. The director chooses to tape several angles of the scene, to be edited together later. In order to accommodate multiple takes, the actors must repeat the scene several times.

(14.5) Jump cut example 1: The glass changes hands instantly at the cut between shots.

(14.6)

But in this case we have a problem. In takes 1, 2, and 3, one of the actors holds the glass in the left hand. Then, the cast and crew take a short coffee break. When they come back to finish the takes, the actor inadvertently resumes the action with the drink in his right hand. No one notices the switch. Later, while editing, no one notices either. The end result is a video in which the glass pops magically from hand to hand with every cut back and forth. The scene displays a glaring error in the portrayal of a real time situation—an illogical flow or, as we defined it, an illogical juxtaposition of shots.

When the budget can afford a larger crew, one may be assigned to do nothing else but pay attention to these details. That person is called the ***continuity person***. They watch for a logical continuity from scene to scene. Did the beer glass stay in the same hand during all the takes? Are people looking in the right directions? Does the clock on the wall show the right time? Does the flow of action make sense? Are there any noticeable flaws in logic?

This potential for jump cuts is characteristic of single-camera production. In a live multi-camera production, it's much harder to distort a real-time flow of action because the action is, indeed, in real time. As long as there is no editing later on, continuity should not be a problem in a live production. It's the process of shooting several takes of the same scene that sets up the possibility of jump cuts.

## 2) Failure to match action.

Assuming that the basic physicality of the scene is correct—that each man is facing the right way and holding the drink in the proper hand, we still have to create a believable flow of action as we cut from one angle to the other. The timing has to be

(14.7) Jump cut example 2: The action doesn't match from one shot to the next. The glass couldn't have advanced that far at the cut.

(14.8)

right between various movements. We call this **matching action**. It means that a movement from one angle is consistent with a cut to the next angle. If you fail to keep the flow of movement constant, then you fail to match action, which appears as an error.

Here's an example. In cut 1, the man is looking at the glass. In cut 2, changing to a close-up, the glass is already in his hand and raised to his mouth. The result is a sudden leap forward in time and a sense of abruptness. The eye is sensitive to these breaks in logical flow. It couldn't really have happened that way. It was a good choice to cut from a medium shot to a close-up, but the change in framing was only part of the criteria for a good cut. The action had to match. Failure to match action usually reads as a jump cut.

Thus, if shot 1, the medium shot, led up to the point at which the man looks at the glass, then the next shot, the close-up, should pick up exactly where the first one left off. In other words, the man should just be ready to raise the glass at the outset of the second shot.

The need to match action is the reason entire scenes are often shot from beginning to end from each angle. That way, the editor has plenty of flexibility in cutting from angle to angle. With all this flexibility, the editor stands a better chance of matching action, assuming the actors replicated their gestures in each take.

The attempt to match action can get complicated, especially when several people are in the scene. One actor's action may match beautifully, but another actor may have done things out of order or at a different pace and compromised the action match for that edit.

We'll talk later about condensing time. In some cases, time can be sped up as a person travels across town or advances through the corridors of a building. But in other cases, the condensing of time will look like a failure to match action. In general, you can condense time between scenes, but must match action within a scene.

### 3) A disconcerting or displeasing juxtaposition of shots.

Sometimes, the flow of action can be logical and the action matches beautifully, but the shot juxtaposition is strange or displeasing. Everything happened in a proper real time flow, but the director's choice of angles and cuts was aesthetically displeasing or even disconcerting.

(14.9) Jump cut example 5: The shots are too similar.

(14.10)

## Displeasing example #1 - Cutting between similar angles.

One version of a displeasing juxtaposition is a transition between similar shots. Any time you cut to a new shot, the change should be substantial. If the change is too subtle—if shot A looks an awful lot like shot B—then the cut is disconcerting. It can be jarring to the eye to see a subtle but instantaneous change when there is no motivation. What is the point of cutting between shots that are almost identical? The cut should either take us in closer, take us out further, change the field of view, or change the scene completely.

Typically, a program begins with a wide shot to establish the scene. Then, the first cut might be to a medium shot of the action taking place. Perhaps people are involved. The next shot may be a close-up of someone talking. Thus, the sequence of three shots takes us into the scene in substantial increments: wide, medium, close. Each shot is substantially different from the previous. The mistake would be to cut from a wide shot to another wide shot of the same scene from the same angle.

So, when planning shots, make sure each subsequent shot does at least one of the following:
• changes the perspective (change angle)
• changes the field of view (change from wide shot to medium, etc.)
• changes the scene

## Displeasing example #2 - Crossing the axis of action.

Another version of displeasing juxtaposition is crossing the line that changes our directional orientation–the *axis of action*.

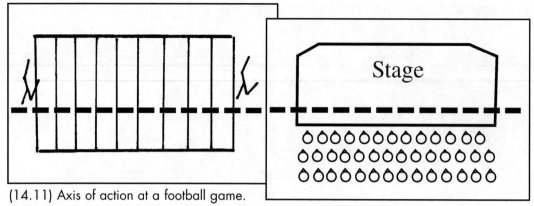

(14.11) Axis of action at a football game.

(14.12) Axis of action in the theater.

Imagine you are at a football game on the fifty-yard line. Your team has the ball and is moving down the field from your right to your left. As long as they have the ball, they should always be moving in the same direction from your point of view. Then, imagine the fans sitting across the field from you. They're on the fifty-yard line on the other side of the field watching the same action. But for them, the teams are moving from left to right.

***Does it matter that you and others across the field have opposite orientations?***

No. Because whatever the orientation, the point is to keep it constant. It doesn't matter which way the teams go, as long as they always go the same way.

Imagine that you have just watched the first down. Just as the second down begins, you are instantly transported to the other side of the field. You quickly have to reorient yourself. Then you are transported back again for the third down. It would get quite annoying and confusing.

In the football example, the axis of action runs down the sideline between you and the players on the field. You can move about your side of the stadium, but as long as you stay on your side of the axis of action, your orientation stays the same.

Another example is the theater stage. When an audience watches a performance on stage, the axis of action runs right along the lip of the stage and separates the performers from the audience. You may be sitting down front on the far left side of the orchestra seating and someone else may be seated down front far right. You each see a different angle of the stage, but both of you are still on the same side of axis of action, so your overall orientation is the same.

The same applies in a TV production. Although a variety of camera angles may be used, they should stay on one side of an axis of action. When shooting scenes for television, be aware of the consequences of shooting one angle from one side of the axis of action, and the another angle from the other side. When you edit these shots together, you will have created a disconcerting series of cuts—a series of jump cuts.

If you're shooting a theatrical performance, you can shoot from different angles in the same way that audience members seated around the room see the stage from different angles. But you need to stay on your side of the axis of action.

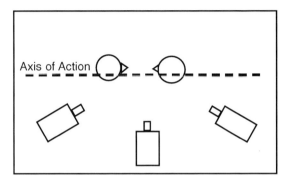

(14.13) In an interview, the axis of action line runs through the two people. Place your camera in as many different positions as you like—on the same side of the axis.

A very common breach of the axis of action rule occurs in the taping of interviews. Let us imagine that one reporter is interviewing one guest. They are facing each other. The axis of action runs right through the two of them. As a director, you will want to shoot an over-the-shoulder shot and then a reverse angle. You can shoot from either side of the axis as long as you remain there for each angle. Otherwise, the orientation of the two people will change on the screen.

In the following figures, we see good and bad examples. In the good exam-

(14.14) When the two interview angles are on the same side of the axis, faces appear to look back and forth. Here, she looks screen left.

(14.15) On the reverse angle, he looks screen right. This makes sense to the viewers.

(14.16) When the two interview angles are on opposite sides of the axis of action, the orientation of each face changes. Here, she looks left.

(14.17) He also looks left. Not logical.

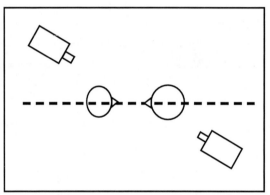

(14.18) If the reverse camera angle is shot from across the axis of action, an illogical orientation occurs between host and guest.

ple, reverse angles maintain the direction each person is facing on screen. We expect to see one person looking right and the other person looking left. But, what if the camera crosses the axis for one of the angles? Then both host and guest will be looking the same way, and that would appear very strange to the viewer.

Even so, all rules can be broken. You may find times when you must cross the axis of action. Perhaps you want to suggest confusion. Perhaps you are creating an MTV-style video with wild montages that do not necessarily make sense. The important thing is that you are aware of your decisions.

(14.19) A cutaway of the car masks the jump cut.

## JUMP CUT AVOIDANCE TECHNIQUES

You can avoid jump cuts with some simple precautions and techniques.

### Technique #1 - Use close-ups to mask jump cuts.

It's risky to shoot and edit only wide shots. Wide shots reveal everything, mistakes and all.

On the other hand, close-ups are nice for aesthetic reasons. And they serve to hide mistakes in overall continuity. Close-ups isolate certain individuals or actions in the scene. The viewer is unaware of any inconsistencies in the broader scene. Close-ups take viewer's eyes away from the wide shot for a moment. For example, if man #1 has a beer glass in his right hand and you cut to a close-up of man #2, then man #1 may have switched hands while we were not looking. The viewer accepts that, for the brief moment of the close-up, the man could have switched hands.

### Technique #2 - Cutaways can help cover jump cuts.

This is really a variation of the close-up rule. Instead of using close-ups of the main subjects, you can use cutaways to other relevant images in the scene: people watching, the clock on the wall, the dog, whatever seems meaningful and not too silly. This technique is very important for condensing long segments such as speeches. If you want to trim the politician's speech, you can cover all the cut points with shots of the reporters, the audience, the cameras in back of the room, the fellow politicians on the podium. Any cutaway that allows the viewer to see something other than the main subject will cover the break in the action.

(14.20)                         (14.21)                         (14.22)

A cut from picture 14.20 to 14.21 would be a jump cut—the shots are too similar. A cut from 14.20 to 14.22 makes sense. The change in framing has meaning—it takes the viewer in for a substantially closer view.

Note—the cutaway should not disturb the audio. The viewer continues to hear the politician's words during the cutaway.

### Technique #3 - Shoot substantially different shots and angles.

The more that a shot changes from cut to cut, the less the viewer will notice any inconsistencies in logical flow or matching of action. When you shoot a scene, tape a wide shot, a medium, and a close-up, or shoot some angles that are very different from each other. Cutting between these will help avoid jump cuts. You don't want to be stuck with all your angles looking the same. You would have a miserable time in the editing room trying to match action.

### SUMMARY

*How do you know if you have a jump cut?*

You can ask yourself two questions:
1) Does the action from cut to cut seem illogical?
2) Does the cut seem disconcerting or displeasing?

If you can answer yes to either of these, then you probably have a jump cut on your hands. Some jump cuts can be fixed in the editing phase simply by readjusting edit points to better match action or to insert cutaways. But some are born in the production phase to haunt the editor—glasses that switch hands, action that changes from take to take and won't match later in editing. These are things to prevent through proper planning.

Finally, be aware that it's hard for even the most professional crews to match action perfectly from take to take. It's common to have small errors. TV productions are inherently full of jump cuts. You see them every time you watch a movie or any single-camera production.

Jump cuts are not always bad, and to hope for a program that is absolutely free of them is usually unrealistic. But the ones you allow should be the small ones that viewers would have to look hard to see. Your job as director is to avoid the obvious jump cuts, the glaring ones, the ones that incriminate you for not having paid attention to this fundamental directorial challenge. As for the little tiny jump cuts—if they don't bother you, they probably won't bother anyone else.

## A REAL WORLD APPLICATION, CONTINUED:

How does the director shooting the lumber mill safety program avoid jump cuts? For the interviews, he makes sure that there are plenty of cutaways to things that the interviewees are talking about. Later in editing, when the editor wants to condense interview bites, creating jump cuts in the process, those cuts can be covered with meaningful and relevant cutaway scenes.

For the general mill activity shots, the director will shoot plenty of close-ups along with the wide shots. Close-ups will always serve to focus the viewer's attention for a moment, allowing some flexibility to change the subsequent shot. The scene may have changed, but the viewer's suspension of disbelief is helped by the momentary close-up. Close-ups also insure that the editor need not cut between similar shots. Instead, the editor can juxtapose wider shots with closer shots.

For the dramatic vignettes, each angle will be substantially different from the others. Framings will vary substantially: wide shots, medium shots, close-ups. The editor will cut between various angles and framings to create pleasing transitions. A crew member will be assigned the role of "continuity person" to watch for logical errors in the flow or continuity of the scene. He or she will watch the action closely to make sure actors repeat movements the same way in each take. Which hand was the glass in? Which way was he looking in that scene? Who raised their glass first? What time did the clock say?

# 15

# Moving Through Time And Space

$\mathbf{T}$V almost always condenses time. An hour-long show usually doesn't span one hour. It tells a story that can span days, weeks, or centuries.

Think about any cop show. Here is a typical scenario. The detective gets an urgent call to go to the location of a crime. He or she puts down the phone, grabs a coat, heads out the door, gets in the car, screeches out of the parking lot, and arrives at the crime scene seconds later.

In reality, this action might take anywhere from five to twenty five minutes. But there's no time for that in the TV show. Who would put up with watching the detective go out the door, down the hall, wait for the elevator, go down the elevator, out to the parking lot, fumble for keys, start the engine, drive out, wait for red lights along the way, etc. etc? There's no time for all this reality. In TV we distort reality and condense the time. We abbreviate action in order to get on to the important stuff.

Just like dealing with jump cuts, the art of moving people quickly through time and space involves some techniques. So, in this chapter we'll explore principles for moving people through time and space.

## SUSPENSION OF DISBELIEF

Thanks to viewers' willingness to suspend disbelief, TV action can be accelerated through time and space. The suspension of disbelief works best when the subject disappears, even for a moment. The suggestion is that, when the subject reappears, he or she could have moved through large amounts of time and space. In other words, the viewer subconsciously agrees that if they can't see the subject for a moment, then perhaps the subject could emerge much further along than real time would allow.

For example, if the subject simply exits Scene A completely, we can immediately cut to Scene B far away and have the subject show up there. This convention is used in almost every action show and movie ever made.

So, when you're directing a shoot that involves people moving from place to place and you want to condense time, make sure you direct your talent to enter and exit scenes in such a way that will allow you to create believable transitions. If you fail to make a subject disappear for a moment, and we see him in two different scenes back to back, you will have a major jump cut and a very unbelievable situation. How could he have moved from one scene to another instantaneously? It can't happen! But a momentary disappearance makes all the difference. There are at least five variations on this rule:

**1) Have the person leave Scene A, then appear in Scene B:**

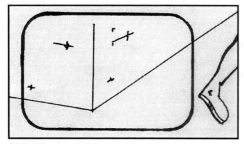 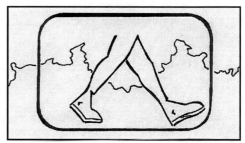

(15.1) Leave A.      (15.2) Appear in B.

**2) Have the person remain in Scene A, then enter Scene B:**

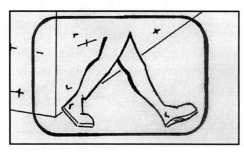 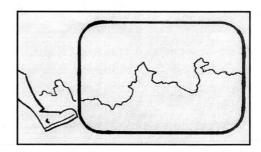

(15.3) Remain in A.      (15.4) Enter B.

**3) Have the person both leave Scene A and enter Scene B:**

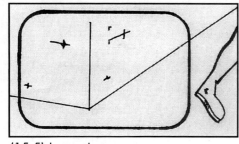 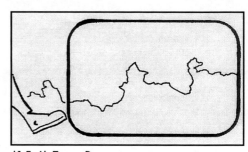

(15.5) Leave A.      (15.6) Enter B.

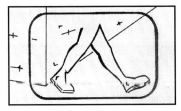

(15.7) Scene A.

(15.8) Cutaway hides the change.

(15.9) New location.

**4) Use a cutaway to bridge Scenes A and B**. By using a cutaway to some other subject, it won't matter whether the subject left or entered either scene. The cutaway will act as a neutralizing agent. For example, Scene A may show the driver on one end of town. The cutaway may show random city street activity. Then, Scene B may show the driver in a completely different part of town. The three or four seconds of cutaway allowed the viewer to believe that the subject could have moved a great distance. Keep in mind that a cutaway should not be purely arbitrary, but should make sense in the context of the scene.

**5) Use a head-on/tail-away sequence**. In this case, the subject does not disappear. Instead, the camera's view changes 180 degrees to reveal a new environment. Scene A shows the subject coming straight toward the camera. Then cut to Scene B. The camera has swung around completely and is watching the subject from the rear moving directly away from the camera in a new location, advancing the subject through time and space.

The head-on/tail-away works because the viewer has no idea what lies behind the camera during the head-on shot. Therefore, the tail-away shot can be anywhere else,

(15.10) Head-on in one location.

(15.11) Cut to immediate tail-away in another location.

even miles away. Perhaps the transition cannot be as drastic as to move the subject from the ice flows of the Arctic to the sands of the Mohave in one cut, but you would be surprised how much you can get away with.

## SCREEN DIRECTION

Along with the condensing of movement, there are a few aesthetic rules to keep in mind. For example, you should pay attention to screen direction from scene to scene. If the subject leaves Scene A to the right, he should enter Scene B from the left. Thus, the subject maintains the same left-to-right flow of movement. Constant screen direction suggests a continuation in the same direction. If a person is travelling, then they normally continue to travel in the same direction. Seeing them change directions from cut to cut feels abrupt and disconcerting. However, there are ways to introduce new directions.

## CHANGING DIRECTION

It may not be realistic to have the subject continue in the same direction in all shots. At some point, you may wish to switch directions. Cutting from screen left to screen right is abrupt. A *neutralizing shot* is needed between the two screen directions— something to distract attention for a moment so that a new direction may be introduced. Here are some options:

1) Use a cutaway to neutralize screen direction. Cut from a man walking screen left to a shot of something he is looking at and back to the man moving screen right.

2) Use a head-on or tail-away to neutralize screen direction. Since these two shots show neither left nor right screen direction, but show movement straight toward or straight away from the camera, they act as neutralizing shots. Edit one of these shots between the two screen directions to create an acceptable direction change.

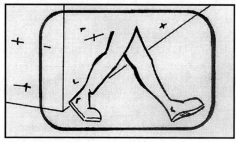

(15.12) Person moves left to right.

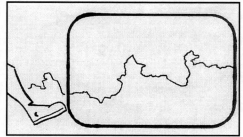

(15.13) Person maintains screen direction in next shot to imply continuous direction.

Screen direction must be considered in both the pre-production and production phases. The director must pay attention to screen direction while shooting. Plan to shoot cutaways and head-on or tail-away shots to use as neutralizing shots which will help later in the editing room.

## EAST OR WEST—WHICH IS RIGHT?

A director at ABC network studios in New York was taping an installment of *All My Children* one day when the episode called for a character to make a cross country flight. The studio had stock footage featuring an airliner high above the clouds. The plane was pointing to the right side of the screen, flying from left to right.

The scene was being rolled into the show during the pretaping session when one of the executives from the back of the room piped up and asked, "Isn't the plane supposed to be flying from the East Coast to the West Coast?" "Yes," was the answer. "Well then, flip it around, it's pointed the wrong way."

One person argued that it made no difference which way the plane was pointing. But the consensus was that most people relate to east and west the same way they look at a map of the U.S.—east is to the right and west is to the left. So, the director asked for the image to be reversed so that the plane pointed left for a westerly flight.

## SUMMARY

When a person is simply moving about within a scene, we don't worry about accelerating them through time and space. We simply worry about matching action as we cut to different angles of them within their environment. Matching action is the main goal as long as the subject stays in the same location.

But as soon as the subject is going to travel distances, the acceleration principles come into play, assuming that time limitations will not allow for a real-time treatment of the travel. The goal is to get that person from location A to location B as quickly as possible and in a manner that seems aesthetically satisfying.

## A REAL WORLD APPLICATION, CONTINUED:

The director considers the scenes in this training video where moving people through space and time will be an issue.

It will not be an issue for the interviews. It may be an issue for the general mill activity and the dramatic vignettes. For example, the director may want to condense time while showing a work routine in action. In reality, a worker may do part of the routine in one area of the mill, then travel across the plant to another area to use a different piece of equipment. The director wants to condense this time period and avoid showing much of the travel from one area to another. So, he uses several methods to help him condense time:

• He directs the subjects to leave and enter scenes appropriately.
• He considers using head-on and tail-away shots to move people through space and time.
• He pays attention to screen direction. If they exit the scene from right to left, he asks them to walk into the next scene from right to left as well, suggesting a constant direction.
• He shoots cutaways of mill activity to use as neutralizing shots.

The director knows that attention to detail makes a big difference in the overall smoothness and professionalism of his production. The success of the final product begins in the planning stages.

# 16

# Directing Talent And Crew

A director coordinates people behind and in front of the camera. Those behind the camera are referred to as *crew*. They include: camera operator, audio engineer, lighting technicians, and assistants. Those who perform for the program are called *talent*. They include: actors, models, narrators, spokespeople, and even non-TV-professionals such as presidents of companies and people on the street.

Both crew and talent look to the director for instructions. That puts quite a responsibility on the director. He or she must have enough "take charge" attitude to keep everyone informed and motivated. Nothing is more frustrating for the talent or crew than to be left in the dark about what to do, what the schedule is, or what is expected of them. So, a good director will think things through, communicate with everyone, and make sure nothing is left to assumption.

When you are the director, expect to be inundated with questions from talent:

•Where do I go to change?
•Who is doing make-up?
•What time am I supposed to be on the set?
•Where is the first shot?
•What time is lunch?
•What is this scene trying to communicate?
• What kind of characterization are you looking for?
• What color shirt should I wear?
• Is my make-up OK?

And questions from crew:

• What time is the crew call?
• Which angle are we starting with?
• Do I have time to adjust this light?
• What time code number do you want to start with?

As you can see, the director has to be an effective communicator. Here are some things a director can do to communicate well with talent and crew:

• Know the material in your script. Be able to answer questions about it.
• Know your vision for the production. Be able to describe it.
• When talent or crew are hired, explain each person's role and responsibility.
• Go over the production schedule. When are people needed?
• Deliver scripts or shot lists to appropriate people as soon as possible. Talent needs time to practice. Crew needs time to understand and prepare for technical needs.
• Provide for a rehearsal if necessary.
• On the days of production, make sure everyone knows the shooting schedule.
• Pay attention to regulations about working conditions. Union actors and crew will have specified break times and length of work days. Even if the personnel are non-union, attention should be paid to breaks, food, and the length of the overall work day. Productions fall apart when people are tired, cranky, hungry, and overworked.

If your budget can afford an assistant director or a production manager, these people can help the director with logistical concerns regarding talent and crew.

## GAINING RESPECT

It is good to realize how many different personal styles exist among directors. Some are mellow. Some are very intense. Some like to give detailed commands step-by-step along the way. Some are more loose in their control.

Whatever the personal style, general leadership skills apply. If the director is self-assured and treats people well, he or she will command respect. However, if he or she is disorganized, unclear, timid, or unkind, then all authority may evaporate.

Crew members will respect a director's authority when the director displays knowledge and understanding of the production's technical concerns. True story—a TV crew was out shooting segments for a nationally syndicated investigative news program. The director asked for a shot that featured the city skyline behind the reporter. Unfortunately, the sun was behind the reporter and the city skyline, creating a harsh backlight and a silhouette of the reporter. The shot looked terrible. The camera operator explained the problem and suggested changing locations. But the director would not hear of changing locations and insisted that the present location would work. Against his better judgment, the camera operator taped the scene which was later rejected as technically unsuitable. How do you think the camera operator regarded the director's knowledge and understanding of the TV medium?

The talent will respect the director who understands the purpose and meaning behind each scene and can explain it well. A director cannot simply rely on spokespeople

(16.1) Director coaches talent.

(16.2) Director coaches camera operator.

and actors to "do their jobs." These people look to a director as the ultimate visionary for the production. If the director does not know the purpose and meaning of a scene, then who does? A narrator may need to know what tone of voice to use while reading a script. Is the narration meant to be funny, straight, sarcastic, or mellow? An actor has similar needs. The director should be able to describe the actor's persona. What is motivating the action in the scene. Where should the actor stand? Which way should he or she face?

The director should expect that good talent and crew will come to the production with good skills and the ability to sense the needs at hand. In fact, actors and crew often make valuable suggestions to the director. But the director is the ultimate authority and when in doubt, the director needs to decide what course of action to take.

## HANDLING PERSONNEL PROBLEMS

What if someone is performing below acceptable standards? Perhaps the actor can't act, can't memorize his or her lines, or isn't being cooperative. Perhaps a crew member does not seem to be skilled at his or her craft. How does a director respond?

The director must consider whether this person is capable of quickly rising to the occasion or whether there is an obvious lack of ability that fast talk won't reverse. If the person has ability, then perhaps the director can work to improve his or her performance. It's a very delicate judgment call. If the director decides that the individual in question is unable to do any better, it is very important that the director continue to treat the person with respect. The hard reality is that actors and crew are fired all the time, but it should be done as tactfully as possible.

Every now and then, someone on the shoot is just not working out and a replacement must be made. There are a couple of important things to keep in mind:

• If the crew person has been contracted to receive a certain amount of money, then they must receive their money even if they are dismissed from the shoot.

• It's crucial to maintain a dignified atmosphere. No screaming and yelling. Just a quiet private dismissal.

The director must ultimately take responsibility for talent and crew selection. That's why directors tend to work with the same key crew members from shoot to shoot because they are known, tried and true. Same with actors. Think about how many film directors use the same actors from film to film. But there will always be situations in which the director will work with new people. That's why auditions are so important. The director must be able to size someone up during an audition and then be satisfied once the choice has been made.

## AUDITIONS

Talent may be selected through auditions. Actors understand that they must present themselves for directors to see and hear in order to make hiring decisions. If an actor is represented by a talent agent, then the agent will work with the director to schedule an audition. The audition may take place anywhere by mutual agreement. In some cases, the agent provides a location to which the director comes. In other cases, the director may request that actors come to his or her studio.

The director should have a clear plan in mind for the audition. The actors may be asked to perform one at a time or in small groups. The director may ask each prospective actor to read a page from the script. Or the actors may be asked to do some improvisational work. The director should not show favoritism during the audition but remain fair and impartial while observing each actor. Actors should be told when to expect final decisions.

The director should communicate any decisions with the actor's agent. Financial arrangements should also be made clearly and in advance. How much will the actor be paid? How much additional money does the agent charge? Most agents charge 10-15% of the total fee paid to the actor. There may be additional fees required for dry cleaning if the actor is asked to supply personal wardrobe.

## CALLING THE SHOTS

The director calls the shots during the production process. Just as the musicians wait for cues from the conductor, the crew and talent await cues from the director. The director decides when to rehearse, when to roll tape, when to call for the talent to begin and how many takes to shoot.

A typical procedure for the director includes the following:

• On the day of the shoot, the director meets with the crew to go over the setup.

• The director leaves the crew to set up while he or she meets with talent to rehearse scenes and go over any questions.

• When the technical setup is ready, the director makes sure that everything looks acceptable. He or she checks in with the lighting person, with the camera operator, and with the audio person to make sure everything is ready and to discuss any changes. The director may evaluate the scene by looking at a monitor and may wish to listen through the headphones to hear the audio during a rehearsal. The director's tone should not imply that the crew members are not able to judge the quality of their individual jobs—rather, that the director simply wishes to see and hear as well. If there are any changes to be made, a good crew person will listen to the director and try to understand and implement those changes without feeling threatened.

• The director calls for a rehearsal/run through. Knowing it will be a first rough attempt, the director needs to see which elements are coming together well and which need attention. The director reminds everyone, "This is only a rehearsal."

• During the rehearsal, the director watches the talent's performance and also checks the TV monitor to see that the lighting, positioning, and framing look good.

• After a rehearsal, the director should address any problems. He or she will address talent about their delivery and separately address crew members to make any technical adjustments necessary.

• Now it's time to record the scene. The director alerts everyone that this will be a take. He or she confirms that actors and crew are ready and calls, "Roll tape." The camera operator engages the VTR record button. The director may call, "slate!" An assistant holds a sign in front of the camera with scene information so that, later, the editor knows which scene is which. Now the tape has been rolling about ten seconds giving plenty of pre-roll time. The director calls, "Action!" The scene begins.

At times, the director will need to forget all the technical concerns in order to concentrate completely on the talent and be sure that the delivery is acceptable. No matter how good the lighting or the audio, if the talent is not performing well, the show may as well come to a halt.

Sometimes the director must work with non-professional talent: corporate executives, politicians, experts, and man-on-the-street interviews. The director should orient the non-professional as much as possible, at the same time being careful not to overwhelm. A non-professional could become quickly intimidated or frustrated if asked to do more than they are willing. Diplomacy and sensitivity are keys to success.

Normally, the director will have spent time alone with the talent rehearsing. The day of the performance should not be the time to discover that the talent cannot do the job. During the pre-production process, either through an audition or a screening, the director should have had the chance to size up the talent and to work with them in an environment free of technical distractions.

Occasionally, the director is also the camera operator. In these cases, the director must handle both artistic and technical concerns simultaneously. The best advice here is to take it slow. If you are in a rush, it will be terribly difficult to maintain a quality production. But with sufficient time, one person can run the camera and take the time to coach the talent.

Some productions don't have any actors or spokespeople. A documentary, for example, may call for a lot of shooting at a particular public event but nobody in particular is supposed to perform for the camera. That frees up the director to pay attention to what's going on without having to coach people.

Remember to be courteous. Thank the talent. Compliment them. And later, compliment your crew. Thank them for a good job. The chances are that you, as a director, have given a lot of orders throughout the day and it's time to be grateful.

## A REAL WORLD APPLICATION, CONTINUED:

For crew, the director picks only those with a proven track record. Either he has personal experience with them or they come highly recommended by close associates. The director picks a camera operator whom he has worked many times before. They know each other's expectations and terminology. The camera operator knows most of the director's personal preferences about shot framing and style of shooting. This crew choice will save a lot of talking and confusion during the production.

For actors, the director relies on a talent agency to provide good candidates for an audition. Ultimately, the director takes responsibility for choosing good people. He picks actors at an audition and now hopes his choices were good. If any of the actors turn out to be worse than he thought, he may call the agency and ask for someone else, even though he will honor the contract and pay for the person he's letting go.

The dramatic vignettes are the only scenes that need rehearsal. The director begins working with actors several days before the shoot. He meets with them twice to go over parts.

Before the shoot, the director makes sure that everyone knows what's going on. He has his assistant pass out a schedule for the three days of shooting listing times, locations, crew, and talent.

The director decides to do most of the interviews and mill activity scenes first. The dramatic scenes will be the most involved, so he saves them for last, figuring that the crew will have solved any problems associated with working in the mill by then.

The director has a forthright manner that commands respect. He is friendly and courteous with all crew and talent. At the same time, he is very clear and firm in his direction so that everyone knows exactly what's expected of them. Both talent and crew sense the director's trust in them, and that makes it even easier to receive direction. If the director wants to change the way a scene is shot, he goes over to the camera operator and has a brief discussion about it. If he wants to simply change framing, he may say, "Change that close-up to a medium shot, please." If he thinks the actor can deliver a line better, he will offer some helpful idea to trigger the actor's imagination.

"Keep in mind that you're exhausted from working all day when the boss comes in the door," the director suggests as a motivation for the actor. "Now let's try that scene again. Camera ready?"
"Ready."
"Audio?"
"Ready."
"Actors in place?"
"OK, roll tape."
"Tape is rolling," comes the response.

"Slate!" The slate of information is held up in front of the camera indicating Scene 31, Take 2. "Action!" The scene begins again.

The day is long and tiring. The director knows that tired actors and crew will fade as the day gets late. He makes sure that people take breaks and have plenty to eat and drink. Catering seems like a luxury at first, but having everyone leave the mill for meals would waste enormous amounts of time. Better to keep everyone nearby. Lunch and dinner are brought in and meals are short but adequate to get people's batteries recharged.

Finally, at the end of the day, the director thanks his talent and crew. As director, he represents the production, the client, and the producer. The talent and crew are the employees. They need to feel appreciated. Morale is yet another area that falls under the director's responsibility, but a few simple gestures along the way make all the difference.

# 17

# Production Formats

In chapter 8, we briefly described a long list of program formats from hard news to entertainment. We could devote a chapter to each, but this book would be too thick. Instead, we'll devote this chapter to four basic *production formats* that are common to any of the program formats listed earlier. These four approaches are the building blocks on which most programs are built. Examine any program and you'll find one or more of these basic production formats at work. By understanding these, the director can decide which apply to the show at hand. In this last chapter of the production process, let's put a lot of previous details into contexts by considering how to execute each of the following four commonly used production formats:

1) *Demonstration*
2) *Interview*
3) *Masterscene*
4) *News and documentary*

We'll define each format, create hypothetical scenarios, and walk through some of the basic decisions a director would need to make. We'll assume that each production uses only one format. In reality, your project may incorporate a blend of these formats.

## FORMAT #1 - DEMONSTRATION

Definition. someone is displaying something to the camera. It may be a salesperson talking about a product, someone explaining a piece of equipment in a how-to program, an artist showing artwork, or a musician playing an instrument. This is a common approach for any educational or training program.

In the demonstration format, the camera represents the viewer standing in one location watching the presentation. There is really only one angle, but there are three fields of view:

• A cover shot to see the whole scene
• A close-up or medium shot of the person who is demonstrating
• A close-up or medium shot of the material being demonstrated

Demonstration format—three or more fields of view from the same perspective.

(17.1) Cover Shot
(head-on)

(17.2) CU demonstrator
(head-on)

(17.3) CU of product
(head-on or OS)

The camera stays in the same place but shoots the action three times, once for each field of view. This represents the viewer who looks up at the presenter and down at the material, but stays at roughly the same vantage spot. You might make an exception on the close-up shot of the material being demonstrated if it's something that can best be seen over the presenter's shoulder—from his own perspective. In that case, the camera can get up and behind the presenter and look down over the shoulder so that the viewer sees the material the same way that the presenter sees it. In each situation, you must evaluate whether head-on or over-the-shoulder makes most sense.

Let's imagine that our sample scenario is a 20-minute art education show for schools. The set is a room with an art table and chair. A man will be sitting at the table presenting some techniques for mounting photographs. Let's see how our three fields of view would apply. The following shots will be used:

1) A cover shot to show the whole setting: the presenter sitting at the table with the material in front of him. We will want to see this view at the beginning and then again periodically throughout the show.

2) A medium or close-up of the man addressing the camera. Why? Because TV is a close-up medium and we want to get in closer whenever possible. The face looks more pleasing when it is easier to see the detail on a closer shot. Just how close is up to the director.

3) A medium close-up of the material on the table that he is working with. Close-ups help us see better. The resolution of the picture is easier to maintain because the image is bigger.

It's time to set up lights and audio. It appears that the table is a little bit too close to the back wall. The director would like more separation between the man and the wall for depth and to allow the shadows created by the lights to fall out of view onto the floor instead of onto the wall. The crew pulls the table a few feet further from the wall.

Once the table is positioned, the crew will set up basic three-point lighting: a key, a fill, and a back light.

Upon finishing the lighting, it becomes evident that the artwork on the table is subject to shadows as the man moves about. So, they take a fourth light and use it specifically for the artwork on the table surface. This "special" light is just for the purpose of highlighting the artwork and minimizing shadows created by the other lights. A scrim is used to soften the light.

The director asks the presenter to sit at the table while the crew checks each light. The crew considers the contrast range. If one part of the scene looks too bright, they may soften the light. If part of the scene looks too dark, they may try to reposition the lights to better illuminate the dark area. By doing these adjustments, they lessen the contrast ratio and thus allow the camera to produce a better looking image. The goal is not to eliminate contrast altogether. On the contrary, some contrast looks good. Some shadowing looks good. The point is to minimize extreme brights and darks.

The camera operator white balances the camera by placing a piece of white paper under the lights, zooming in on that paper, and pushing the white balance button on the camera. The nearby color monitor confirms that the colors in the scene all look true.

Next, the director asks the audio person to set up a microphone for the presenter. What type of mic would be most appropriate? Certainly not a hand-held, because the presenter needs to have hands free. A shotgun on a fishpole could work. But it would mean having a crew person hold the fishpole over the presenter's head. In this case it may not be a good idea because he will be continually looking down at the artwork and will thus be turned away from the shotgun.

The audio person decides on a lavaliere clipped on the presenter's lapel. The mic requires a common A-76 battery available at any drug store. Fortunately, the mic comes with a couple of extra batteries. The audio person will monitor the audio using headsets to make sure the host's clothes do not rub up against the mic as he moves about. It would be awful to find out later that the audio was distorted by the constant rustle of clothing.

The director asks the crew members if they are ready to begin rehearsing. Before actually rolling tape, the director asks the presenter to practice part of the presentation. This gives the crew a chance to check lighting and audio. It also gives the director a chance to see how everything is working and to make technical adjustments before rolling tape. The director checks a waveform monitor to make sure the video level is proper. The brightest parts of the scene peak at 100 units on the waveform.

The director notices that the presenter's eye glasses are causing a bad reflection from the lights. A minor movement of the key light solves this problem.

The director feels that the pace of the presentation is going a little too quickly. The director and host discuss it for a few minutes. They agree that the audience will not be familiar with the subject matter and it may be best to slow the pace some and spend more time on key points.

The director must assume that the presenter does not understand the production process—specifically the need to shoot the scene three times. He explains that the presentation must be videotaped three times, once to frame a wide shot, once for the medium shot of the presenter, and once for the close-up of the artwork. This three-take approach will require some repetition by the presenter. The advantage is to allow flexibility in the editing room to edit from angle to angle.

Noticing that the presenter is a little nervous, the director has a clever idea. First, he asks the presenter to rehearse which helps relax nerves. Then, the director considers the order of shooting. He decides to begin shooting with the close-up of the artwork. That way the camera will not see the presenter's face in case some nervousness still shows. By the time they get to the wide and medium shots, the presenter should be warmed up, confident, and relaxed.

After shooting each angle and a few false starts, the crew has recorded about seventy minutes worth of tape. This tape will go off to the editing room where an editor will choose portions of each of the three camera angles to sequence the entire twenty minute presentation as if three cameras were running simultaneously. Whenever the presenter is working on something, the editor will choose the angle that shows the artwork. When the presenter is addressing the camera, the editor may either use the wider front shot or the medium close-up of the presenter. Thus, the finished show will appear to have been shot by three cameras.

Later, when the editor pieces the three angles together, care will be taken to match action from cut to cut. If the presenter's right hand is reaching for scissors in the wide shot, then the cut to a close-up should continue the action at the same point. If such a match becomes impossible, a close-up of the presenter's face can serve to bridge the jump cut.

### *If the presenter stumbles, is it necessary to start all over?*

No—not from the very beginning. However, the director should pick strategic places to resume. To avoid a jump cut, the director chooses to do a *pickup* at a point where the close-up view of the artwork is most likely on screen. In other words, the cut is masked by the visual close-up.

### *Does the talent really have to run through the entire presentation three times?*

If possible, record the three angles in their entirety. However, you may find that to be impractical in some situations. Just remember that the fewer angles you tape, the more you limit your options in the editing room. You may find you are stuck with a jump cut and no options to cover it.

In summary, the demonstration format's most distinguishing feature is that the camera stays in one place, yet provides a variety of framings, simulating a multi-camera coverage. This combination of wide and close framings from one point of view is fundamental to a variety of television programs.

## FORMAT #2 - INTERVIEW

Definition—two or more people talking to each other face to face. It could be a news show, a talk show, documentary, or drama.

Interview shooting involves framing equal and opposite over-the-shoulder shots, one favoring the interviewee, and a reverse angle favoring the interviewer. This over the shoulder format also applies to dramatic dialogue, any situation in which two actors are talking face to face.

An interview format often features both the interviewee and the interviewer on camera. However, in some cases, reporters prefer not to be seen in the context of the interview. As a director, you must know whether to exclude the interviewer and shoot the interview so that the interviewee's responses stand alone as complete thoughts. In such a case, the interviewer has no presence in the final program. His or her role during the shoot is only to prompt the interviewee for statements.

(17.4) Matching OS shots          (17.5)

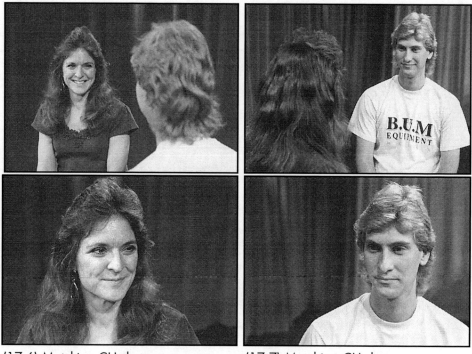

(17.6) Matching CU shots          (17.7) Matching CU shots

Ideally, the best way to shoot a real time conversation would be to use a multi-camera setup, two cameras and a switcher. Talk shows are done with multiple cameras. In fact, some field productions are shot with two cameras. The Barbara Walters specials, for example, which are usually shot on location, employ multiple cameras and a switcher. It's a much more expensive way to go, but it saves time and ensures good continuity. Most of all, it allows the director to cut back to the star host/interviewer more often. However, for most news and documentary productions, it would be highly impractical to take two crews on location. Thus, the interviews are done with a single camera.

Using a single camera, one way to capture a real-time two-person conversation without editing would be to shoot a 2-shot—profiles of the people looking at each other. The problem is that profiles are not the best way to view faces. Three-quarter profiles are much preferred. In lieu of a multi-camera setup, the single-camera style must involve shooting first the interviewee over-the-shoulder and then changing angles to shoot the interview as he or she repeats key questions, comments, transitions, opens and closes. The editor will later create the illusion that there were two cameras.

Whereas the presenter in the demonstration format addresses the camera, in an inter-view, people are instructed to avoid looking at the camera. "Just look at each other while you talk," the director coaches. The only exception is if the interviewer has opening and closing remarks delivered to the viewer—an introduction, transition, or sign off at the end.

### Why shoot the interviewee first?

• Because the interviewee may not have time to stick around.
• Because the interviewee is fresh and spontaneous the first time.
• Because the interviewee may not understand the reason for shooting both angles and may give inappropriate responses.

It is common for interviewees to precede the answer to every question the second time with, "As I said before..." Or they give painfully abbreviated answers the sec-ond time such as, "Yeah. That's right."

When shooting the reverse angle—the host's questions and transitions—the guest does not even need to complete the answer. It's already on tape from angle one.

Imagine a scenario in which a news team is going to city hall to interview the mayor. We'll assume that the interviewer wants to be included since she has an identity as an on-camera reporter for the TV station. The interview will be shown on the evening news as a special five-minute segment. The mayor was not free to come down to the TV station, so the station sent a single-camera crew to the mayor's office. The reporter/interviewer from the station plans to deliver an open and clos-ing statement to the camera. The reporter has certain key questions already in mind to ask the mayor. She expects that they will tape about ten minutes of interview and edit the best four-and-a-half minutes, leaving 15 seconds on either side for her open and closing remarks.

In this case, the camera operator is acting as director. Since the reporter knows the content to be discussed, the director's role is mainly to insure that everything is working well technically. That's why the news station felt that it was not necessary to send an additional person to act as director. Along with the reporter and cam-era/director, an assistant helps with lighting and audio.

The crew arranges to show up at the mayor's office at least a half hour before the interview to set up and light. Typically, news crews have to run and shoot quickly. They would never take that much time to set up. A politician on the move is not

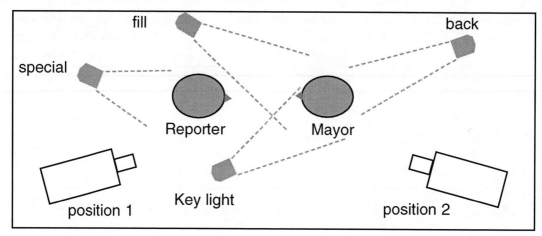

(17.8) Lighting setup for camera position 1. Besides basic three-point lighting, a special is used to light the back of the reporter. Camera position 2 shows where the camera will be placed later for a matching reverse angle. The lighting will be reversed as well.

about to wait around for lighting adjustments. But since this is not a rushed situation, the crew gives themselves the extra time and the mayor's office cooperates by letting the crew come in early for setup.

The crew arranges with the mayor's office to use a conference room that will be vacant prior to the time of the interview. No site survey was done ahead of time, but the director knows the room from prior shoots. Upon entering the room, the director/camera person recognizes a huge window all along one side of the room. Lots of sunlight is filling the room. The crew considers whether or not to work with the sunlight and balance the TV lights for sunlight by using blue gels.

However, the sun is so strong that it's causing a lot of harsh shadows and contrast. And the sun will change minute by minute. So, the crew decides to drop all the blinds, pull all the curtains, and block out most or all of the sunlight. They then work exclusively with their own TV lights which are balanced for 3200 Kelvin.

The crew must anticipate two angles: one of the mayor and a reverse angle of the reporter. Each angle will be set up as an over-the-shoulder shot with the potential for the camera to zoom in past the OS and into a CU of the featured person's face.

One compositional goal in an interview is to match angles. The OS of the mayor should look a lot like the OS of the host. Angles, elevations, and distances should look similar.

When shooting the reporter—the reverse angle—the director will not want to run through the entire interview a second time. That would create a nightmare for the editor since nothing ever comes out spontaneously the same way twice. Answers will vary. Matching exact dialogue would be impossible in an unscripted discussion. Instead, the director will simply ask the reporter to do three things:

1) Ask key questions, the ones she is quite sure she can repeat much the way she asked them the first time.

2) React a little for the camera for use as possible cutaways that may be helpful later to bridge jump cuts. The host nods, smiles, listens as the tape records.

3) Recite opening and closing remarks. The host presents a scripted welcome and a goodbye, thanks for being with us.

The crew sets up three-point lighting first for the mayor. They also set one *special* light for the back of the reporter as seen in the OS shot. Later they'll reverse the three-point lighting to light the host and use the special on the mayor's back.

For audio, the assistant sets up two lavalieres, one for the reporter and one for the mayor. The record VTR has two audio channels, so one mic is plugged into each channel's input. There is no attempt to hide the mics. They are placed on lapels free and clear to avoid clothing rustle. The wires leading from the mics are discreetly run inside the jackets to keep them hidden. This is called *dressing the cables.*

The assistant will monitor the audio using headphones while the director/camera person runs the camera and gives any needed directions to the reporter and mayor.

The crew gets ready as quickly as possible, knowing the mayor is on a busy schedule. When all is ready, the crew lets the mayor's assistant know.

The mayor enters and chats for a minute with the reporter. They get seated right away so that the crew can check audio and lighting. The reporter asks the camera person/director if they can begin. The camera person starts the tape rolling, nods, and they begin the interview.

While the interview is going on, the camera person does some shot variation. He uses the OS shot on some questions and then zooms in to a close-up for other questions. This offers visual variety and helps the editor avoid jump cuts.

When the interview is finished, the director/camera person asks the mayor to stay for another five minutes while they shoot reverse angle questions and reactions of the reporter. The mayor says fine. The crew does a quick readjustment of lighting and moves the camera around to the opposite angle, but is careful to stay on the same side of the axis of action. The camera person is careful to remember what the two people looked like in relationship to each other from the first angle and works to match angles on the reverse.

When set, the camera person rolls tape, waits a few seconds for pre-roll time on the tape, and cues the reporter. She repeats each question, sometimes a few different ways to make sure that the tone and delivery match well to the tone in the first angle. The better the match, the better the illusion of two cameras.

If the director does a good job shooting the interview, then the editor can piece together shots that match well, that have good conversational flow, in which any jump cuts can easily be covered by host reaction shots, and which all culminate in a presentation that looks as if it were shot by at least two cameras.

## FORMAT #3 - MASTERSCENE

Definition—shooting multiple angles of a single scene, beginning with a cover shot and then repeating the scene with the camera repositioned for each new angle in order to simulate multiple cameras.

*Masterscene* shooting is a more complex version of the demonstration format and interview. It employs numerous angles in order to create the illusion of multiple cameras cutting back and forth within a scene. Whereas the interview and demonstration formats might have only used one, two, or three angles, masterscene shooting might use many more. A scene with three or four people might require six to ten different angles and framings.

Masterscene shooting is the style used by feature film productions shooting dramatic scenes. Actors understand that their job is to repeat a scene over for each angle. In most cases, they will repeat the entire scene for an angle. In some cases, they may only repeat part of the scene.

The word "masterscene" refers to the first angle shot by the camera—a wide cover shot of the entire action. The term implies that a number of other angles will be shot after the masterscene: over-the-shoulder shots, close-ups, any angles that would let us see the various members and actions within a scene.

(17.9) Masterscene

(17.10) OS Bob

(17.11) OS Mary

(17.12) CU Bob

(17.13) CU Mary

(17.14) Cutaway of book

(17.15) Mark enters room

(17.16) CU Mark

In our hypothetical example, we'll shoot a three-minute dramatized scene to be used in a corporate training program. The scene is an office. In this scene, two people, Bob and Mary, are seated and talking. The woman refers to a book on her lap. Toward the end of the scene, a third person, Mark, comes in and joins the group.

These eight angles constitute the various angles to be cross-cut in the editing room, giving the illusion that there were multiple cameras on the set. The actors will run the entire scene from each angle, except perhaps for the cutaways which happen very quickly. Running through the entire scene over again offers some advantages:

1) The actors are able to re-establish the full flow and rhythm of the scene each time.

2) Full run throughs on tape give the editor the choice where to make edits.

The director found the actors by auditioning them through a couple of different talent agencies. These agencies represent models, spokespeople, voice over narrators, and actors. The director met with the agencies to go over the casting requirements. The agencies put together audition sessions with about five people for each part. The director wanted to see how well each one could act, but was also concerned about the right ethnic mix. Ideally this team of actors would display some racial and gender diversity. Once the cast was selected, the director contracted with the agency to use them for one rehearsal session and a day of shooting. The director supplied scripts to the actors ahead of time, then rehearsed with the actors a few nights prior.

Now, on the day of the shoot, the crew has come in to set and light. They are working on a rented *sound stage* at a local production studio. The sound stage is a large soundproof room with curtains, a curved seamless wall and floor that looks infinitely large, called a *cyclorama*, and a lighting grid to hang lights. The advantage of the sound stage is that it provides a completely controlled environment. No noise and interruption from the outside world. It is also well equipped with electricity and hardware. A set has been constructed for the scene.

### Why build a set when you could go shoot in a real location?

Dramatic scenes can be done in real locations. However, the director knows that things are better controlled on a sound stage. Even though an office set must be constructed, there are other factors that actually save money: the fact that the crew will be in control of the environment at all times, that the surroundings will be quiet, that lighting and electricity are reliable, and that the room is soundproof and fairly dead. The set will be used for many scenes in the program, so the production will get its money's worth. Finally, movement of cameras—the ability to truck, dolly, arc, and do moves up and down on cranes—is much easier on a sound stage.

It's 7:00 am, the morning of the shoot. The set builder brings in a few final pieces for the office. While the builder builds, the grips hang lights, the audio people prepare a boom, and the camera person sets up the tripod and camera on a dolly and track. The director is in the back room doing a run-through with the actors.

By lunch time, the set is ready. After lunch it's time to do some run-throughs and record the scene. The actors also get checked over by hair and make-up assistants.

The audio person uses a shotgun on a boom. Lavs might rustle in the clothing or be seen. He tries to keep the boom as close to the actors as possible without dipping the mic into the picture. He also tries to keep the shotgun just in front of and pointed directly at the face of whoever is talking. The boom operator practices getting the mic over to the third person as he enters and speaks from the doorway.

The director runs the rehearsal. The camera is set for position 1, the masterscene angle. Lighting and audio people use the time to make minor adjustments.

Finally, it's time to roll tape. The director calls for the first take to be the masterscene—a wide cover shot. The director calls for the videotape to roll. An assistant calls, "Scene 14a, Take 1" out loud so that there is a verbal record on tape. The director waits a few extra seconds for pre-roll so that the scene does not begin too close to the beginning of the tape. The director calls "action" and the actors begin the scene. They do four takes of Scene 14a before the director is satisfied with the masterscene.

Next, the crew sets up for the second of the eight angles, an over-the-shoulder shot of one of the people seated at the table. They do three takes from that perspective and slate it as Scene 14b to indicate a new angle. Then, keeping the camera where it is, they do Scene 14c, a close-up of the same person.

Scenes 14c and d are OS and CUs from the opposite side, facing the other person seated at the table.

Scene 14e is a medium shot at the doorway when the third person enters. Since that third person is only at the door for a few seconds, the director stops the scene shortly after the actors leaves the doorway since nothing else happens there.

Scene 14f is a close-up of the third actor once he is seated at the table next to the other two.

The actors have repeated their scene about 24 times: eight angles and three takes each. It may seem a bit tedious, but they are used to it. They understand the discipline needed to make a single-camera shoot happen. They understand the masterscene style.

All the raw footage will go to the edit room now. Tomorrow, the director and editor will make decisions about when to cut to which shots and angles.

## FORMAT # 4 - NEWS AND DOCUMENTARY

Definition—news stories and documentary productions are lumped together in this format because they share qualities. Both formats are usually handled by small crews—one to three people. Both formats are typically on location and on the move. Both formats have days when subject matter can be well scripted or days when nobody knows how events will unfold and shooting must be spontaneous.

It's the spontaneity of fast-breaking news that gives the news crew a special challenge. The trick is to get broadcastable footage in the most adverse of conditions. Setups must be fast. At times the crew hops out of the van with tape rolling.

*How does the production crew handle the challenge of being ready to shoot at a moment's notice?*

• The crew checks all equipment before leaving for the shoot, making sure everything is working and ready.
• They use batteries only. No time or place to plug in.
• Lights can be run off heavy duty batteries for short periods of time if need be.
• Videotape is already loaded in the VTR and extra tapes are handy.
• They try to use only the best in broadcast cameras. The high-end cameras produce the best pictures in dark conditions and in high contrast conditions. Since a news crew may have no control over lighting and locations, at least the better camera will help alleviate the problems of low light and high contrast.

Like news, a documentary production typically takes a crew to many different locations and may involve many interviews. The documentary tells a story about people or events. The events may be current or recreated from historical photos and films. The pace may be fast like a news story or slower like a feature, depending on the subject matter.

In our example, the documentary will be about a current news story. This type of documentary presents a challenge for the director because nobody really knows how the story will unfold. The writer and director try their best to anticipate the subject matter. They research and write a script, even though there are many unknowns. This forces them to imagine how the story will flow. As events change, they will update the script.

In this case, the documentary is about the aftermath of the failed savings and loan institutions and the attempts of the now defunct Resolution Trust Corporation to sell off assets in order to make up for the billions that were lost. The makers of the documentary want to show how big a crisis the savings and loan scandal was and how inept the Resolution Trust Corp. was in handling the asset sales.

This production has a director and an on-camera reporter. The crew of two include a camera person and an audio person who doubles as a lighting assistant. The team of four will be together for one month of travel and shooting. They're going to visit four cities and interview more than 20 people.

Some people don't want to be interviewed. If they perceive that they will be made to look like fools by the media, they may be reluctant to speak on camera. Gaining people's trust is an ongoing challenge for the director and reporter.

The production team scheduled as many of the interviews as possible. However, some interviews have to be spontaneous. Sometimes the crew encounters people who they did not know existed, but who would make good contributions to the show.

Thus, the crew has to be fast. Sometimes the set-up time is brief. The crew configures themselves to be ready to roll tape in a few minutes' notice. In many cases, interviews are grabbed quickly. No time for three-point lighting. In other situations, there is time to create a nicer looking environment for the interview.

In the interest of speed, audio is best applied with the shotgun and fishpole. No time to pin mics on people. The audio person swings the fishpole into position and the crew is ready to roll.

Besides interviews, the crew needs to get shots of buildings, homes, vacant lots, and other real estate. They even rent a helicopter to get some aerial shots of housing developments that were affected by the savings and loan scandal.

In addition to shooting, the director spends time locating existing news footage from several years ago when the scandal was at its peak: political speeches, news headlines, and other media coverage at the time. In some cases, the production team must purchase the rights to use other people's footage. Other old footage is made available free of charge by TV stations affiliated with the production team's network.

In this documentary production, the reporter is the writer. The story was well researched before production began. But every day's interviews are shedding new light on the story. Every night, the reporter and the director talk about where the show is heading and what scripting changes need to be made. The reporter then rewrites sections of the script based on the actual content of that day's interviews.

This reporter prefers to be on-camera. He is seen in the interviews, which necessitates reverse angles for questions and reactions. And he narrates the show. Some scenes involve the reporter doing news-style stand-ups. The crew finds a suitable location for the reporter to stand and face the camera to deliver opening and closing comments for various segments of the show. At the end of the production process, the script should be finalized and the reporter will record voice-overs to fill in the rest of the narration.

All the elements—interviews, outdoor scenes, news footage, reporter stand-ups, and voice-over narration—will go to the editing room to be woven into the final edited program.

## SUMMARY

These formats comprise some of the most commonly used styles of single-camera production. Often the styles will be combined. For example, a documentary may include some interview or demonstration segments. Or a demonstration may be combined with an interview. Thinking about these formats helps you plan for the types of production techniques you wish use.

---

### A REAL WORLD APPLICATION, CONTINUED:

The director knows that the production incorporates several formats:

• The interviews are shot in the interview format and will not feature the interviewer. The questions won't be heard later. Instead, the interviewees will be prompted to respond with complete, stand-alone statements—sentences that begin with "I think that..." rather than just, "Yes, I do," which makes no sense without hearing the question. The director will explain this concept to each interviewee before taping. Usually, people understand and comply easily. In the final edit, these interview comments will be used in various spots throughout the program.

• The scenes showing general mill activity use some documentary format and some demonstration format shooting. In some cases, employees will be asked to demonstrate specific tasks or procedures. In other cases, the video crew is in a more spontaneous mode, watching for actions around the mill that might naturally illustrate some of the concepts in the safety program.

• The dramatic vignettes incorporate the masterscene format. Shooting is done from a variety of angles to be edited later, creating the illusion of multi-camera coverage. Each vignette is taped in its entirety from each angle.

---

## Section V

# Post-PRODUCTION

Post-production is the third phase of the single-camera production process.

The term *post-production* encompasses more than just editing the scenes together. The post-production process also includes music selection, audio effects, narration, and graphics. The final chapter will discuss distribution options for the finished video product.

# 18

## PREPARING TO EDIT

It's the morning after. All the scenes have been shot. Numerous video cassettes are now full of field footage. It's time to begin the post-production phase, otherwise known as editing.

The tapes, known as *source tapes*, *field tapes*, or *original footage*, will not be altered in the editing process—there will be no physical cutting or pasting. It's more like a cloning process. In editing, the electronic signal is electronically cloned off the source tape and onto a new tape—a controlled copying process.

In the *linear editing* mode, scenes are transferred from one videotape machine to another. In the newer *non-linear editing* mode, the scenes are transferred into a computer environment using PC or Mac-based editing software programs and large hard drives to store the digitized video. After editing in the computer environment, the finished material is transferred back to videotape for distribution.

By contrast, film editing involves the physical cutting of the original film. In the early days of video editing, videotape, too, was cut and spliced. Eventually, the more efficient electronic cloning method put an end to physical cutting.

### WHY PREPARE TO EDIT?

The premise for this chapter is that the editing process should be efficient. Editing can be extremely expensive per hour. Ill-preparedness means a large waste of money. Also, editing, which is inherently time-consuming, goes faster with some up-front preparation.

Here are four preparation steps toward an efficient editing session:

1) Tape log
2) Script refinement
3) Paper edit
4) Gathering of materials for the edit

---

**TAPE LOG**

*TAPE 1*

1:00   Scene  14a  Take 1   masterscene - bad take
3:00   Scene  14a  Take 2  OK
6:00   Scene  14a  Take 3  OK
10:00  Scene  14a  Take 4  good
13:00  Scene  14b  Take 1  over-the-shoulder (OS) of BOB - good
18:00  Scene  14b  Take 2  better

*TAPE 2*

1:00   Scene  14c  Take 1   OS Diane - good
3:30   Scene  14c  Take 2   OK
6:30   Scene  14d  Take 1   CU Diane - OK
11:00  Scene  14d  Take 2  good
13:00  Scene  14e  Take 1  Jim at the door - good
15:00  Scene  14e  Take 2  better

---

(18.1) An example of a tape log from the first two source tapes.

## TAPE LOG

One of the first things to do—if it hasn't already been done—is create a printed record of all the scenes that were shot on location. Otherwise, time is wasted searching high and low for desired scenes while editing.

The log can be made by an assistant during the shoot. The assistant references clock time numbers or time code numbers on the VTR to indicate locations on the tape for each scene. Or, if taking notes on location is too much trouble, the tape log can be made later while reviewing all the footage.

This log will help the editing process. It's also helpful to keep the tape log in the file for future reference. When someone calls up and says, "Do you have a shot of the front of the bank building?" you don't have to go looking through all your tapes. You can just pull out the tape log. Tape logs kept on word processing computer files are particularly handy because you can do word searches to find scenes. You'll also find tape logging software programs on the market that offer some useful features such as the automated creation of still images to serve as visual scene references.

## KEEPING TRACK OF TIME

Most VCRs have a way of showing a running time. But there are different methods and it is very important to understand the difference between each one. For example, if a scene is logged at "23:44," that number could represent any of three types of numbering systems. It's important to know which is being used and which is most accurate. (See chapter 4 for more information on frame and frame measurement.) Let's look at three types of time keeping.

## COUNTER TIME

On a VHS player, a time counter may be a three or four digit readout, for example: 3455. Unfortunately, this is an arbitrary number that does not correlate to any standard measurement. It does not relate to the clock or to the time of day. There is no way to be precise. Therefore, counter numbers are the least reliable.

## CLOCK TIME

A clock time counter is found on many newer VCRs and on professional videotape equipment. The clock time displays hours, minutes, and seconds just like a digital clock.  In addition, a clock time used in video will usually have an additional set of digits to measure frames. Remember, there are 30 frames per second.

Unlike the arbitrary counter time, clock time is a standardized form of measurement that we all know. When a scene begins at 1:01:30 and goes until 1:02:00, you know that the scene lasted 30 seconds. Or, if a scene lasts from 1:01:30:15 to 1:02:05:20, the scene is 35 seconds and five frames long.

## TIME CODE

Time code reads the same as clock time: hours, minutes, seconds, and frames. The difference is that a system using time code records the numbers on a track of the videotape. Time code is a permanently encoded signal on the tape created by an electronic time code generator within the recording VCR. The track gets laid down as the tape is recorded.

If the clock time readout were 12:02:10:29, that would mean: 12 hours, 2 minutes, 10 seconds, and 29 frames into the tape. The next number in the sequence would be the next frame, or 12:02:11:00. The frame digits advanced from 29 to 00 and the seconds digits from 10 to 11. Similarly, the following frame would be 12:02:11:01.

The time code can be set to start at whatever time the operator wishes. For example, source tape #1 can be set to start at 1:00:00:00. Tape #2 can be set to start at 2:00:00:00. That makes for easy logging. When tape #2 is played, for example, the time code shows the entire sequence of numbers starting with "02" in the hours column. The editor knows that all shots starting with hour #2 come from tape #2—assuming the source tape does not exceed one hour in length.

## LOGGING TAPE IN A NON-LINEAR ENVIRONMENT

Non-linear editing requires the user to first catalog clips from the source tapes according to time code numbers. Rather than digitizing all footage on all source tapes, the user scans through the material and marks in and out points for the desired scenes, thus logging the tapes. As the user marks the in and out points for each clip, the non-linear editor will show the chosen clips as little picture icons on the computer screen. In each case, the icon can be named, for example "Scene 1a," and the icon is associated with a time code number for the beginning and end of the scene.

After this logging step, there is still no actual video information in the computer's hard drive—only the icons that represent the user's selections appear on the screen. But the time code numbers associated with those icons have been recorded so that later, when digitizing is ready to begin, the computer knows exactly where to find the selected scenes as it transfers video information into the computer hard drive.

## SCRIPT REFINEMENT

Even though the script was prepared before shooting began, changes are often made later in the process. Perhaps some lines in the dialogue need to be rewritten. Or, in a documentary, the story may take some unexpected turns and the script may undergo major rewriting.

The script should be revised as much as possible before the editing begins. The script is the roadmap for editing just as it was for shooting. The goal is to keep decisions to a minimum in order to maximize the time.

## PAPER EDIT

The *paper edit* is a tool to help you make decisions before entering the editing room. A paper edit involves figuring out on paper the way the show will be pieced together. One method is to choose time code numbers from the tape log and mark them on the script or on the tape log where they should occur.

A more detailed approach is to create a list of "in" and "out" times for each scene. This is more time-consuming, but it's a huge time saver in the editing room.

One approach to the paper edit is shown in figure 18.2. In this case, the director simply uses the tape log and indicates which scenes will be used and in what order. In this figure, the first five edits have been tentatively chosen using only the tape log.

The advantage to marking the tape log is that it's quick and easy and doesn't involve additional paperwork. The disadvantage is that it is not extremely precise. You still have to determine in and out points for each shot.

Figure 18.3 shows the more detailed approach. In this case, exact in and out points are determined for each scene. This requires spending more time watching the raw footage and noting the beginning and end of desired scenes.

---

**PAPER EDIT**

TAPE 1

|      | 1:00  | Scene 14a Take 1 masterscene - bad take |
|      | 3:00  | Scene 14a Take 2 OK |
| #1   | 6:00  | Scene 14a Take 3 OK |
| #2   | 10:00 | Scene 14a Take 4 good |
|      | 13:00 | Scene 14b Take 1 OS of BOB - good |
| #3   | 18:00 | Scene 14b Take 2 better |

TAPE 2

|      | 1:00  | Scene 14c Take 1 OS Diane - good |
| #4   | 3:30  | Scene 14c Take 2 OK |
|      | 6:30  | Scene 14d Take 1 CU Diane - OK |
|      | 11:00 | Scene 14d Take 2 good |
| #5   | 13:00 | Scene 14e Take 1 Jim at the door - good |
|      | 15:00 | Scene 14e Take 2 better |

---

(18.2) Paper edit, example #1 - The simplest way to create a paper edit is to number the scenes on a tape log in the anticipated order for editing.

**PAPER EDIT**

| EDIT # | REEL # | DESCRIPTION | IN POINT | OUT POINT |
|---|---|---|---|---|
| #1 | 1 | Scene 14a | 1:00:06:35 | 1:00:07:00 |
| #2 | 1 | Scene 14a | 1:10:22:20 | 1:00:35:10 |
| #3 | 1 | Scene 14b | 1:18:20:00 | 1:18:30:00 |
| #4 | 2 | Scene 14c | 2:03:48:02 | 2:04:15:00 |
| #5 | 2 | Scene 14e | 2:13:30:20 | 2:13:35:10 |

(18.3) Paper edit, example #2 - A more specific approach is to create a paper edit that looks like an edit decision list. Each anticipated scene is put in order on a list along with time code in and out points.

Other details may be added to this paper edit:

• The kind of transitions preferred for each edit—cuts, dissolves, or wipes

• Notation of any graphics, names, and titles that will be needed for editing.

**GATHERING OTHER MATERIALS**

Besides the tape log and paper edit, there are other preparations for editing.

• *Stock footage*. There may be other types of footage that you did not shoot but that you need for the edit. Perhaps you need World War II archival footage from the library, or a film clip from Paramount Pictures, or a shot of Big Ben from a stock footage provider in New York. The premise here is that some shots are cheaper to obtain from someone else than to go out and shoot yourself. Whatever the need, round up the additional videotape ahead of time. Go into the edit room with everything ready to go.

• *Product shots*. Some items may need to be shot during the editing process: graphic cards, photos, products. Some edit studios have graphics cameras whose signals are wired into the editing system in order to capture images of objects or artwork. Consider whether you are able to shoot any of these items during the production phase or whether they must be brought in to shoot during the edit session, requiring extra time.

• **Music.** Consider the use of music in your show. Will it be original music? If so, you must contract with a composer. Will it be licensed library music off a tape or CD? If so, then listen and choose the cuts you think will work. (More on music in the chapter on post-production audio.)

• **Narration.** Is there going to be a narrator? If so, begin to think about who that will be. Man or woman? Union or non-union? Someone you know? Or do you need to audition them?

• **Graphics**. Do you have the means to create titles? Names and titles to identify speakers? Maps or charts? Do you have the resources to get graphics made? Do you have a character generator in your editing system to type names and titles? Can graphics be created ahead of time in order to be all ready for your edit session?

## SCHEDULING THE EDITING ROOM

Scheduling is critical in the TV business. Facilities get used so much, the only way to keep order is to schedule. Plan ahead. Book your time.

Sometimes the client wants to be there to watch the editing process. Or it's important to have the client there in order to get immediate feedback on shots that may require the client's expertise or judgment. In any case, decide if the client should be present for some or all of the edit session and make necessary arrangements.

## SUMMARY

Editing can be very expensive. Professional editing suites charge anywhere from $125/hour to $500/hour. If you have to spend time searching around for scenes and calling around for things you forgot to secure ahead of time, the hours spent in the edit room are sure to multiply at an alarming rate. If you can walk into an editing session with plenty of advance planning, you are sure to have a quick and efficient time getting the show completed.

## A REAL WORLD APPLICATION, CONTINUED:

After the shoot, the director reviews all the tapes in preparation for editing. He makes a tape log to note the time codes for all the scenes. Using an asterisk, he notes which takes he likes best. He also notes the "out" times as well as "in" times for scenes which, after adding up the times of all the selected scenes, gives him some idea of overall program length.

As he reviews the interviews, he notes which comments work well from a content standpoint, but also which comments are short enough and concise enough to be suitable for the video. Interview bites always eat up a lot of tape time. Lengthy comments, though rich in ideas, are usually too long for a brief video presentation. Yet each interview is full of good material. It's often hard for the director to select among all the good sound bites. He would like to use more than time allows. But he does his best to pick responses that will be both brief and meaningful.

After logging the scenes, the director tries to imagine the overall way in which these scenes flow together. Referring to the script, he imagines where each scene will go and makes a tentative list of time code numbers in the order they would appear. This is his paper edit. He makes a copy of the paper edit for the editor. The editor can refer to the paper and see which tapes and scenes will be needed.

The director collects other materials for the edit session:
• A logo created by a computer animator, delivered on a BetaSP tape,
• A list of names to identify graphically in the video,
• A voice-over narration recorded at an audio studio, and
• Music selections from a music library on compact disc.

By the time the director goes in to the edit room to begin, he is well prepared. He knows that edit rom time is expensive and he must stay within budget or the production company may not hire him again.

# 19

## Editing Mechanics—Linear And Non-Linear

Today's editor can choose whether to edit on a linear or non-linear editing system. This chapter will explain both. Even though the newer non-linear method is the cutting edge of technology, it's important to understand the linear method as well for two reasons: 1) many traditional linear editing concepts form the basis for non-linear editing, and 2) linear systems are still prevalent in the TV industry and the director should understand how they operate.

This chapter will cover the editing process in three sections:
• Overview
• Linear editing
• Non-linear editing

### OVERVIEW

Editing is very much like the writing process. When writing a story, it's best to plan ahead, to have an idea clear in your mind and a structure for the story. That way, when sitting down to the typewriter or computer, you will have some direction already in mind. While writing, you choose what to say, how much to say, and in what order to say things. It's the same with video editing. Except, in this case, you compose not just words, but sounds and pictures.

Directors do not necessarily have to know all the mechanics of editing. One can hire an *editor* to assemble the program. The editor may function in a purely technical capacity or as an artistic consultant as well. In most high-end editing suites, the equipment is so complex that a staff editor normally operates the equipment. The director acts as client, supplying source tapes and instructions as he or she supervises the edit session.

The director's relationship with the editor, as with other crew, varies from person to person. Some directors extend enormous amounts of creative latitude to editors. They may go over the material and then leave the editors to work alone. Other directors supervise the edit sessions from beginning to end. Since there is no official term to distinguish the creative editor from the one who is supervised, the director must decide and make clear what kind of working relationship he or she is to have with an editor and choose the best person for the job.

## EDITING MECHANICS

With tapes, tape logs, a paper edit in hand, and a strategy in mind, it's time to enter the editing room. But wait! There are different kinds of editing systems from which to choose.

Some editing systems are linear. Some are non-linear. Some are digital. Some are analog. Different editing systems may be set up to use specific tape formats. It can be confusing. So before we start editing, we need to make some distinctions about the types of systems available. Three types of distinctions help categorize them:

1) linear versus non-linear
2) digital versus analog
3) component versus composite

These are a lot of terms to be hit with all at once. But they are important, so let's define them one at a time.

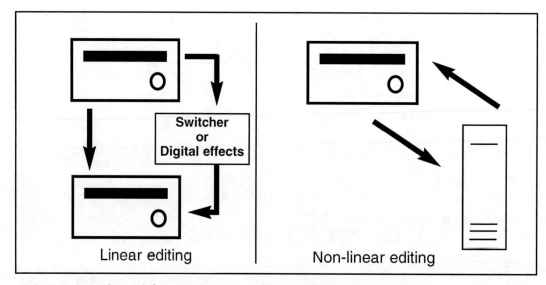

(19.1) Linear editing, left, involves dubbing scenes from a source tape deck to a recorder tape deck. Along the way, the video may pass through a switcher or digital effects computer to manipulate the images. Non-linear editing, right, involves digitizing scenes from a tape player to a computer, then editing and creating effects within the computer's random access environment, and finally transferring the finished program back to tape for distribution.

## 1) Linear versus non-linear

Linear editing is from tape to tape. Non-linear editing is from tape to computer and eventually back to tape after editing is finished.

Traditional linear editing is comparable to typing on the typewriter. If you want to insert a paragraph in a page that has already been typed, you start the page over from scratch. Similarly, if you want to add ten seconds of video in the middle of an existing show, you will have to re-edit the later portion of the show in order to position the scenes further down the videotape. You can't just slide the signal down the tape in order to make more room.

The newer non-linear editing is comparable to word processing. The video is stored on a computer where it can be manipulated in a random access style with the click of a mouse. Once scenes have been clicked and dragged around the computer screen, the sequence can then be "printed" or dubbed back to videotape for distribution.

## 2) Digital versus analog

Besides linear and non-linear systems, we also need to consider the terms *digital* and *analog*. These terms are explained in chapter 3. It's helpful to know what kind of system you are using and its pros and cons.

All computer-based non-linear editing is digital because all computers process information digitally. But traditional linear editing, which uses videotape machines, can be either analog or digital. In other words, the video signal can be processed and recorded on tape in either a digital or analog format, but the function of the editing system is still linear if the signal goes from one tape machine to another.

If the editing system is using the analog method of recording a signal, then this cloning process causes a loss in quality on the new recorded tape. The new tape cannot retain an image as clear as the original source tape. With every copy of an analog tape, a little more electronic noise is introduced to the picture. This inherent drop in quality is called *generation loss*. With every generation or copy, there is a small loss in resolution.

The better the quality of the videotape, the less noticeable is the generation loss. A broadcast quality BetaCam tape copied to another BetaCam tape will reveal much less generation loss than a consumer grade VHS tape copied to another VHS.

|  | **LINEAR** | **NON LINEAR** |
|---|---|---|
| **ANALOG** | • uses videotape machines as source and recorder<br>• subject to generation loss<br>• no random access | • no such thing<br>(would require scissors to move scenes around!) |
| **DIGITAL** | • no generation loss<br>• uses videotape machines<br>• no random access | • computer based<br>• scenes get digitized into the computer<br>• random access<br>• no generation loss |

(19.2) Basic comparison of linear and non-linear systems.

Digital processing has revolutionized the generation loss issue. As binary code gets passed back and forth through digital processing, there are almost no signs of generation loss. Digital images can be passed back and forth many times within a digital processing environment with negligible degradation of the picture quality.

*How do you know whether your system is analog or digital?*

All non-linear editing systems are digital because all computers are digital. However, if the system is linear, using videotape machines to perform edits, then it may or may not be digital. A videotape can accept either digital or analog information. You must determine whether or not your videotape machine is made to process digital information.

*How do you know whether your system is linear or non-linear?*

If the system passes information from one VTR to another, it is linear. If you could cut the tape and rearrange it, then it would be non-linear. But the tape, like the typed page, stays intact and, therefore, requires a linear approach to editing. Each scene, once placed in order, is immovable unless re-edited.

A note about computers—just because there is a computer in the room, does not mean the system is non-linear computer-based editing. Most editing systems use computers somewhere in the system to control the equipment. But these computers are not processing the video signal. They are simply being used as edit controllers to stop and start the videotape machines and to create edit decision lists. If it is truly a computer-based editing system, there will be no videotape machines involved in the actual editing process. The footage is on the hard drive and stays in the computer environment while editing occurs.

### 3) Component versus composite

Composite video—the traditional method—means that all aspects of the TV signal are combined into a single electronic signal and sent through a single cable. In other words, the one signal is a "composite."

Component video processes brightness (luminance), and portions of the color (chrominance) information separately. Specifically, component video is separated into three parts of the TV signal throughout the processing. This method maintains a better signal-to-noise ratio than composite video. The result is a crisper, cleaner picture. Copies in the component mode yield less noticeable generation loss. For these reasons, component video is always preferable. Look for editing systems that are wired using component inputs and outputs.

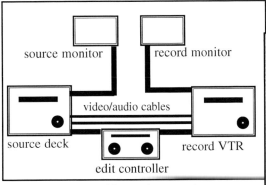

(19.3) Diagram of basic linear editing system. Video and audio pass directly from the source VTR to the record VTR. Or, the video may be routed through a switcher to control transitions and the audio may be routed through a mixer to control volume and equalization. The edit controller is wired to the machine control functions of each VTR in order to log in and out points. The edit controller also initiates preview and edit functions—it does not alter the video or audio information.

(19.4) Linear editing system. The source and record BetaCam VTRs are rack-mounted on the right. The edit controller sits on the console and can access both VTRs An audio mixer is found on the left of the console. There is one video monitor for each VTR. Audio speakers and a waveform monitor sit above the video monitors.

## I. LINEAR EDITING

The process of linear editing is much like making a copy from one videotape to another. If you want to make a copy, you connect two tape machines, push "play" on one and "record" on the other. The player machine feeds a signal to the recording machine, yet the player tape remains perfectly intact. The signal has been electronically cloned onto the other tape. Editing is just a more sophisticated and controlled way of making copies between tapes. The editing process allows you to be very precise about how many minutes, seconds, and frames you are copying. It lets you manipulate individual tracks: Video, Audio Channel 1, and Audio Channel 2.

The most basic linear analog editing system will have the following:

1) A player or "source" videotape machine. This machine is used to load and play the source footage shot on location.

2) A record machine. This machine is used to record new signals as they are cloned off the player via the editing process.

3) An edit controller. This unit goes in between the two machines. It is used as the keyboard to control the editing process. The edit controller allows the user to control the accuracy of the edits, choose beginning and ending times for each scene, and choose which tracks will be affected: audio, video, or both. On a simpler system, the edit controller is not much more than a keyboard. On a fancier system, the edit controller is actually a computer. The computer controls the tape machines. The presence of a computer as an edit controller does not make the system non-linear since it still uses tape machines.

4) A player or "source" monitor. The player machine needs a TV monitor and audio monitor so that the user can see and hear the source tapes while selecting scenes.

5) A record monitor. The record machine needs a monitor for the same reason.

6) Wiring to connect the machines. The player and the recorder are connected by video and audio cables. Other cables connect each videotape machine to the edit controller. Finally, wires connect each machine to their respective monitors.

Let's identify the basic steps in the process:

## PREPARING THE EDIT MASTER

With source tapes in hand, you need a fresh new tape on which to build your show: the edit master. A new videotape just out of the box has no signal on it. Perhaps you are familiar with how a TV screen looks when there is no video signal. The picture looks like snow or static and the audio sounds like a hiss.

In the editing process, we will begin to create tracks of video and audio information on the edit master. The following tracks on the master tape may be affected:

• *Video track* - The picture information goes to the video track.

• *Audio track* - The audio information goes to the audio track.

• *Control track* - The record machine generates a special track called a control track. The control track consists of a steady pulse that the video machine needs to keep itself timed and regulated. When there is no control track, the machine loses a reference and may speed up, slow down, or the picture may distort. Video without control track is considered unusable. When you choose edit modes, the control track gets created automatically as you edit.

• *Time code* - Another track is for the time code. Whereas all tape machines require control track, not all video systems use time code. It's an optional feature, but a very useful one.

If the editing system uses time code, then the clock time readout on the VTRs will show time code numbers. If, on the other hand, the system does not use time code, a clock time will still appear on the readout, however the time is arbitrary, and can be reset like a stopwatch. In short: time code numbers are permanently encoded. Control track numbers are arbitrary and changeable. Either way, you can use the numbers to measure transitions, scene lengths, and overall program lengths.

Note—some edit controllers can reference either control track or time code. Others can only reference time code. Therefore, time code must be a feature of the VTR in order for certain edit controllers to function.

Now we know that our goal is to fill an empty master tape with signals assigned to various tracks. The linear editing system offers certain modes in which to edit. Each mode has important implications.

## EDIT MODES: ASSEMBLE AND INSERT

To start editing with the linear videotape system, we must choose an edit mode. The linear editing system offers two choices: *assemble mode* and *insert mode*. The mode selection button is on the edit controller, the panel that connects the source and the recorder videotape machines. Depending on which mode you select, something different happens electronically:

*Assemble Mode* - In the assemble mode, new control track is generated on the record tape along with all tracks of video and audio.

*Insert Mode* - In the insert mode, no control track is generated. Video and audio tracks can be selected individually or all together.

*How do you know which mode to select?*

Since a fresh new tape has no signal, it needs to have control track along with the picture information. Since the assemble mode is the only one of the two modes that generates control track, then the assemble mode must be used when editing over unrecorded sections of videotape.

The insert mode is designed to help make changes over existing control track. The insert mode allows the user to selectively make changes on the video track only, either of the audio tracks, or any combination of the three. The insert mode will not disturb the existing control track.

## IN AND OUT POINTS

For every scene, we have to tell the edit system where the scene is coming from and where it is going. We search the source tape until the preferred beginning point has been found. This is called the *in point*. To mark an in point, find the scene by advancing the tape until the exact spot appears on the screen. Then, select that spot with the push of a button on the edit controller. Remember to select in points on both source and record machines. By doing so, we've answered both questions: Where is the scene coming from on the source VTR? Where is it going on the record VTR?

*Out points* can also be selected. Choose one out point on either the source or record VTR. Once an out point is selected, the other machine will follow with the same duration. If you do not wish to pick an out point, start the edit with in points only and stop the edit manually whenever you wish.

## PREVIEW

The *preview mode* simulates the edit without recording it to the master tape. If the editor is not happy with the timing of the edit, he or she can modify the in and out points on either the playback or record machine and preview again until satisfied. Then, the "edit" function on the controller panel finalizes the edit by actually recording to the master videotape.

## PRE-ROLL

The videotape machines cannot perform an edit immediately from a standstill. They must be up and running at full speed when the edit occurs. Therefore, the process begins with a *pre-roll*. When the user pushes the edit button on the controller, each machine automatically backs up its tape five seconds prior to the in points. Then, the machines roll forward. During the five seconds of pre-roll, the machines get up to speed, the picture signal stabilizes and the machines synchronize with each other. At the end of the five-second pre-roll, the machines will be right on the in points and the edit will take place. Information from the player will start transferring to the recorder.

Here are a few technical rules that will help you understand the process.

*The first scene on a brand new master tape cannot be edited.*

Since a pre-roll requires control track, what do you do for the very first scene when there is no video to roll back over? The answer—the first action taken cannot be an edit. Instead, the first edit can only be recorded the same way a tape is copied: by pushing play on the player, and record on the recorder. The consequence of doing this action first is that the beginning of the scene will not be clean. Instead of a clean stable edit, the beginning will be an unstable transition between static, where there was no video, to picture, where you began recording. Therefore, a program should not begin at the very beginning of the tape. Instead, a black signal is recorded for about 30 seconds, creating a safety margin, after which the program can begin.

*An "in point" must be selected at a place on the tape where there is existing video and control track to allow for "pre-roll."*

If there is video for the first five minutes of the tape, but the remainder of the tape is unrecorded, then any edits past five minutes must be assemble edits which will lay

| | ADVANTAGE | DISADVANTAGE |
|---|---|---|
| **ASSEMBLE** | • creates control track<br>• only choice for new tape | • end of edit breaks control track<br>• only records all tracks |
| **INSERT** | • isolates tracks<br>• won't disturb control track | • won't create control track |

(19.6) assemble edit versus insert edit.

down new control track over the unrecorded portion of the tape. Each new in point must be placed over the tail end of the existing video.

If the edit occurs over existing video and control track, then it can be an insert edit. The insert mode will not interfere with the control track.

***Assemble edits are clean in and dirty out.***

An assemble edit only needs enough existing video on the master tape to initiate the pre-roll and the edit. As the edit continues, the assemble mode paves new control track as it lays down the source video onto the edit master.

However, a major disadvantage to an assemble edit is that it makes a mess at the end of the edit. The control track will be disrupted on the last few frames of the edit. If there was existing control track on the video master, it will be disrupted at the end of the assemble edit. Therein lies the danger of doing an assemble edit over existing

| *IN* Assemble edit *OUT* ⨌ | *IN* Insert edit *OUT* |
|---|---|

(19.5) These two graphic representations of edits are meant to show how assemble and insert edits have different affects on control track. Assemble edits are clean in, dirty out—the control track is disrupted at the end. Insert edits are clean in, clean out—the control track stays intact. Assemble edits actually generate new control track. Insert edits do not generate control track and leave existing control track alone.

control track. It's no problem if you're always pushing ahead with your editing, but you'll have a major problem if you use the assemble mode to do an edit in the middle of an existing program. If, however, you should damage control track by doing an assemble edit in the middle of a program, the only way to fix the problem is to make a new in point just prior to the disruption and do another assemble edit, thus reediting all material from that point forward.

Here's an analogy. Imagine an earth mover clearing the dirt for a new highway. It lowers its shovel into the ground and precedes forward. The "in" is clean—the push forward is clean. But when he stops, there's a pile of junk in front of the shovel. The only way to continue is to back up just a bit, dig in, and press on ahead.

If you decide to go back and add a scene in the middle of the program, use the insert mode. Remember that insert edits do not generate control track. So they cannot be used to repair damaged control track. If you happen to use the insert mode on an area devoid of control track, your system may either not work or it may cause an unstable edit—a picture that rolls or shakes.

*Every new tape should start with a TV black signal.*

Because of this necessity to do the first scene as a copy and not as an edit, the standard practice in the TV industry is to always begin any new tape with the color black. This black is considered a video source and would be copied onto the beginning of the tape for at least 30 seconds.

Black is a video source that can be generated and recorded on tape the way any graphic or color can be generated by a graphics computer. TV black is a standardized color—official black registers at 7.5 units on the waveform monitor—and is used throughout the TV industry as a video "curtain" on either end of a program or segment. You have seen TV black every time a TV show fades down before a commercial break. In your edit room, TV black may be available as a source on a videotape or from a graphics generator.

*Every show should be bookended by TV black, at least 30 seconds on either side.*

The black signal provides both a technical and aesthetic advantage. It provides a video signal with control track for the first edit. And it provides a "curtain" before the program starts. Your master tape should have a minimum of thirty seconds of black before the program starts. Tape machines need a extra tape length to thread. You don't want your program too close to the beginning or it may get cut off.

Given all the rules, there are a couple of different ways to approach your editing.

### Option #1 - Assemble as you go.

To begin, copy 30 seconds or so of black. Then, start doing assemble edits one at a time. Each time you start a new assemble edit, back up into the previous video to log a new in point. Proceed until the last shot, then assemble 30 seconds or so at the end of the show to bookend the program with black. Then, if there are any inserts of video or audio such as cutaways, narration, or music, you can go back and edit those in the insert mode. Make sure you switch to insert mode on the edit controller. If you go back and accidentally perform an assemble edit in the middle of your show, the edit will be good at the beginning but will disrupt the control track at the end. In effect, it will have punched a hole in your control track, leaving you with the unfortunate task of re-editing from that point on.

### Option #2 - Record black. Then insert edit.

To begin, copy video black throughout your tape. Then go back and do all edits in the insert mode. This is the easiest and most commonly used method.

In summary, a new master tape needs a signal on it before any editing can be done. The very first signal must come from a "play/record" function, not an edit. Once some signal is on tape, we choose whether to keep editing in the assemble mode or the insert mode. Choose assemble if you need to keep paving the tape with control track. Choose insert if you are editing over existing control track and wish to leave it untouched.

## WATCH FOR BAD EDITS

A bad edit, technically speaking, is one in which the editing system fails to place the edit cleanly between frames of video. The electronic accuracy of the edit controller has failed. It is not the user's responsibility to know exactly where the beginning and end of a frame occurs. The edit controller takes care of that. The user simply locates a frame and marks it for an in point. The edit controller will determine exactly where the beginning or end of that frame is. A series of bad edits could mean the equipment needs repair. But often, a bad edit just happens intermittently. Therefore, it's important to check each edit afterward by playing back the record tape. Watch for any noticeable glitch or break in the picture where the edit occurred. If you find a bad edit, make a new in point prior to the edit and try again.

## TRANSITIONS

Any change from shot to shot is considered a transition. Editing video might be considered the job of creating transitions between scenes.

*Cut* - The most basic transition is a cut. A cut is an immediate transition between shots—the shortest possible transition. A cut stops one scene and begins a new one on the very next frame. The edit controller senses where the beginning of a frame is on the player and where the end of a frame is on the recorder. When the edit occurs, the frames will be butted together neatly so that there will be no break in the flow of frames.

The cut is the only transition that requires just one video source. The following transitions all require two or more video sources combined.

*Dissolve* - A dissolve is a crossfade from one scene to another. As one scene fades in, the other fades out. The *crosspoint* is half way through the transition where each image is at 50%.

The dissolve is measured in seconds or in frames. For example, you may request a 2-second dissolve, which would be the same as requesting a 60-frame dissolve. A dissolve can be any length.

A very quick dissolve will be about 8-10 frames in duration, or about 1/3 of a second. A one-to-two-second dissolve is considered medium, and more than two seconds will be considered a slow dissolve.

The dissolve requires two video sources. Often, the two sources are videotapes, but not necessarily. One of the sources could be a graphics generator, a character generator, a camera, or any other source of video.

The record machine can only accept one video input. It cannot handle the mixing of sources. So a new piece of equipment will be introduced to execute the dissolve—the switcher.

## THE SWITCHER

Some effects—dissolves, wipes, and fades—require multiple video signals to be combined into a single picture. During a dissolve, for example, two images are seen crossfading on the screen. During a wipe, one image may be squeezed into a box and

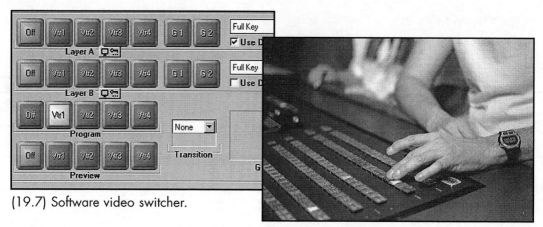

(19.7) Software video switcher.

(19.8) Hardware video switcher.

keyed over the other image. During a fade, one image is crossfaded with the color black. The video *switcher* is the tool that combines video sources in order to produce such effects. The output of the switcher goes into the recorder. That way, the recorder only has to accept one video signal.

In linear editing, the multiple video sources come from various pieces of hardware—usually two videotape playback machines. In non-linear editing, the multiple video sources come from video already digitized onto the computer hard drive.

So, let's imagine a dissolve or a wipe in the linear mode between source VTR-A and source VTR-B. The output of both machines is routed into a video switcher. The user loads a source videotape into each VTR. An in-point is selected on each of the two sources VTRs. When the user initiates an edit, the edit controller will cause each machine to pre-roll simultaneously, pause, and roll for the edit. Once the edit begins, the switcher is used to dissolve or wipe from one VTR's image to the other's.

*Fade -* The next transition is called a fade. The fade is a dissolve from black to picture or from picture to black used at the beginning and end of shows and segments.

*Wipe -* A wipe is similar to a dissolve because it also involves two video sources. But instead of a cross fade, a wipe uses geometric shapes to conceal one scene and reveal another. The shape may be a line moving across the screen, a circle getting smaller, a star growing out from the center of the screen. One video source is on one side of the pattern getting covered up while the other video source is on the other side increasing in size.

(19.9) In the past, wipes were two-dimensional. In this example of a 2-D wipe, the square is getting smaller, but the man's face is merely cropped—it isn't squeezed proportionally.

(19.10) Digital technology allows for wipes that perform three-dimensional and proportional moves and manipulations.

Computer-generated wipe patterns, called digital effects, lend a great deal of sophistication to the wipe transition with the options of 3-dimensional patterns: flips and page turns, etc.

*Key* - A key is an electronic cut-out of part of one image imposed over part of another. For example, if a person's name appears under his or her face while hosting a show, the letters that spell the name are electronically inserted in the picture of the host. The letters come from a computer that generates type that can feed directly into an editing system. The person's face comes from the camera signal. The two images are combined using the "key" feature. The switcher will cut a hole in one picture and insert the key signal in that hole. How is this done?

## LUMINANCE AND MATTE KEYING

In one method of keying, the letters in the host's name are surrounded by black. The switcher ignores the black area and responds anywhere it sees the brighter video of the lettering. It cuts out the letters and cuts identically sized spaces out of the other picture. Then, the switcher inserts the images of the letters into the other picture. The result is a composite picture—one source keyed over the other. When the switcher responds to brightness levels placed over black as just described, the key method is called a *luminance key*. Another method uses an electronic stencil that matches the outline of the keyed image. The stencil is cut into the background image and the keyed image, also called the fill image, is placed inside the stencil. This stencil method is called a *matte key* and is further explained in chapter 20. (See figures 19.11, 20.10, and 20.11.)

(19.11) Example of a matte key. Both the woman and the name graphic begin as video inputs on the switcher. The name graphic has an embedded matte key signal which is automatically and simultaneously cut into the background image by the switcher into which the name graphic is inserted. The result is the ability to key graphics of any luminance level with a clean, crisp result.

## CHROMINANCE KEY

The switcher can also refer to color instead of brightness for deciding which part of the key signal to use. If the color blue is selected as the key color, then all but the color blue will be keyed over the second picture. Knowing this, the user can place a subject to be keyed in front of a blue background and ask the switcher to ignore blue. This approach is used when the weatherperson delivers a forecast in front of a computer-generated map. The person actually stands in front of a blue screen. The map comes from a graphics computer. The switcher ignores the color blue and keys the person over the computer-generated map. Why blue? Because the color blue is a distant hue from skin tone. This insures that the person is not accidentally keyed as well. Of course, the weatherperson should avoid blue suits, ties, or scarves or they may appear as part of a weather map!

## OFFLINE AND ONLINE EDITING

As director, you want to avoid spending a lot of money editing, only to find out that the client wants major changes made. So, an *offline edit*—also called a *rough cut*—is the editor's first and less expensive stab at piecing the show together.

An offline edit may be done on a low-grade editing system in order to save money. There may be less attention paid to fancy transitions. The main goal is simply to piece the show together for approval without spending money unnecessarily.

Once approved, the director can apply the finishing touches in an *online* editing session. An online edit suite will have the best equipment, the most elaborate effects, and will cost the most per hour. The online edit should go quickly because all the creative decisions have been made during the offline stage.

The terms "offline" and "online" have no exact definitions regarding quality of the editing system or the work involved. These terms loosely define an approach that attempts to work quickly and cheaply during the initial drafts and save most of the technical wizardry and fine tuning for the final version.

## CUTS-ONLY EDITING

The simplest editing configuration consists of two VTRs, linked together with an edit controller. This configuration is called a ***cuts-only*** or a ***machine-to-machine*** editing system. This most basic setup allows one type of transition only—the cut. Any other type of transition—fade, dissolve, or wipe—would require more than one video source routed through a switcher.

There are times when a very simple cuts-only editing system is adequate or even preferred. For example, a news team editing on location must bring minimal equipment along in a van or truck. Or someone who cannot afford more equipment may get by with a simple system and then go to a fancier facility near the end of the editing process to add bells and whistles that aren't available on the simple system.

## A/B ROLLING

A dissolve or a wipe requires two simultaneous video sources rolling together while the dissolve or wipe crosses from one to another. The use of two source machines is termed *A/B Roll* editing.

The term A/B Roll comes from the film industry. In film editing, all transitions are set up by creating two separate edited films in checkerboard style. Scene 1 is on reel A. Scene 2 is on reel B. Scene 3 is on A again, etc. Wherever there is a scene on one of the films, there is black leader film on the corresponding section of the other film, thus creating the checkerboard.

These two films are aligned in a machine called an optical printer. Both films are exposed onto a new master film, thus creating the composite finished product. Wherever there is a dissolve or wipe that requires seeing both images at once, the checkerboard scenes are cut longer so as to overlap each other for the duration of the transition. For a two-second dissolve, Scene B would begin a second before the crosspoint and Scene A on the corresponding film would last one second beyond the crosspoint. The optical printer is programmed to execute a transition between the two reels.

Similarly, in video editing, when two source VTRs are used, we call the two source tapes A and B Rolls. During a wipe or dissolve, both machines roll, providing two images which are combined in the video switcher to create the desired effect.

Note—dissolves, wipes, and fades do not always require that the video source comes from a VTR. One or both of the sources may come from another type of video output including: graphics generator, frame store computer, or character generator.

## DYNAMIC TRACKING

When a video picture is *tracking* well, the picture is stable. The tape is running properly over the mechanical guides and drums inside the machine. When you pause your VCR, or shuttle it fast or slow, the picture loses its stability. While you shuttle or pause, the picture has lines through it. Perhaps there is enough image to recognize where you are, but the picture is by no means stable or usable.

However, some playback machines are built with a feature called *dynamic tracking*, which allows the picture to remain stable at any speed—or while paused.

Dynamic tracking is a necessary feature in videotape machines if you wish to perform slow motion, fast motion, reverse motion or still frames. The dynamic tracking machines allow you to program a speed. For example, dial in 150% speed and the machine will playback at 1–1/2 times the normal speed for a fast motion effect. Or dial in 0% for a still frame—the machine stays on the desired frame and does not move. Or dial in 30% for a slow motion playback.

## SPLIT EDITS

Remember—in the insert mode, the video and audio tracks can be edited independently. An edit can be programmed to affect the video or audio channels one at a time or in any combination.

A *split edit* takes this independence one step further and allows the user to begin an edit with one track and delay another. The edit may begin with audio and delay video. Or the other way around.

For example, perhaps you have already edited a scene of video (Scene1). You don't want to disturb it. But you want the audio—perhaps a voice—from Scene 2 to begin under Scene 1. So, you program a split edit. Mark an in point where the new audio begins under Scene 1. Then, program the edit controller to enable the new video as soon as the first video has finished, thus completing a transition to Scene 2 one track at a time.

This concludes the explanation of linear editing In the next portion of this chapter, we'll cover non-linear editing. As you'll see, many of the concepts covered to this point will serve as a basis of understanding for the newer non-linear method. In the meantime, here is a handy summary checklist for linear editing:

## SUMMARY CHECKLIST FOR LINEAR EDITING

__1) If using a brand new tape for a master, decide whether to black the tape first or to assemble a scene at a time.

__2) The first edit is a "play/record" dub function with a video source feeding the record machine. Dub about 30 seconds of black if you intend to assemble, or black a few minutes beyond the projected length of your program if you intend to insert.

__3) Choose the appropriate edit mode: insert or assemble.

__4) Find the desired location on the record machine for the first scene and mark an in point. The first in point should be at least 30 seconds past the beginning of the tape.

__5) Find the desired scene on the player and mark an in point.

__6) You can mark an out point if you want or simply push the "end" or "stop" button on the fly as the edit occurs.

__7) Once the points are marked, preview the edit.

__8) While the edit is previewing, check for acceptable video and audio levels.

__9) Trim the in and out points if desired.

__10) Preview again if points were trimmed. Make sure you are happy with the preview.

__11) Then execute the edit by pushing the "Edit" button on the controller.

__12) When the edit is finished, play back the edited scene. Make sure the edits going in and out are clean—no glitches or breakup.

__13) If a glitch occurs, try the edit again. If it occurs frequently, check for equipment malfunction.

## II. NON-LINEAR EDITING

Up to this point, we've discussed editing in the context of videotape machines. Non-linear editing is computer-based. A videotape machine is only used to transfer video into the computer before editing begins.

A non-linear system consists of:

• A VTR to transfer source tapes onto the computer.

• A computer with appropriate speed and RAM.

• Editing software.

• Large hard drive storage capacity for holding and accessing video clips.

Following the analogy of the typewriter and the word processor, editing is done on the computer and then "printed" back to the videotape when finished. In the non-linear system, certain traditional terms no longer apply:

• No more assemble/insert modes. All editing done in the computer environment is characteristic of the insert mode. However, when the final edited product is transferred back to a videotape, then the insert/assemble choice may apply.

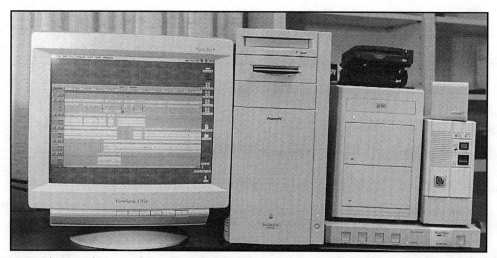

(19.12) This non-linear edit suite includes (left to right): a monitor, a computer with editing software, a large hard drive for video file storage, and a power supply unit. Not pictured is a VTR for digitizing footage from source tapes and for final mastering back to tape. The monitor shows the timeline from a video edit session.

• No more pre-roll. While editing in the computer environment, pre-rolls do not apply. They may apply when transferring back to videotape at the end of the project..

## DIGITIZING

The non-linear editing system requires you to start with raw footage shot in the field on videotape. You may then digitize any or all of your raw footage into the computer system. Once digitized, you may organize and choose clips to sequence on a timeline. The problem you face is limited hard drive storage space. There may not be room enough to store all your footage. So, you have two options to maximize space on the hard drive:

• Limit the number of clips that you digitize by doing a paper edit first.

• Digitize all your clips at a high *compression ratio*. (See chapter 3 for an explanation of compression) The resolution will be poor, but the clips will then take up less room on the hard drive.

## COMPRESSION RATIO

Non-linear editing systems allow the user to choose a compression ratio. The compression will be applied to the video clip as it is digitized from the source tape into the computer hard drive. The less compression, the better the resolution, but the more hard drive space will be used. A common strategy is to digitize at a high high compression ratio to begin editing. Then redigitize only those clips that made the final cut for the final output of the program at a low compression ratio for high picture quality.

## CLIPS AND BINS

As scenes are digitized into the computer, they may now be referred to as *clips*. The clips are organized in screen windows called *bins*. As editing begins, clips can be clicked and dragged from the bins onto a *timeline*. The timeline represents the linear progression of the program—it replaces the master tape in the traditional linear editing method. It is the palette on which the show is created. And, since the timeline is part of a computer software program, it is randomly changeable, allowing the user to click, drag, and rearrange clips at will.

Clips can be trimmed at either of two points in the editing process: 1) while they are still in the bins, or 2) once they are on the timeline. While still in the bin, the non-linear system offers a preview box in which to trim the length of any clip.

Remember that a clip can not be stretched out any longer than the amount of material originally digitized. So, when digitizing, it's a good idea to allow a little extra material at the beginning and end of any clip. The clip can always be trimmed shorter while editing. However, if you find that you did not digitize a long enough clip, you may have to go back to the first step and redigitize from the source tape. Most non-linear systems automatically add a second at the beginning and end of each clip as it being digitized in order to give the user a little bit of extra leeway.

## TRANSITIONS AND EFFECTS

The non-linear system uses a software-based switcher. Menu icons represent transitions such as dissolves, wipes, and fades. Choose the icon for your preferred transition and drag it to the place on the timeline where the transition should occur.

The computer can play back the developing timeline in the same way a VTR can play back a tape, thus allowing you to view your progress. Changing your mind is easy compared to linear editing. After playing back a dissolve transition, you may

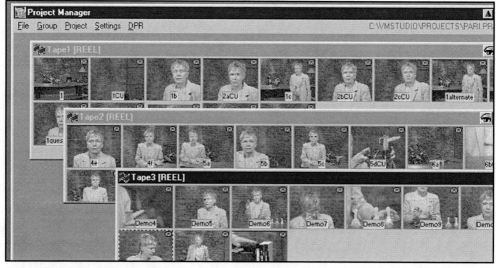

(19.13) Video clip bin. Clips are digitized into the computer from videotape sources, then cataloged and stored in bins. In this example, each bin corresponds to a source tape. Bins 1-3 contain clips from source tapes 1-3.

(19.14) The clip editor is used at two points in the non-linear editing process: first, to operate and view the source VTR in order to select and mark time-code ins and outs from the source tape for desired clips before digitizing, and second, to play back an already digitized clip from the hard drive and trim its length before placing it on the timeline. Notice the overall clip length under "clip-in" and "clip-out." Just above, notice the slightly trimmed section called "mark-in" and "mark-out" showing the actual trimmed portion that will be transferred over to the timeline. The same clip can be accessed and trimmed to different lengths as needed. Various brands of non-linear editors may vary slightly from this example, but the concept stays the same.

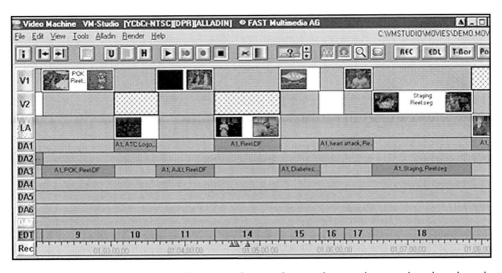

(19.15) Non-linear timeline. Clips are dragged onto the timeline and ordered and reordered as desired. In this example, the upper three tracks are for video. There are six active audio tracks beneath. The EDT line shows the number of edits in the program. The lowest line shows the running time.

decide you prefer a wipe instead. Simply substitute a "wipe" icon for the "dissolve" icon on the timeline. Then play back that portion of the timeline to make sure you are satisfied with the new choice.

## REDIGITIZING

To clarify, as you edit on the non-linear timeline, all scenes come from the computer hard drive where they have been digitized and stored. However, the original scenes reside on source tapes stored safely on a shelf. Don't lose those original tapes! They may be useful again soon.

For example, the hard drive must be periodically cleared for new projects. There's only so much room to store video clips. Video may be erased from the hard drive and *redigitized* later using the original source tapes. The reference icons for each video clip remain in your project file and take up little room. They tell the computer which tape numbers and time code numbers are necessary to redigitize the actual video material associated with that icon. Thus, if you have cleared the video for your project off the computer and later wish to do further editing, you may redigitize your scenes back into the computer system. That involves retrieving the original source tapes and inserting them in the VTR, then allowing the computer to replay each clip to transfer the video information back into the hard drive. It's a quick and simple process.

Non-linear editing is an important advancement in video editing technology. However, the two main drawbacks with non-linear computer editing are:

• Computers crash periodically. Save your work often as you go. Your work is saved in files just like any other computer program.

• Storage space is limited. Depending on how much hard drive space you have, you may have to load and unload projects fairly often to allow other people to work on their own projects. You might try selecting a high compression setting which allows the video to take up less space on the hard drive.

## THE PROGRESS OF NON-LINEAR EDITING

When non-linear editing first came on the market, it was used primarily as an offline editing system—the resolution was only good enough to do rough cut edits. The final online edit would have to be done on a conventional linear system. The reason for this was simply that computers could not store or process bits fast enough to keep up with the demand for broadcast quality video. Compression ratios were so high that the video quality suffered.

As computers got faster and hard drives got bigger, non-linear editors started being used for final output editing that could go straight to a TV station for broadcast or straight to an industrial edit master.

In fact, computers are getting so fast that compression is becoming less necessary. Some non-linear systems already offer compression-free editing.

## III. EDITING DECISIONS

As the technical functions of linear and non-linear editing systems become familiar, the editor can concentrate on strategic and artistic thoughts, including all the aesthetic principles discussed in earlier chapters: jump cuts, matching action, and the best ways to move people through time and space. Just as these principles were important in the shooting stage, they are equally important in the editing stage.

Even though we now focus on the role of the editor, it is still important to understand the role of the director in the editing process. The director's relationship with the editor is similar to his or her relationship with the camera operator and the writer, all key people in the creative process. In each case, the director may take a strong hand, may be very easy going, or anywhere in between. The important thing is that the relationship is understood going into the process.

An editor can serve either of two job descriptions:

• An artistic creative person who not only carries out the technical function but also makes many of the creative decisions for the director.

• A technical operator whose main task it is to understand the equipment and carry out editing functions under the artistic direction of the director who might be sitting in the same room throughout the process.

In a multi-million dollar editing suite, the equipment may be more than any director has the time to learn. Resident technicians run the systems. However, in a simple editing room, or one in which the director is skilled, he or she may do their own editing if desired.

In feature film productions, the role of the director in the editing process is a con-tractual specification. The director's role in the editing room is negotiated. Often, the director's authority is limited by the studio executives.

On the other hand, small productions have small crews and staffs. The director works very closely with an editor and reserves the right to request changes through-out the editing phase. Or, the director and editor may be the same person.

Throughout the rest of this chapter, we'll refer to director and editor interchangeably, since both are really faced with the same kinds of aesthetic choices.

## SHOT SELECTION

The editor is given material to work with: all the raw footage that was shot on loca-tion. It is the editor's job to chose the best scenes and piece them together on a new edit master tape.

The editor's work is affected by the shooting ratio that occurred during the produc-tion stage—the amount of tape shot compared to the amount actually needed for the final show. If the director conducted an average of five takes per scene, then the *shooting ratio* is at least 5:1. The editor has to sort through five times the amount of footage that will actually be used.

So, what's the first shot going to be? The answer should normally be determined by the script or by the paper edit. The script should indicate what comes first. The script or paper edit should have notes made by the director with the time code numbers or clock time numbers for the preferred scenes. Otherwise, the editor is left to choose the best takes of each scene.

The script won't answer all the questions. For example, if the script calls for a tran-sition, it may not specify a dissolve, wipe, or cut. Who will decide? If a dissolve is chosen, what will the duration be? One second? Two seconds? There will be many artistic decisions for the director/editor to make.

To get the process underway, the editor puts black down on the master tape and is ready to begin. A first scene is selected. The editor selects an in point on the source and an in point on the master. The in point on the master must not be at the begin-ning of the tape. The editor allows at least 30 seconds of black to roll before mark-ing an in point, providing some margin up front for pre-roll and creating a "curtain" of black before the show starts. Typically, the transition to the first scene would be a "fade in" from black to first picture. The fade in from black requires a switcher since a fade requires two sources: 1) black and 2) picture. In a cuts only system, the editor can simply cut from black to first picture.

Once the first edit is made, the next question is, "What is the second scene going to be?" This question is more important because it deals with the biggest aesthetic challenge and the most fundamental aspect of editing: shot juxtaposition—how shots look next to each other, what it feels like to go from one shot to another. The pace. The rhythm. The change of angle. The style of transition.

## TRANSITIONS

With every edit, the editor chooses a transition: cut, dissolve, wipe, or fade. Let's consider the reasons for choosing each. (See figures 4.5 through 4.8)

## WHEN TO USE A CUT

Cuts are best for real-time transitions within a given scene. For example, when two people are talking to each other, the normal thing to do would be to cut back and forth, not to dissolve or wipe back and forth.

A cut suggests that the transition to the next shot has not changed time or place but is sequential within the same scene and the same time frame. Transitions within a given scene or within a given time frame are usually cuts.

## WHEN TO FADE OR DISSOLVE

Fades and dissolves suggest passage of time or change of location. The transition might be to dissolve from one scene to another or to fade to black for a brief instant and fade back up to the next scene. Fades and dissolves might transition in and out of dream sequences (change of location), from one scene to another later that day (change of time), etc.

## WHEN TO USE A WIPE

Wipes were gimmicks when they first appeared decades ago as 2-dimensional geometric patterns: a circle growing bigger to reveal a new scene, or a line moving across the screen as a transition. Wipes have become extremely sophisticated today in 3-D computerized form, but they are still gimmicky. Feature films rarely use them. In TV, they can be practical, for example, to place a box of information over the shoulder of a newscaster. Local car commercials are notorious for over-using digital wipes. Everything flips and tumbles until your stomach flips and tumbles. There probably isn't a show on TV using wipes that couldn't achieve the same result with traditional dissolves and cuts. Yet, you see them all the time: pictures over someone's shoulder, page turns, pushes, revolving doors. There is no rule for when to use wipes. Just be careful not to overuse them.

## AVOIDING JUMP CUTS

We considered the jump cut during the shooting process (chapter 14). Now, we consider it again when editing because the editing process provides plenty of opportunities to create nonsensical shot sequences. To review, the jump cut is an illogical juxtaposition of shots. Here are some typical jump cuts that happen while editing.

### *Failure to match action.*

The masterscene and subsequent angles may have been shot properly, but, as an editor, you still need to choose at what point to cut back and forth between angles. If you let one shot go right up to the point at which the man is reaching for the glass, then edit to another shot beginning with the beer glass already raised to the man's mouth, then you, the editor, have created a jump cut in the form of a bad action match. The cut jumps ahead in time resulting in some degree of discontinuity at the cut point. The subject leaps forward in time, if only by a few frames and the result is more than noticeable.

Now, if you trim back a second or so on the source machine for shot #2, you can redo the edit with the source starting when the man's hand is just about to lift the glass off the table.

### *Failure to cover breaks in action in order to condense time.*

One of the most common things an editor must do is shorten the time of a given scene. Reality just takes too long! Often, little leaps forward in the action are absolutely necessary to shorten the overall time of the scene.

For example, you may have to trim the political speech from ten minutes down to four minutes, choosing a few of the best statements. By necessity, you are going to have to link some scenes together that occurred in various places on your source tape, thus creating potential jump cuts at every edit point. Even though the subject remains a constant, he or she is never in exactly the same spot. Even if they moved an inch or if the camera changed framing by one degree, the juxtaposition of two shots would reveal a slight but noticeable shift. So, what are your options?

1) Use cutaways. Edit a cutaway scene over the cut point, thus hiding the juxtaposition. The cutaway takes the viewer's eyes away from the subject for a couple of seconds. By the time the viewer sees the subject again, following the jump cut, they don't know whether this was a real time flow or not. You fooled them!

2) If the change of framing is substantial, the cut may work without a cutaway. Dissimilar shots alleviate the perception of bad match framing. The viewer's frame of reference changes so dramatically that a slight shift in the subject's stance is hardly noticed.

Note—that doesn't mean cut from extreme wide shot to extreme close-up. It may seem abrupt. Rather, move into the scene with deliberate incremental changes in framing—from a wide to a medium, from a medium to a close-up.

Let's put this into practice. Assume that the camera operator changed framing throughout the speech. At one point the camera was on a close-up. A few minutes later, the camera moved to a waist shot. The editor may be able to cut directly from one to the other. Even though the cut will not represent the real-time flow of the action, at least it will be aesthetically acceptable to the viewer. The variation of framing will help to hide the subtle changes in the speaker's stance.

A third option may be considered: leave the jump cuts. In the old days of television, a jump cut was a greater sin. These days, we make many exceptions. It's as if the magic of television is not as potent as it used to be. We all know (more or less) how the system works.

The David Lettermans of the world have demystified the technology by taking us behind the scenes and revealing the tricks. Sometimes, journalists leave jump cuts in documentaries as if to say, "We're not trying to doctor this presentation." In other cases, advertisers may use intentional jump cuts in commercials: the woman talking about how good Folgers Coffee tastes. Her quick comments are each jump cuts. The effect is to say, "This is raw footage, undoctored, therefore truthful."

*Failure to observe the axis of action rule.*

If the camera team broke the axis of action rule, it may be pretty hard to get around that in editing. A face-to-face interview in which both heads are facing screen right, for example, will look ridiculous and there is nothing the editor can do to reverse the problem.

## PACING

How long should a shot stay on the screen? When is it too abrupt? When is it too long? Pacing, like a lot of other artistic considerations, is a judgment call. You need to evaluate your own work and consider the issue of pacing.

When you begin to edit a scene, think about whether the shots need to move quickly or slowly. Then, when you've finished several edits, review what you've done. Evaluate your work periodically by replaying the last few edits you've done. It's best to evaluate before you've gone too far, in case you want to do some scenes over again. When you are laboring over an edit, it is easy to lose touch with the overall rhythm of the scene.

In the linear mode, it's a tedious job to restructure the order of scenes after they have been edited. Such changes may involve a lot of re-editing. With a non-linear system, scenes can be taken out, added in, and rearranged easily.

### Rule of thumb #1

Any scene shorter than two seconds feels abrupt. You may purposely want an abrupt cut and therefore choose to edit a shot that lasts only ten frames or even one frame! That's fine. But you must be satisfied with an effect that most viewers will experience as abrupt. Normally, for cutaways and other short shots, think about making your shot a minimum of two seconds in length.

### Rule of thumb #2

If there are words on the screen—character generated titles, credits, or anything that needs to be read—consider letting the scene go on long enough for the material to be read very slowly. Don't assume that people can read quickly. Some directors exercise a rule that any words should be able to be read three times over at normal speed to accommodate the slow readers. Again, there are always exceptions. Look how fast credits go by on many TV shows, much too fast for people to read. And it's often a source of frustration if you truly want to read every word.

## CREATING A STRUCTURE

Just as the chess player cannot simply focus on the move at hand, but must think one, two, or several moves ahead, so must the editor think several edits ahead. The end result will not be judged on the basis of any one shot, but how those shots were juxtaposed and the rhythm and pace they created. Just as any piece of writing can be analyzed by it's structure—how the various elements are sequenced, the way the events flow, and the pace of the action—so can a video program be analyzed by its structure.

The structure of the show would have been considered back in the concept stage, reflected in the script, and carried out in the production phase. Now, the editor figures out the best way to support the structural concept through the shot juxtaposition and pacing that is created in the editing room. If the script was extremely detailed, the editing structure may already be decided by the writer and the editor's job is simply to carry out the instructions. On the other hand, some scripts do not go into such detail and leave many structural considerations to the editor. In either case, here are a few examples of editing structures:

## PARALLEL ACTION

Some stories have parallel plots—two or more stories happening in different places. Consider a commonly used structure of editing called *parallel action*, also called parallel development. This structure is used in almost every cops and robbers program ever made, in westerns, in action dramas, anywhere that multiple plots occur. In one scene, the police plan their strategy. Cut to the location of the bad guys planning their strategy. Cut back to the police on the move. Cut back to the bad guys on the move. The motion picture medium allows us to watch the parallel development of action as two scenes occur simultaneously in different places.

## FLASHBACK

Another structural approach is the *flashback*. The story may be based on jumping from present to past and back again. Normal chronology is purposely avoided.

## MONTAGE

In the *montage* approach, scenes need not follow a linear or predictable order. The editor may sequence a variety of shots from many times and places. Pacing may be fast and jarring or slow and fluid. Jump cuts may be used intentionally.

## CINEMA VERITE

Another structural approach is called *cinema verite* (ver-i-tay). In this style, the camera does little more than observe. The role of the editor is minimal. The camera records long scenes as they occur and there is little or no attempt to manipulate the action in the editing room. It is an approach that seems tedious by today's standards of quick cuts and fancy effects.

## STRUCTURAL CINEMA

Based on the cinema verite approach, *structural cinema* is an experimental form in which a scene is shot and presented in a long unedited form. Andy Warhol played with this structure in his film *Sleep* which featured an uninterrupted scene of a person sleeping for several hours.

## MASTERSCENE EDITING

As detailed in chapter 17, the masterscene is the most common form used in dramatic presentations. A scene is shot several times from a variety of angles and then pieced together in the editing room to simulate multiple cameras.

## SHOT SEQUENCE EDITING

In *shot sequence editing*, the editor pays close attention to the progression of shots and the impact that it can offer—for example, the progression from wide shot to medium shot to close-up can build tension or increase intimacy.

## INVISIBLE EDITING

*Invisible editing* attempts to hide the edits by placing them during certain actions— a person getting up to leave, a car rounding the corner, or someone passing in front of the camera—in order to draw attention to the action and away form the edit.

**EDIT DECISION LIST**
Program Title: Mutiny on the High Seas
Edit date: 2-28-97  Editor: Williams

| EDIT | TRANS / DUR | | MODE | DESCRIP | SOURCE IN | REC IN | DUR |
|------|-------------|---|------|---------|-----------|--------|-----|
| #1 | FADE IN | 60 | VA1 | Scene 14a | 1:00:06:35 | 1:00:00:00 | 05:00 |
| #2 | CUT | | VA1 | Scene 14b | 1:10:22:20 | 1:00:05:00 | 10:00 |
| #3 | DISS | 60 | VA1 | Scene 14c | 1:00:06:35 | 1:00:15:00 | 05:00 |
| #4 | CUT | | VA1 | Scene 14d | 1:11:21:20 | 1:00:20:00 | 07:00 |
| #5 | CUT | | VA1 | Scene 14e | 1:00:07:00 | 1:00:27:00 | 05:20 |
| #6 | CUT | | VA1 | Scene 14f | 1:15:12:20 | 1:00:32:20 | 10:00 |
| #7 | CUT | | VA1 | Scene 13a | 2:00:14:35 | 1:00:42:20 | 05:00 |
| #8 | CUT | | VA1 | Scene 13b | 2:10:23:20 | 1:00:47:20 | 03:00 |
| #9 | WIPE | 60 | VA1 | Scene 13c | 2:08:06:35 | 1:00:50:20 | 05:15 |
| #10 | CUT | | VA1 | Scene 13d | 2:10:22:10 | 1:00:56:05 | 02:15 |
| #11 | DISS | 60 | VA1 | Scene 13e | 2:07:06:35 | 1:00:58:20 | 03:00 |
| #12 | CUT | | VA1 | Scene 14a | 3:00:22:20 | 1:01:01:20 | 09:15 |
| #13 | CUT | | VA1 | Scene 14b | 3:00:16:35 | 1:01:11:05 | 04:00 |
| #14 | CUT | | VA1 | Scene 15a | 4:06:22:20 | 1:01:15:05 | 20:00 |
| #14a | CUT | | V | CU Man | 4:07:00:00 | 1:01:35:05 | 08:00 |
| #15 | CUT | | VA1 | Scene 15b | 4:08:06:35 | 1:01:43:05 | 13:00 |
| #16 | CUT | | VA1 | Scene 15c | 4:10:22:20 | 1:01:56:05 | 10:00 |
| #17 | CUT | | VA1 | Scene 15d | 4:04:06:35 | 1:02:06:00 | 03:15 |
| #18 | CUT | | VA1 | Scene 16a | 4:11:22:20 | 1:02:09:15 | 10:0 |
| #19 | CUT | | VA1 | Scene 16b | 4:13:06:35 | 1:02:19:15 | 03:15 |
| #20 | CUT | | VA1 | Scene 17a | 4:14:10:00 | 1:02:23:00 | 5:00 |
| #21 | FADE | 60 | VA1 | Scene 17b | 4:15:10:00 | 1:02:28:00 | 2:00 |

(19.16) Edit decision list for a two and a half minute program.

## EDIT DECISION LIST

The editor keeps a record of the edits using the ***edit decision list*** or ***EDL***. The EDL should show the in and out numbers for all edits. The purpose is to have exact information handy when making changes to an edited master. It's common to re-edit shots later. The EDL shows exactly what edits were made. All the information is there to re-create any edit. Computer-operated edit controllers automatically generate EDLs while editing. Or, you can take notes while editing to construct your own EDL.

## AUDIO

Audio during the editing process deserves its own chapter. See chapter 20.

## STOCK FOOTAGE

You may need shots that are difficult to get on your own. A shot of Big Ben would require a trip to London which may not be in the budget. However, there may be footage available. Any outside footage procured from another party is referred to as stock footage. The other party may charge you for use of the footage, or you may find footage that is public domain or available for classroom use. Copyright laws allow students to use almost anything within the context of classroom use.

## FADES OR PAD?

Many single-camera productions end up as segments on the nightly news, in talk-shows, entertainment programs, variety shows, or other broadcast programs. If your video project is to be used as a segment in one of these shows, you must decide whether to bookend your show with "fades" or "pad." You can either fade up from black at the beginning of your segment and fade to black at the end. Or, you can lead into the first shot with a few extra seconds of video "pad" and end the show with a few extra trailing seconds of video.

The decision depends on the type of transition that the director of the broadcast program intends to use. If the director intends to fade to black before your segment, then your segment should fade up. But, if the director plans to wipe or dissolve to your segment, then you need to add several seconds of video pad to allow time for the transition to occur with video on the screen.

For example, imagine that you are preparing a news package. The director plans to wipe from the studio to your VTR package. The wipe duration is two seconds. Therefore, you must put at least four to five seconds of extra video pad up front to give time for the director to see the package begin, execute the wipe, and allow the transition to complete before any action begins in the segment.

Commercials are usually created with fades because program segments usually fade to black before commercials begin. News packages are usually created with pad because newscasts usually wipe or dissolve to packages.

## A REAL WORLD APPLICATION, CONTINUED:

The director has his own "cuts only" offline editing system. In the past, he would transfer original Beta SP footage to S-VHS and do a rough cut in his office. Then, he would go to a studio for final online editing.

Now, with the growing popularity of non-linear editing systems, he has decided to edit the entire project on such a system. He begins by deciding which scenes need to be digitized into the non-linear system, thus creating a rough tape log.

He brings his Beta SP source footage to the editing studio and gets all the scenes digitized. He decides to digitize at a low resolution level in order to save room on the hard drive.

The scenes now appear as clips in a bin. A freelance editor steps in at this point to begin arranging the clips in order on a timeline. The editing system allows him to create transitions: cuts, dissolves, wipes, and fades.

When the first draft of the show is finished, the editor records the sequence of shots in the timeline to videotape. The director submits the program to the client for review. There are various changes the client would like to see: some interviews that don't quite say what they'd like to hear, some shots they'd like to change. The director makes notes and goes back to the edit room. With the non-linear system, moving and deleting clips is easy.

This process goes back and forth until the client is satisfied. Finally, the director and the editor redigitize all the scenes at a high resolution level. Now the hard drives are full of huge video files. They make the final corrections and print to videotape.

The video clips can be deleted from the hard drive. Should they need to be used again in the future, they can always be redigitized.

# 20

## Graphics and Animation

Not all images come from the real world. Some pictures must be created artificially. For examples: a cutaway of the human body to show the respiratory system, a three-dimensional title for a program, a bar-chart to show a company's year-end profits, an arrow pointing to the item being discussed, or credits rolling up the screen at the end of the show. None of these are natural occurrences, so each of these must be created with traditional art supplies or with the use of a graphics computer. The creation of an individual frame of artwork for is called a *graphic*. A sequence of graphics designed to move is called *animation*.

For decades, television graphics were created by hand using paint and other conventional art supplies. Animation was also created with physical materials—either two-dimensional drawings or three-dimensional objects such as clay. These physical objects, once created, were photographed with a video or film camera. In other words, art was created in the physical environment—ink and paint—and then transferred to the electronic environment—videotape or disc storage.

The 1980s saw a complete change in approach to graphics creation. With the advances in computer technology, many graphic art applications switched from physical creation to computer creation. Computer technology bypasses the physical stage and allows the artist to create in the digital realm. Therefore, anyone learning to create television graphics today will rarely touch traditional art supplies. Some programs make typography for word, names, title graphics. Some programs allow the user to create 2-dimensional graphics and animation. Other programs specialize in programming three-dimensional objects.

Just because the computer has taken over the world of graphic design does not mean you always have to use it. One can always choose to create art by hand and place it in front of the camera to become a graphic. For example, someone may wish to create unusual credits by drawing with colored chalk on a brick wall.

## ASPECT RATIO

If an image is extremely tall or wide, it may not fit well on a TV screen. It may be cut off or it may have to be rendered extremely small in order to fit within the TV screen dimensions. The TV screen dimensions are known as the *aspect ratio*.

The traditional TV screen uses an aspect ratio of 4:3, four units wide by three units tall. In 1998, a new format was introduced called "wide screen" which has an aspect ratio of 16:9. High Definition Television will use this new ratio.

The graphic artist should consider the aspect ratio and design art to make efficient use of the screen dimensions. By doing so, images will be as large as possible, yet will fit well on the screen.

## SAFE TITLE / SAFE PICTURE

Each television monitor crops a picture slightly differently. If you position essential graphic information near the edge of the frame, one monitor may include it fully, another may cut it off a little, yet another monitor may crop it completely. Therefore, two different margins of safety are recommended outside of which no essential information should reside.

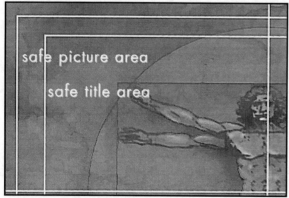

(20.1) Safe picture/safe title boundaries.

*Safe picture area* is the more liberal of the two safety margins. Outside of this margin should be no essential picture information. That's one reason why headroom is important when shooting a person.

*Safe title area* is a more restrictive safety margin inside of which should stay all written information such as titles, character generated word graphics, name identifiers, and informational graphics.

Some TV camera viewfinders display safe picture and safe title screen markers to use as guidelines while creating and framing graphics. If your equipment does not show these screen markers, then you must imagine a safe picture and safe title margin and try to work within those boundaries.

(20.2) Once an illustration is drawn or digitized into the computer environment, it can be manipulated and retouched using software "paint" and "3-D" programs.

## COMPUTER GRAPHICS

Computer graphics offer advantages over traditional physical art objects:

1) The electronic art is already in the environment where it will end up. Thus no conversion from physical to electronic is necessary.

2) Art created in the computer environment is digital and therefore can be manipulated. Changing the size, retouching the colors, adding elements are all accomplished through software program commands. All parameters—size, hue, saturation, luminance—are stored numerically in order to be precisely replicated.

Computer graphics programs come in several commonly used applications:

• **Frame store** - the ability to import and store images from outside sources

• **Illustration** - rendering individual graphic frames

• **Animation** - the sequencing of frames to depict movement

• **Typography (Type)** - words used in titles, name IDs, and other informational graphics

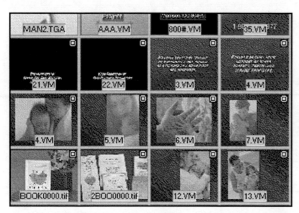

(20.3) Graphic frames stored and cataloged as thumbnail icons on a frame store computer.

## FRAME STORE

TV stations use various still graphics over and over: logos, station identifications, underwriter credits, to name a few. Stations may use these many times each day. They need a simple way to store and recall individual graphics frames as they are needed. The *frame store* is a digital computer library of individual graphic frames—each stored as a separate file.

Using the frame store alleviates the need for additional cameras or VTRs. Tonight, when you watch the news and see a station ID with a colorful graphic displaying Channel 7 ABC, that graphic is most likely a stored image being recalled off a frame store computer.

Physical art objects may be shot with a camera and kept in the frame store prior to a live show. It's a convenience for the director because that camera will have one less job to do later during the show. For example, a guest author for an interview may bring in a copy of her book to display during the program. Rather than actually displaying the book in studio, the director will probably choose to shoot the book ahead of time with a video camera, store the image, and call it up during the show as frame store source on the video switcher.

(20.4) Computer paint systems offer many paint-brush-like features—brush size, color, density—operated with electronic pen and tablet or mouse.

## COMPUTER ILLUSTRATION AND ANIMATION

The process of creating an illustration in the computer environment is called a *paint* process. A computer graphics artist will paint a picture on the computer using iconized forms of traditional painting materials: an icon of a paint brush, parameters for brush size, color, and texture. Using the mouse or a computer pen and tablet, the artist "paints" on screen.

The term "paint" also comes from the fact that the Quantel company produced one of the first widely used high-end graphics systems called the "Paint Box."

## 2-D AND 3-D ANIMATION

Animation is the sequencing of individual graphic frames to simulate movement. Traditionally, animators hand-drew every frame in an animation sequence. A two-second animation required the creation of 60 graphic frames. Today artists still draw the overall parameters, but computers do much of the repetition and thus save count-less hours of frame-by-frame drawing and redrawing.

The word *render* is a generic term for drawing or creating a picture. But in comput-er graphics, the term "render" describes the tedious process the computer must go through to create every frame in an animation once the overall parameters have been established by the animator. The animator may design the objects, colors, textures, and moves. Then, the computer fills in the details of all the in-between frames. If the animator determines that an object will move from point A to point E, the computer figures out and renders points B,C, and D based on the mathematical trajectory of the first and last points.

In many cases, the computer renders slowly—anywhere from a few seconds to a few minutes per frame. Therefore, the rendering of all frames must occur over an extend-ed period of time before viewing the final playback at 30 frames per second. For the artist, render time is often the opportunity for a lunch break while the computer cranks away, rendering all the in-between frames of an animation.

The output of the graphics computer can be fed directly into the editing system via the switcher for use in an editing session. Or, graphics from the computer can be transferred to a videotape, a hard drive, digital disc, or an internal drive. Older com-puter disc drives could not play back video in real time. The frames had to be trans ferred to videotape before complete playback could be viewed. Today's faster drives can play sections of animation sequences back in real time.

Movement may be depicted two-dimensionally or three-dimensionally. An example of a two-dimensional animation might be a red line that moves across a map to depict a route of travel. An example of three-dimensional animation may be an object spinning through the air. The computer must know the shape, color, and tex-ture on all sides of the object so that it can render each frame in the sequence of movement. This 3-D process is more time-consuming and requires more rendering time.

(20.5) A frame from a 2-D animation. We never see all sides of the helmet. The computer only has to render a 2-D movement.

(20.6) A frame from a 3-D animation. The helmet rotates. The computer must learn all sides of the object in order to render a 3-D move.

In earlier days, animation computers were limited. A computer/software package could handle either paint functions or 3-D animation functions but not both.

For example, if you wanted to fly a baseball through the air, the 3-D computer would be used to create the ball and assign it a trajectory of movement. But the paint system would have to be employed to create the leather texture, lacing, and color. The two treatments were then combined to create the composite effect.

Today, however, computers handle information much faster. Thus, it is common to find both paint and 3-D features on a higher-priced computer and software package. Lower priced systems may still separate paint and 3-D functions.

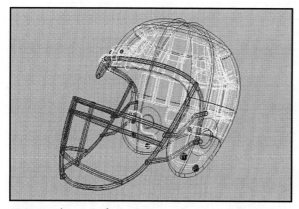

(20.7) The wireframe preview can quickly test computer 3-D animation without the time-consuming task of full rendering.

## WIREFRAME

It takes time for the computer to render an animation sequence. You may wish to make alterations at steps along the way without having to wait for the entire process to finish each time.

A helpful tool is called the *wireframe animation*. It's a feature of the 3-D computer graphics system that allows the artist to quickly preview the animation in a rudimentary form before all the colors and textures are added.

For a wireframe, the computer draws a simple skeletal outline of the object. No detail. No color. Since minimal information needs to be computed, the computer can quickly create and move the wireframe through the animation path in real time. Later, when it's time to render the animation frame by frame, the computer will have to work at a much slower rate to add all the color and texture. The wireframe allows the user to quickly preview the animation, make corrections, and preview again, before doing a final full-detail rendering.

As computer storage and playback functions get faster and faster, the need for wire-framing diminishes. Some computers can bypass the need to wireframe and can show real time playbacks of fully rendered images. Only a few years ago, this would have been unheard of. No computer could process information that quickly.

## TYPE

(20.8) Character generator operator creates type to be keyed over a source tape.

A computer that creates type for titles and credits is called a *character generator* or *CG* for short. The CG enables the user to choose from a variety of type styles and sizes. The words are then typed on the screen and saved as a file. The CG is treated as a video source in the edit room, just like any VTR, and gets routed through the video switcher. The CG graphic can be used alone or in combination with other video sources.

Some CGs have limited animation functions. They can create credit rolls or crawls across the screen. However, when sophisticated moves are needed for type, such as flying logos and titles, an animation computer is used instead of a CG.

(20.9) A key works by cutting out all information over a certain brightness level and keying that information over the second source image. Notice that the letters have a drop shadow. This is a feature of the video switcher that performs the key.

## KEYING

In many cases, the images from the CG or animation computer are combined with other video sources to create a composite picture. Consider the opening animated logo on a number of current TV programs in which a three-dimensional title flies in over the studio. The viewer sees the title as well as the studio behind the title. The graphic title from the computer is keyed over the camera's shot of the studio.

How is this done? Remember how a key works? (See chapter 19) Keying is done through a video switcher which electronically cuts out one image and places it over another. How does the switcher know what to cut out? In the case of a *luminance key*, any video over a certain brightness or luminance level is cut out. All the darker levels within that picture are left behind. So, for example, a name ID made of white letters over a black background can be luminance keyed over another image—most likely of the person being named.

## MATTE KEY

A more preferred and cleaner method for keying a graphic is called a *matte key*. It's used when the graphic has too many luminance or chrominance variations to produce a good luminance or chrominance key. So, an outline is created by the graphics system that is an exact replica of the perimeter of the object. That shape can then be used effectively as a luminance key to cut out the hole in which the real image will be then be placed. The cut out hole is called the *key signal*. The image is called the *fill signal*. The advantage of the matte key process is that the key signal shape is high contrast and therefore capable of allowing a good quality key. Since the matte key is cleaner and sharper than other types of key signals, it is often the key of choice.

Thanks to digital technology, the non-linear editing process has simplified the process of creating a matte key signal. Whereas traditional linear editing method requires a switcher to combine the key signal with a separate fill signal, the computer-based non-linear editor allows the key and fill signals to be combined into a

(20.10) This figure shows the rendered object. Its brightness and range of color may make it hard to do a luminance or a chroma-key.

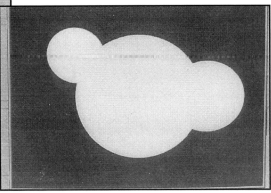

(20.11) A matte is created to do the keying. The rendered art will then be inserted in the matte hole.

single graphic file. An electronic process called an **alpha channel** provides a means of embedding the key signal in the same computer file as the main graphic. The alpha channel uses some of the bits that make up the file to hide the key information as a separately accessible signal.

## ANTI ALIASING

*Alias* refers to the breakup of curved lines in the television picture. Since TV is made up of 525 scan sweeps of the screen, the resolution is poor. Any curved edge, such as the letter "O," will not maintain a fluid line as its arc descends though numerous TV scan lines. The image will break up into a choppy stair step pattern, known as aliasing.

A feature of higher end graphics systems is the ability to **anti alias** curves in the picture. This feature applies a slight smudge to each step in the stairs. This smudge helps soften the curved lines and make the Os look rounder instead of jagged.

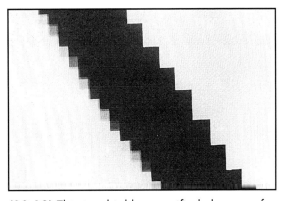

(20.12) This is a highly magnified close-up of a diagonal line on a TV monitor. The jagged stair-step on the right shows alias–very jagged. The stair step on the left has been anti-aliased to smooth out the line. At normal size, the line looks crisp and clean.

## AN ANIMATION IN THE MAKING

Let's follow the steps in the graphics process as it might occur during an actual post-post-production scenario:

1) The concept phase. The director wants an animation for a corporate logo. This logo will appear at the beginning and end of the video program as a signature.
In this case, the company logo uses an abstract American flag with a prominent 5-point star. The director dreams up an idea—a real flag blows in the breeze. From that flag, an animated star pops off the field of 50 stars and tumbles toward the viewer, finally coming to rest. The abstract red and white stripes behind the star dissolve into view and the name of the company appears on the bottom of the screen.

The director does a rough storyboard of the idea and sends it out to several computer graphic artists for bids. Each bidder looks over the sketches and comes back with a slightly more detailed storyboard which demonstrates their proposal. They also offer price quotes for completing the project.

2) The client chooses an artist based partly on price but more on the creative ideas presented.

3) The artist begins by fleshing out the storyboard, adding detail to the overall treatment. He wants the client's approval before starting work.

4) Once approved, the artist begins creating the physical objects involved in the animation: the star, the real flag, the abstract stripes, and the 3-D title.

5) Next, the artist programs in the computer how and where the objects should move. Using a wireframe shape, he builds a path for the movement.

6) The artist wants the director to approve the motion before adding all the detail of color and texture. The artist shows the director a wireframe animation of the basic movement. This gives the director and client a chance to see the movement and to sense the timing. They may decide that the path of the movement needs to be altered. Or that the motion is too fast or slow. The artist reprograms as necessary.

7) The artist uses the paint function to add color, texture, and highlighting to the objects to make them come alive.

8) Now that each frame has shape, color, and texture information, the 240-frame sequence is so loaded with information that the computer must render slowly. It may take the computer several minutes per frame. On a more complex job, the artist might let the computer render overnight. In this case, the rendering takes only a few hours. The faster computers are able to process, the faster rendering occurs.

9) As the computer finishes rendering each frame, it transfers the finished frame to a storage medium. In the past, that storage medium was videotape. In fact, the computer used to be so slow that it had to edit one frame at a time to a videotape editing machine just to free up enough memory to render the next frame. Now that computers are faster and hard drives are larger, the storage medium is usually a disc drive.

10) Once all the rendering of each frame is finished, the complete animation can be played back in real time, then copied from computer to videotape or disc, or networked directly to a hard drive in the editing room.

## THE ARTIST'S PLIGHT

In the past, a graphics person had to be well grounded as a visual artist with skills in illustration, design, and freehand drawing.

With the advent of computers, the graphic artist put down the airbrush and picked up the computer pen or the mouse, transferring his or her illustrative skills to the computer environment.

A paradoxical problem is that computer software packages have made many artistic functions accessible to anyone. But the question is, how much can the computer replace the artist? How much can the hacker create with no particular artistic training?

Software programs try to replace the need for artistic skill in certain areas. For example, a trained artist knows about shading—how a light source creates shadows and highlights on an object which helps accentuate its three-dimensionality. However, graphics programs now have the ability to make these determinations. Create a sphere, for example. Tell the computer where the light source is coming from, and the computer figures out the highlights and shadows on all sides of that sphere, making up for the user's lack of knowledge about shading.

*Clip art* is another product that helps turn the novice into an artist. Software programs offer hundreds of prepared generic images that the user can select and incorporate. No need to draw. It's been done for you.

Although the computer graphics software has enabled a lot people without any graphics background to create illustrations and animation, there is still a great advantage to having a user with formal artistic training. There are likely to be needs that only a trained illustrator can fulfill; for example, a freehand drawing as the basis for a graphics treatment. Even more importantly, a trained artist will be more likely to offer good design ideas. The ability to assess a project and make recommendations about design, color, and illustration is a skill that cannot be programmed into a computer.

---

**A REAL WORLD APPLICATION, CONTINUED:**

The director considers the graphic needs for the program:

• Titles. He will use a character generator to create titles.

• Name/title CGs. Each interviewee will be identified with a name keyed over the lower third of the picture. The director calls them "name supers." These name supers will be created on the character generator in the editing room.

• Animation. Some of the mill equipment operation is best seen through an animation sequence. The director hires a computer graphic artist to create a 3-D animation sequence. The artist goes over information and diagrams with the director, then does a first draft of the animation and shows it to the director using the wireframe mode. The director is able to see the basic movements without having to wait for the complete rendering. Once approved, the artist tells the computer to render the entire animation frame by frame.

All graphics files are imported into the non-linear editing system which can then access them as clips in the bin.

---

# 21

# Post-production Audio

$A$udio deserves special attention in the post-production phase. In some professional editing facilities, you will find two operators: the main editor accompanied by an audio engineer who monitors audio levels during each edit. In other cases, one editor handles both video and audio. One way or the other, audio quality must be monitored. The editor should not regard audio as something that just happens automatically. This chapter will explore audio considerations during the editing process.

## SOUNDS THAT GET ADDED LATER

Typically, the production phase—the shooting phase—is used to record essential location audio. But, many other sounds—special effects, narration, and music—get added during the editing phase. It would be too much trouble to handle these during the production phase.

For example, if the scene involves a dramatic dialogue between two actors with church bells ringing in the distance and music playing, then the sound of the spoken words is the only essential sound to record on location. The church bells and the music can be added later and controlled more easily in the edit room. In fact, were they actually ringing during the location shoot, they would probably be an annoyance, chiming at the most inappropriate moment.

In the real world, cars honk when they want to. In the editing room, cars honk when you want them to. That's a big difference. Given the choice, production teams will usually choose to add secondary sounds later.

## TYPES OF SOUND TREATMENTS

The following types of sound treatments might be employed in your production:

## MUSIC

Music, abbreviated MUS in script notation, is a common audio treatment. Music typically comes from any of four sources:

1) Commercial
2) Natural
3) Licensed library
4) Original

*Commercial Music* includes any music currently on the market, from Billy Joel to the Boston Pops. Any of this music can be used, but commercial use requiring licensing will no doubt be costly. Licensing companies such as ASCAP and BMI handle the arrangements. To find out how much it would cost to use a well-known popular song, simply call one of these organizations and ask for a quote. Just make sure you're seated when they respond.

Although licensed music may require permission, according to copyright law there are special exemptions which fall under the term *fair use*. One example of fair use under the law is music used in a classroom/educational situation. Music used in a student project does not require licensing or permission. However, once the music is used for a commercial production available to the general public, then the production team needs to make sure that permission has been secured. (Other forms of fair use are listed in the International Copyright Law.)

*Natural Sound Music* is that which is recorded on location in the context of shooting. Someone in the scene may be playing the guitar. The director may choose to employ that in the show. For student production, permission would not be necessary under the law, however, it's always a diplomatic gesture to ask the performer for permission to shoot the performance and use the music in the production.

*Licensed Library Music* is music composed and provided for sale by private companies. Music libraries are usually sold as sets of compact discs and used under contract for agreed upon periods of time. In some cases, the user pays a blanket fee to use as much of the music as they wish during the contract period. In other cases, the user only pays for the number of times that music is used.

The advantages of library music are:
• The licensing and permissions are all taken care of under contract.
• The price is most likely far less than the cost of hiring a composer.
• The library should offer a wide variety of music styles.

*Original Music* is composed especially for you by the composer of your choice. The pace and emotion of the music can be customized to your production. A good way to locate a composer is to inquire with a local music recording studio. Once you find a composer, you may draw up a contract. In your agreement, you should state that this music belongs to you once it has been composed. That way, the music is yours alone and won't be heard in any other productions. Original music is usually a preferred choice, if it is affordable. There is no rule of thumb on price except this—the more famous the composer, the more you should expect to pay.

Let's continue with types of sound treatments in editing.

## AMBIENT SOUND

Abbreviated *AMB* in script notation, ***ambient sound*** refers to the sound that occurred in the environment where the scene was shot. In other words, if a microphone were on during the shooting, what would it hear? If the scene takes place at the zoo, then the ambient sound would be the noise created by any animals or crowds of people in the area.

Some ambient sound is desirable. Some is not. In the case of the zoo, the sound of animals and people seems fitting. But what if there was a construction site nearby with the sound of a jackhammer? Or what if a plane flew overhead? These sounds have nothing to do with the subject.

In the editing room, you must decide whether to use ambient sound as part of your sound track. It's always preferable to use some—it adds a sense of reality. But if your ambient sound is too full of unwanted noise, consider your options next time you're out shooting:

• Wait until an unwanted sound, such as an airplane, goes away before taping.

• Ask someone to stop making the noise: "Sir, could you take a break from mowing your lawn and go have a beer for about 20 minutes please?"

## NATURAL SOUND

Abbreviated *NAT* in script notation, ***natural sound*** is synonymous with ambient sound. You may see it noted either way.

## SOUND EFFECTS

Abbreviated *SFX* in script notation, ***sound effects*** refer to any sound added in post-production that did not occur naturally on location. If no horns honked in the scene, but the sound of horns honking is desired, then the editor may find a recording of horns honking and add them to the sound track. In such a case, the horns would be considered SFX. Had they occurred on location, they would have been considered NAT or AMB.

## SYNC SOUND

*Sync sound* refers to any audio that must match the timing of an associated picture. An obvious example is the voice that must match the lips of the person talking. Or the slam of a door that must match the timing of a door closing in a scene.

## WILD SOUND

*Wild sound* refers to any sound that does not need to match any action, or would not be perceived to match any action—non-synchronous sound. For example, the sound of traffic, the sound of wind rustling in the leaves, or the sound of rain falling. These sounds may be added as sound effects, or they may have been recorded on location, but there is no precision required when adding these sounds in the editing process. The advantage of wild sound is that it can be recorded separately—at another time or place.

## VOICE OVER/NARRATION

Abbreviated *V/O* in script notation, a *voice over*, also called *narration*, is any voice track that is not sync sound. With a voice over, the viewer never sees the person behind the voice. A program may use a combination of an on-camera spokesperson and voice over. For example, a news reporter may be on camera for part of the story, for which the audio would be considered sync sound. In other parts of the story, that same reporter may record voice to be used behind various other scenes. That portion of the audio would be considered voice over.

## MIXED TRACKS VERSUS SPLIT TRACKS

Imagine a singer accompanied by a piano. If both the vocal and the piano are recorded using one microphone, the audio is considered *mixed*. Both sounds are combined on one track of the tape. One sound cannot be affected—increased, softened, or eliminated—without affecting the other.

Now, imagine that the pianist records the accompaniment first, sending the signal to Channel 1 on the record deck. Next, the singer sings while listening to a playback of the piano recording. Her voice is routed and recorded to Channel 2. Now the tracks are considered *split*. They can be played back in unison, but the advantage is that either one can be manipulated without affecting the other.

Typically, an editor will build the soundtrack one sound at a time. Each sound gets added as an audio insert edit. Perhaps the editor will start with narration, then add natural sound, and finally music. As long as these sounds are recorded separately from each other, then each can be changed later without affecting the other tracks.

When sounds are left separate on different tracks, the audio is referred to as *split track*. If the sounds are all mixed together, having been processed together through an audio mixer, then the soundtrack is referred to as *mixed track*.

The disadvantage of mixed track audio is that anywhere the individual sounds are overlapping—music behind voice, for example—these elements can no longer be edited individually.

The advantage of a mixed track, on the other hand, is that the relative sound levels are permanently protected and cannot be tinkered with by an unknowing viewer. In other words, with split tracks, someone could inadvertently have channel one turned up loud and channel 2 turned down low and hear an unintended imbalance of sound levels.

So, which way to go? Split track or mixed track? It is customary for an original edit master to maintain split tracks. That makes it easier to change elements on one track or another at a later date. If, for instance, narration occurred on Channel 1 and music on Channel 2, then either music or narration may be independently modified at any time. If those two tracks are mixed, then nothing could be done to one sound without affecting the other.

However, a copy of the master is typically made for distribution while the original master sits safely at home under lock and key. The duplicate master typically has mixed audio tracks. Then, when it falls into the hands of the end users—mass duplicators or broadcast stations—nobody can unintentionally disturb the relative playback levels between tracks. A mixed track prevents volume imbalances, or, even worse, failure to play back one of the two tracks.

## AUDIO LEVELS

The only objective way to measure audio volume is with a *VU meter* (VU is an abbreviation for Volt Unit). The VU meter measures volume—also called sound *pressure level*. The unit of measurement is called the ***decibel (db)***. The higher the sound pressure level (volume), the higher the decibel rating and the higher the VU meter displays its measurement. Some VU meters display with a needle on a numerical scale. Others use a series of LED lights.

If the sound gets too loud, the needle or LED light will enter the "red zone," indicating that the decibel rating is too high for the recording medium. If the sound is louder than the recording medium can handle, the sound will distort. Therefore, it's important to keep the audio within an acceptable range—below the red zone.

On the other hand, it's important to avoid letting the audio level drop too low. If the sound pressure level is recorded too low, then playback levels must be turned up to compensate. This increases the amount of hiss on the tape as well as background sound.

## AUDIO SWEETENING

*Audio sweetening* is TV industry slang to describe the process of adding sounds to the audio track.

Most videotape formats have only two audio tracks. Most digital non-linear systems have eight or more tracks of audio. But in either case, it may be necessary to work with numerous tracks for a complicated sound treatment. Since audio recording studios can handle dozens of audio tracks, the video editor may make use of the audio studio process.

To sweeten audio tracks 1 and 2 from a videotape master, they are first dubbed onto a multi-track system in an audio studio—either a multi-track tape machine or a non-linear audio editor. Next, additional sound tracks are added—music, sound effects, narration. Finally, the whole multi-track finished product is mixed back to the video-tape master.

Imagine that tracks 1 and 2 of the video master tape are dubbed to tracks 1 and 2 of a 24-track system. A third track is designated to hold time code. That leaves 21 tracks remaining on which to add music, sound effects and more. When the work is done, the entire 24 tracks can be mixed back down to two tracks and placed back on the video master tape. Time code allows the transfer back and forth to stay perfectly synchronized.

Traditional linear editing systems were limited to two audio tracks. That's why audio sweetening was so often a necessity. Today, however, the need to transfer an audio track into another environment is less and less needed because non-linear video editing systems come with eight or more tracks already on the timeline. Only the more complex audio treatments would require that the work be done elsewhere.

## MAKING DO WITH ONLY TWO AUDIO TRACKS

What if multi-track audio sweetening is not an option in your setting? What if you don't have multi-channel non-linear systems? You may have a traditional linear editing system with only two channels of audio available. How can you maximize the use of only two tracks?

First, take stock of the sound elements in your production. For example, imagine a news report. The sound includes the reporter's voice and ambient sound. Simple enough. The voice goes on track 1, the ambient sound on track 2.

If the reporter is on the scene of a new story doing a stand-up report, you already have ambient sound as background to the reporter's microphone. (Hopefully it won't be too distracting.) In that case, you automatically get voice and ambient sound mixed on one track. Then, if you need to add any sounds, such as music, you have another track to work with.

Now, imagine a feature story that uses music, narration, and ambient sound. That's three audio sources and only two tracks. What to do?

Option #1 - Don't use music and ambience simultaneously. That way, you can do both on the same track. For example, narration goes on track 1. Music opens the show on track 2. Ambience occurs in various scenes following the music, also on track 2. And music comes back in for a transition or for the closing.

Option #2 - Mix music and ambience as you edit. An audio mixer can be used to combine a CD player or cassette recorder with the ambient sound coming off a VTR. Recommendation: If narration plays a major role in your show, dedicate a track to the narration and do not try to mix other sounds with it. Why? Because it is very common to make changes in the narration and having to remix the other sound elements each time you change a narration segment makes life difficult.

## AUDIO RERECORDING

The term rerecording refers to any spoken words that must be dubbed over because the sound quality in the field was inadequate.

Perhaps a scene had to be shot near a noisy airport or construction site. It was impossible to record the actors' dialogue without an unacceptable level of background noise. So, the production team shot the scene anyway, but later had the actor come into the post-production studio to watch a playback of his or her scene and lip sync the words, now recorded in a quiet environment.

Obviously the actual environment in the scene would not be totally quiet. Thus, the actor's voice coming from a noticeably quiet room would sound unrealistic. The remedy is to mix sounds back into the soundtrack. Although this may seem like a lot of trouble to go through, it's the only way to make sure that horns honk between sentences, that noise levels are low enough so as not to interfere with the actor's voice level. This method puts the editor in total control of audio.

Recording actors' dialogue is an art. Actors must be able to watch themselves on tape while rerecording dialogue. If not done well, the result can be comical. You must experiment to see what types of sound environments and microphone placements work best for a given scene. As a rule, natural audio on location is always preferable over rerecording, as long as good mic presence can be maintained.

## MONITOR LEVEL VERSUS RECORDING LEVEL

Do not confuse monitor level with recording level. The "monitor level" is simply the volume of your speakers in the editing room. You may turn the volume up and down to suit your comfort, but that has nothing to do with the volume being recorded onto your master tape. The "recording level" is the actual volume going onto your record master. On your record deck are VU meters, one for each channel of audio. VU stands for "volt unit." This meter measures the volume of sound coming into the record deck. You should always pay attention to the VU meters. If the VU meter peaks too high, the sound will be distorted. If the meter peaks too low, the sound is not loud enough. Make adjustments using an audio mixer, or by adjusting the audio input controls on the record deck, or by audio output controls on the source deck.

## EQUALIZATION AND NOTCH FILTERING

The term *equalization* refers to the attempt to balance all the frequencies—to raise the bass if its too low, to lower the mid-range if it's too high.

Equalization (EQ) is familiar to most anyone with a modern stereo system. EQ controls allow the user to accentuate or deaccentuate frequency ranges within the overall sound.

(21.1) EQ controls on an audio mixer. Each EQ knob controls a different frequency range.

For example, if the music sounds too bass, the EQ can be used to quiet the lower frequencies and raise the volume on the higher frequencies, thus giving the music a brighter sound.

A *notch filter* is an EQ system that can zero in on a specific frequency or narrow band of frequencies for enhancement. The problem with typical EQ controls is that they affect large frequency ranges. However, you may want to zero in on a specific frequency without affecting the others. With the notch filter, the user can isolate a narrow frequency range and either raise or lower the volume on just that range.

If a recording has certain specific undesirable noise like a high-pitched hum or a low rumble, a notch filter may be able to isolate the sound and notch it out. The problem occurs when the unwanted noise falls within the frequency range of speech.

## NOISE REDUCTION

Audio, just like video, can be processed in the analog or the digital mode. When the audio is processed digitally, there is much less noise or hiss as a natural outcome of the process. But in the analog mode, there is always some noise level present.

There are various types of noise reduction systems on the market. These are electronic systems built into the audio processing mechanism of the given VTR or audio recorder. Noise reduction systems attempt to minimize the noise and hiss levels in analog audio.

There are various brands of noise reduction systems. Since Dolby is the most common, and since SONY has incorporated Dolby into the professional Beta videotape format, let's examine how it works.

Dolby uses a two-part process, part one during the recording, and part two during the playback. When Dolby is employed, the overall frequency range is amplified. Both the sound and the associated noise levels increase. The audio signal is now said to be "encoded."

Then, when the Dolby is played back or "decoded," the overall frequency range volume is reduced and, along with it, the noise level. The result is that the percentage of noise level is lower than it would have been originally.

## CONCLUSION

A director can plan for the kind of natural sound to record on location and the additional sound treatments to add in the post-production phase. Remember not to get fancier than your equipment can accommodate. If you don't have a multi-track system, you may not be able to work with numerous simultaneous discrete sound effects. But try to employ as much variety as possible, for an interesting sound track adds a rich dimension to any video production.

---

**A REAL WORLD APPLICATION, CONTINUED:**

The director considers his post-production audio needs:

• He will hire a narrator to record a voice over narration for the program. The audio will be recorded in a digital format and imported as a file into the non-linear editing system.

• Music will come from a CD library that the TV production pays a yearly license fee to use. The library contains hundreds of cuts of varying styles. The director will spend a couple of hours listening to cuts and choosing the best themes for the production.

The non-linear system offers eight tracks of audio on the timeline. The director and editor can decide where to assign the various audio sources. Narration is assigned to channel 1. Interviews to channel 2. Music to channel 3. Sound effects and ambience to channel 4.

When the timeline is printed to videotape, the multiple audio tracks will all get mixed to one channel on the tape. Should there be any problem with the balance between the various sounds, the editor can go back to the non-linear timeline, adjust levels on any track, and reprint the timeline to videotape.

---

# 22
# Distribution

What happens to the television program after it has been edited? Is the job over? Does the show sit on the shelf? If not, where does it go?

For a student production, the end result may be submission for a grade. Beyond that, the student may wish to distribute copies to friends and family on VHS cassettes. In addition, the student's work may get added to a resume reel to show prospective employers for internships or summer jobs.

In the commercial world, a production is not meant to sit on a shelf, rather to be seen and used in the marketplace, be it broadcast or private applications. In today's diverse world of video, there are many ways for the show to get distributed.

Any production team working in the business world must maintain a perspective that keeps the end use of their project in sight. Who is the program for? How is it being distributed? For example, a program prepared for broadcast may be marketed differently than a program that will be packaged and sold as a home video cassette.

As the leader of the production process, the director takes a concern for the distribution of the final program. The director may not be directly involved in distribution, but must be aware of any decisions needed along the way to make sure the product is suitable for its intended use.

Early in the pre-production process, the director should understand the intended distribution. If the show is for broadcast, the director may choose higher resolution equipment to ensure broadcast standards. Closer attention may be paid to white and black levels, making sure they are within broadcast legal limits. If the show is intended for commercial television then the length of each segment may be critical.

If the show is intended for VHS cassette distribution, then the length may be important. Simplicity of images may be helpful to overcome VHS' poor resolution. Finely detailed graphics, for example, may not read well on VHS. The color red tends to "bloom" on VHS, so the director may avoid bright red clothing for the actors.

Let us consider a list of possible ways in which a television program may get distributed.

1) **Broadcast** - The program is transmitted by a TV station.

2) **Closed circuit** - The program is routed over the wires of a private system—a cable company, a hospital system, a school district, etc.

3) **Bicycled** - "Bicycling" is an industry term that means sending videotape copies of a show to a list of TV stations. As each one receives the tape, they either broadcast the show or make a copy of the tape for later airing and send the original on to the next station on the list. Satellite services have reduced the need for bicycling.

4) **Satellite Uplink** - The program is uplinked to a satellite and downlinked to a network facility, a cable company, a private teleconference, or a home satellite receiver.

5) **Direct mail** - The program is promoted through telemarketing and sold and shipped as a home video packaged cassette product.

6) **Store point-of-purchase** - The show is packaged for retail and appears on store shelves.

7) **Premium, promotional** - The show is given away as a free offer, either as a bonus for buying something else, or as a free advertisement for a product.

The important thing is to see how the pre-production, production, and post-production phases can serve the end result by anticipating the form of distribution.

For each form, we want to answer the following questions that may have an impact on the form of distribution:

*a) Who is the audience?*

The audience should have been identified way back in the concept stage. Now, consider the audience again as you package the show for distribution. Is this video going through the proper distribution channels to meet its intended audience? For example, a show that is intended for an extremely specific market, such as a training program for plumber's apprentices, may not be suitable for broadcast. Or a home video training program for pilots may not be effectively marketed through ads in Better Homes and Gardens. Certain language may not be suitable for certain audiences. Programs for general audiences may need introductions and explanations to orient them to the program that might not be necessary in a niche market presentation. A video designed to teach coast guard licensed boat captains how to upgrade their licenses, may make perfect sense to the intended audience, but may be nothing short of confusing for another audience or a general audience. So, the first distribution consideration is this: Is the program going to be niche marketed to a specific audience, or will it be distributed to a general audience?

### b) What needs to be spelled out in a contractual agreement?

If the show is for home video distribution, does the client want an FBI copyright warning at the beginning? Are any disclaimers required for legal purposes? If it's for broadcast, what are the station's rights? How many times may the show be aired? Stations often require proof of your rights to use music or any other material in the show that may be subject to royalties.

### c) Whose technical standards must be met?

Sending a show out for distribution may involve meeting other people's technical standards. Broadcast TV, for example, has certain technical standards. The higher the authority, the tougher the standards tend to be. Networks will scrutinize the technical quality of a tape moreso than a local station might. Network affiliate stations will be tougher than independent stations because they are required to uphold network rules and regulations.

For example, video levels must not exceed 100% on the waveform monitor, nor should they dip below 7.5%. A network or national cable distribution company may reject a show based on one scene in which the levels went outside of prescribed boundaries. Small stations or independent stations are not usually so strict.

### d) Who requires the edited master tape?

When you finish editing the program, you have a master tape in your hand. The question is: who needs it? Before you give the master to anybody, it is wise to make a backup master. Simply copy the master onto a new tape. If someone accidentally drops your tape in a mud puddle or if a VTR eats the tape for lunch, you're back to the editing room unless you made a safety copy.

The two most common places for a master or backup copy to go are: 1) a broadcast station for airing, and 2) a duplication company for dubbing.

In the case of broadcast, the station will want the tape on the highest grade video format possible. If the master was created on professional BetaCam, for example, then it should be given to the station in that format. The station will not want a lower grade version. Stations hate getting tapes submitted on consumer VHS, for example, since this format is far below the normal professional standards and has a much lower resolution.

### e) Duplication for consumer distribution and retail—VHS and DVD

The traditional way to distribute a program to the general public was through various low grade, cheap videotape formats. The two formats most common in the 1980s were Panasonic's VHS format and Sony's BetaMax format (not to be confused with Sony's professional grade BetaCam format). VHS won the marketing war and became the commonly used duplication format. VHS is a poor quality format. Programs created on high quality professional formats such as BetaCam SP, one-inch, and D-2, loose a tremendous amount of resolution in the transfer to VHS. In other words, the VHS tape cannot handle the signal with justice to the original master. The picture is grainy and the video noise is greatly increased on VHS.

To help solve the problem of poor grade duplication to VHS, the **DVD** is offering distributors better quality options with interactive menus. Similar in size and shape to a CD-ROM or music CD disc, the DVD can play on a computer disc drive and on a TV set top player that resembles the home VCR.

A DVD program has twice the resolution of a VHS tape and six to ten times the capacity of a CD. A DVD program can incorporate menu and track selections similar to a music CD. The user can switch to different chapter points on a DVD program through the use of a remote control or keyboard function. Hence, the tedious task of shuttling a tape back and forth to find a location is no longer necessary.

## VHS DUPLICATION

The VHS duplication company takes the video master in order to make mass quantities for consumer retail distribution. The duplication company will always want the best possible format from which to make dubs. It is best to provide a broadcast quality master. The signal from the master tape is amplified and split out to numerous consumer format decks. The better the master, the better the copies will look.

Large duplication companies will dub as many as one thousand VHS machines simultaneously. The high quality master serves as a source tape. The signal goes through a process called *distribution amplification* which boosts the level of the video and audio signal so it does not weaken as it gets split out to the numerous recording decks.

The customer can choose to have the VHS recorded in SP or EP modes. SP (standard play) is the normal speed and produces the best quality. The EP (extended play) mode slows down the tape, tripling the play time but producing a rather poor picture quality. In the past, a third option was available called LP (Long Play) which was an intermediate speed, poorer quality than SP but not as poor as EP. VHS decks used to offer all three speeds but more and more offer only the SP and EP. Since VHS is inherently poor in quality, its best to hang onto whatever image quality one can by recording in the SP mode.

## VHS COPY PROTECTION

Nobody wants their VHS copies to be bootlegged by others. Another option for the customer is to request a copy protection process while the duplication is made. Some duplication companies can provide a process that de-stabilizes the signal to the record machines just enough so that the the tapes play well, but when someone attempts to make a copy, the picture breaks up on the copy. This process is marginally effective. Some tape machines will effectively copy the tape anyway.

## DVD ENCODING, AUTHORING AND REPLICATION

DVD has some additional optional steps compared to VHS duplication. Whereas a VHS copy can be made by dubbing directly from the master tape, the video going to DVD must first be *encoded* into the MPEG-2 format while the audio must be encoded into a WAV or Dolby Digital format.

Encoding the program into MPEG-2 or other file format requires running the video signal through an encoding process. Encoders may be software based, hardware based, or a combination of the two. Software encoders are the slowest. A 10-minute show may take 40 minutes to encode. Hardware encoders are faster. More expensive ones not only encode in real time but use a technique called "multipass" encoding in which the encoder surveys the master tape to optimize a variable compression rate before doing the actual encoding, using more compression where necessary, and less where able.

At this point, an MPEG-2 file is ready to be transferred to a DVD disc. However to make a DVD, a few more steps are required.

The next step is called **DVD authoring**. The purpose of DVD authoring is to add menus and other forms of interactivity to the video presentation. DVD authoring requires a software package that is similar to a non-linear editing program. The MPEG-2 file is placed on a timeline to be edited for interactivity. Menus and associated links may be placed throughout the program. For example, if the lumber mill training program has three main sections, then the person authoring the DVD can create a menu with three choices. Each menu button can link to a target location in the program. A marker is placed on the timeline at the point where a section begins. That marker is associated with the button on the menu.

DVD authoring offers other advantages. The DVD specifications allow up to eight selectable audio tracks and up to 32 selectable "sub-character" channels for subtitling. So, the lumber mill training program could have alternate language tracks for employees in different countries and a subtitle track for the hearing impaired.

Once authoring is finished, the next step is to **mux** the files—a process in which all the appropriate video, audio, and graphic files are organized into proper file types and folders. At this point, the operator can preview the playback of a DVD program using DVD playback software associated with the authoring program.

If the playback looks good, the next step is to create a disc **image file**. This is a composite of all the muxed files into one large file that will be written to the DVD disc. Again, the authoring software provides the appropriate tools to create a disc image.

Finally, the disc image can be written to a DVD-R burner or saved on a digital linear tape and sent out for mass production. In DVD lingo, mass duplication is called **replication**. The DVD replicator will first create a glass master from the digital linear tape and then produce multiple DVDs. The DVD discs may be single-sided, double-sided, single-sided/double-layered, or double-sided/double-layered.

In short, DVD offers many advantages:
• the ability to play on a computer drive as well as a TV
• higher resolution than VHS
• the ability to be authored with interactive menus
• 8 audio tracks
• 32 subtitle tracks

## f) What are the packaging requirements of a VHS or DVD program?

If the program is distributed as individual cassettes, what are the packaging require-ments? If the video appears in a store as a point-of-purchase item, it needs to look good. A 4-color box with sharp graphics is essential in the competitive marketplace. Often, a client will not consider the packaging needs until the project is done, mean-ing they did not budget for graphic design or printing, and the distribution gets delayed while all this takes place. These things need to be considered early on.

To create packaging for the video, a graphic artist must design the cover. The cover must be printed. Like any printing, black and white art is cheaper to design and print than color. Video boxes come in a variety of styles. Some are plastic boxes with printed inserts. Some are die-cut cardboard printed sleeves that get folded and glued to form a box.

In the case of DVD, packaging is similar to a CD-ROM or music CD. The plastic "jewel" box is commonly used which simply requires a printed insert and a label to go on the actual disc.

## g) What is the ongoing responsibility of the production team?

If the master tape goes to the client, then the production team can consider the job over. However, if the production team is also involved in broadcast or duplication, then the team should keep careful track of tape storage.

What if the client wants to make changes later? Perhaps a phone number needs updating, or some information in the video becomes obsolete. It is common for a client to come back to the production team and ask for changes. The smart solution is for the production team to keep edit decision lists, source tapes, and notes so that changes can be made easily in the editing room.

## CONCLUSION

Distribution is an easily overlooked area, especially when it comes to budgeting. A client must consider the cost of duplication, packaging, and any other costs that are involved in getting the finished program to the marketplace. You, as the director, can be of help by raising these concerns and shaping the program throughout the pro-duction process so that it is suitable for its intended outlet.

## A REAL WORLD APPLICATION, CONTINUED:

The lumber mill executives want a copy of the safety video to be seen by every employee. They also want it to be used in all training classes throughout the nationwide locations.

They discuss the advantages of VHS versus DVD duplication and decide to do some of each. Not all the offices throughout the company have DVD players yet. But they all have VHS machines. However, the company executives know that DVD will become more and more prevalent.

The VHS copies are made by simply sending a dub master of the finished program to the duplicating company. The director works with a graphic artist to create attractive printed labels and inserts to slide in the plastic box covers This will give the program a polished professional appearance on the shelves of trainers and managers throughout the company. The combined total of printing and duplicating comes out to about $2.50 per VHS copy.

The program master is also sent to a DVD authoring station where the program is encoded into the MPEG-2 format. The program is put on a timeline similar to editing on a non-linear system. In this case, the timeline is used to add interactivity to the program such as menus to allow the user to jump to different sections of the video at will. When the DVD authoring is finished, the entire MPEG-2 program is transferred to a digital linear tape (DLT) which is sent to a DVD replicator. The discs will be made and placed in plastic boxes using the same graphic design as was used for the VHS boxes.

Thus ends the distribution phase, the post-production phase, and the entire production process. Different crew members have come and gone, but the director has seen the job through from beginning to end. The producer of the program receives a final word from the director that everything is completed. Now the producer, representing the TV production company's executive team, can contact the client, confirm that everything is satisfactory, and bill the client for final payment. Meanwhile, the director goes home and clears his mind. He's ready for a break, but he also can't help wondering what the next project will be.

# Section VI

The following are suggested exercises. Some work well as in-class workshop exercises. Others make good in-the-field assignments. Even if you do not actually carry out the exercise, read over each one and consider the concepts and ideas.

# Exercises

## EXERCISE 1 - BUDGETING A SINGLE-CAMERA SHOOT

**Purpose:**
To become familiar with all the items that can go into a budget for a simple video production. Also, to get a sense of what the professional world is charging for services.

**Description:**
What does it cost to do a video production? You may not have to worry about budgets when you're working on a class project, but it's interesting to know what a shoot would cost if you were doing a professional project. In this exercise, you will discover some current real-world prices for equipment and services.

**Assignment:**
Go over the list of items on the next page. Get a basic understanding of what they are. If any terms are unfamiliar, use the glossary in this book, or go over them in class. Then, call local companies and price each item or service. You can look them up in the yellow pages.

**Suggested sources:**

CREW: TV production service companies

TALENT. Talent agencies

EQUIPMENT: TV equipment rental companies

EDITING: TV production service companies

Using the list of items below as a starting point. Call various production companies and request their rate cards for equipment and services. This exercise will give you an idea of current prices in your market.

|  | PRICE / RATE | AGENCY / COMPANY |
|---|---|---|
| **CREW:** | | |
| CAMERA OPERATOR | _____ | _____ |
| AUDIO ENGINEER | _____ | _____ |
| LIGHTING GRIP | _____ | _____ |
| MAKE-UP PERSON | _____ | _____ |
| TELEPROMPTER | _____ | _____ |
| | | |
| **TALENT:** | | |
| MODEL | _____ | _____ |
| NARRATOR | _____ | _____ |
| ACTOR | _____ | _____ |
| SPOKESPERSON | _____ | _____ |
| | | |
| **EQUIPMENT:** | | |
| CAMERA | _____ | _____ |
| MICROPHONES | _____ | _____ |
| VTRS | _____ | _____ |
| LIGHTS | _____ | _____ |
| DOLLY | _____ | _____ |
| TRIPOD | _____ | _____ |
| BATTERIES | _____ | _____ |
| FIELD TAPE | _____ | _____ |
| | | |
| **EDITING SERVICES:** | | |
| OFFLINE EDITING | _____ | _____ |
| ONLINE EDITING | _____ | _____ |
| MUSIC LIBRARY | _____ | _____ |
| COMPUTER GRAPHICS | _____ | _____ |

# EXERCISE 2 - A SITE SURVEY

## Purpose:
To gain an appreciation for the things to look for when sizing up a location for production.

## Description:
In actual EFP shooting, you may not always have the luxury of doing a site survey. For example, a news team can't evaluate the location in which a robbery is about to take place. However, whenever possible, you can save yourself a lot of agony and ensure a more successful shoot by surveying the sites first.

For this exercise, evaluate two locations of your choice, one interior and one exterior. Use the questions provided to analyze each location. Once you've finished, decide whether either of the locations will work or whether you should find others.

## PART 1 - Evaluate an interior location:

Pick a room. It could be your classroom, your room at home, or any other room. Assume you are going to tape an interview in this room.

*1) Evaluate electrical power sources.*

You need electrical power for lights and for your camera and deck. The camera and deck draw very little power. But your lights may draw anywhere from 5 to 25 amps, depending on how many lights you use and the wattage of your bulbs. The lights will most likely have three-prong plugs which include a ground wire.

Does your room have three-prong grounded outlets? If not, you'll need adapter plugs.

What amperage capacity are the circuits? Most newer homes have 15 to 20 amp circuits, so that two lights that each draw 6 amps could work off of one circuit without tripping the breaker.

If you have too much wattage for one circuit, are there more circuits in the room? Or can you run an extension cord to a nearby room that's on another circuit?

If you happen to trip the breaker and all the power shuts off, do you know where to find the circuit breaker box to turn things on again. How would you reroute the wires to keep the problem from happening again?

Findings:_____

*2) Evaluate the space in the room.*

To do an interview, you need enough room for two people to sit face-to-face with ample space around them for the camera to get reverse angles. You also want to avoid having either host or guest backed up against a wall. You want enough space behind them to allow for some depth in the shot and to allow for shadows from lights to fall off behind them. Is there enough room?

Findings:_____

*3) Evaluate the aesthetics of the room.*

Does the background look acceptable from each angle? Keep in mind that you'll only see a small portion of the room in your field of view. The whole room doesn't need to look good—just the part you'll see. Is the background a mess? Is the wall unpleasant to look at? Is it all white or all black, something that would cause unwanted high contrast?

Findings:_____

*4) Evaluate the color temperatures in the room.*

Every light source has its own color temperature. The sun coming in through the window is around 5600 degrees Kelvin. The tungsten reading light is about 2800 degrees Kelvin. The fluorescent lights are around 3800 degrees. But your camera can only handle one temperature at a time. You can white balance for one at a time. So a mix of light sources will cause a problem. As much as possible, you need to establish a uniform light source.

Do you think you will light the room with 3200 degree Kelvin TV lights? If so, are there any light sources in the room that will interfere? If so, can you turn them off? If there is a window letting in sunlight, can you close the curtains? If a big picture window has no covering or curtain, can you balance your lights for daylight by using blue gels? Do you see any other problems?

Findings:_____

*5) Evaluate the sound environment.*

You don't want a lot of nearby noise to interfere with a nice clean audio recording. Are there any noise sources that cannot be controlled?

Is there a loud air conditioning system? Can it be turned off? Is there a lot of traffic noise coming in from outside? Is there noise from people working nearby? If there is an uncontrollable noise, is it intermittent enough that you can work around it?

Findings:_____

**PART 2** - Evaluate an exterior location for an interview.

*1) Evaluate power sources.*

Is there AC electrical power available? If not, do you have enough battery power to complete your interview?

Findings:_____

*2) Evaluate the space.*

Is it a reasonable place in which to do an interview? Will it work better to stand or sit? Can you get both angles? Can you keep each subject at least several feet away from any wall or other background in order to create more depth?

Findings:_____

*3) Evaluate the aesthetics.*

What do you see in the background of each angle? Is there anything undesirable? Too much commotion? Something too dark or too bright?

Findings:_____

*4) Evaluate the lighting.*

When you're outside, you generally want to take advantage of natural light. Will the position of the sun at a particular time of day work well for you? Are you under trees or other objects that might throw unwanted shadows? Is the background too bright compared with your subject?

Can you anticipate light cloud cover that would keep the sun from appearing too bright? Or can you shoot in early morning or late afternoon so as to avoid harsh direct sunlight? If you need to shoot in direct sun, can you get scrims or reflectors to help even out the light?

Findings:_____

*5) Evaluate the sound environment.*

Stand in the space and listen. Is there too much traffic noise? Are there any other distracting sounds in the environment? If so, would moving somewhere else nearby minimize the noise?

Findings:_____

# Exercise 3 - CAMERA MOVES AND FRAMING

**Purpose:**
1) To learn and execute basic camera moves.
2) To frame basic shots of a single face and two people facing each other in a conversation.

**Description:**
You've probably used a video camera before and perhaps you've tried panning around and zooming in and out. But now you want to hone your skills, develop a precise vocabulary and a precise working knowledge of types of shots.

Using a video camera, shoot any subject you like and execute the following list of shot types.

Remember, always bookend each move with several seconds of static framing. In other words, a zoom in is not just a zoom in. The full move would consist of: static for several seconds, then zoom in, then static for several seconds. You always want to see a move in the context of a beginning and an end. This "bookending" concept applies to any camera move.

Too many moves will make the viewer dizzy. So, along with pans, tilts, trucks, and other moves, it's always good to get a purely static framing where the camera doesn't move.

Shoot one example of each item on the following list.
1) __a static shot (no camera movement)
2) __pan (left or right)
3) __tilt (up or down)
4) __zoom (in or out)

For the next set of shots, you'll need wheels. They could be wheels on the base of a tripod. Or you can improvise with a shopping cart, a skateboard, or anything else you can come up with.

5) __truck (left or right)
6) __arc (left or right)
7) __dolly (in or out)

The next group of shots will help you practice framing people. Your task is to get some friends to pose for you while you frame each of the following shots and record about ten seconds of each composition. Evaluate in class.

Single face:

8) __head-on
9) __profile
10) __3/4 profile

Two faces in conversation:

11) __2 profiles
12) __over the shoulder, 2-shot and CU
13) __over the shoulder, reverse angle, 2-shot and CU
14) __2 Faces East

# Exercise 4 - Audio Presence

## Purpose:
To get familiar with audio presence from a microphone.

## Description:
Microphone presence refers to the distance between the microphone and the subject. Close presence means that the subject sounds very close. Distant presence means that the subject sounds further away. There are times when you may want to create a distant presence. But the general rule of thumb is that you want the microphone as close as possible, because once you start pulling it away from the subject, all the other sounds of the environment start blending in and competing with the sound of your subject.

Experiment with microphone presence. Have a friend read or recite a short poem or paragraph three times, each time with a different microphone presence.

1) __Use the internal shotgun mic on the camera for a distant presence.

2) __Use a remote mic on an extension cable to get about 2-3 feet away from the subject for a medium presence.

3) __Use the same remote mic just in front of and below the subject's chin for a close presence.

Play back each take and note the difference of each sound.

# EXERCISE 5 - THREE-POINT LIGHTING

**Purpose:**
To learn and practice basic three-point lighting on a subject consisting of one person.

**Description:**
In this exercise, you can take some time to experiment with positioning a key light, a fill light, and a back light.

The key light should be positioned about 45 degrees above and 45 degrees to the side of your subject.

The fill light should be 45 degrees up and 45 degrees to the other side. The fill should be about half the intensity of the key. You can achieve this by using scrims or by flooding out your light (an adjustment on the instrument makes the light more diffuse). This 1/2 intensity is not an exact science. What you're mainly trying to achieve is a face that doesn't look too evenly lit from both sides, therefore not too flat.

The back light should be about 45 degrees up and directly behind the subject. A light stand would be in your picture if it is directly behind the subject, so move it a few feet to one side. The back light should highlight the hair and shoulders.

**Assignment:**
Have your subject sit in a chair. Frame a chest shot or a loose head and shoulders shot. Set up your three lights. Turn on each light individually to evaluate. Look at the back light alone. Are the hair and shoulders highlighted?

Look at the key and the fill separately. How does each look? Is the light too bright, washing out the face? Is the light too harsh? Do you need to add a scrim or flood out your light? If it's still too harsh, do you want to try a reflector for a much softer light?

How do shadows look on the face? If the subject has deep set eyes, are the lights too high, causing him or her to look like they are wearing sunglasses?

If the subject is wearing glasses, are the lights throwing shadows onto the face? You can adjust the placement of your lights a few feet one way or the other.

Perhaps most important of all, evaluate the nose shadow. Is the nose shadow going across the cheek? Is it dropping down over the mouth? Ideally, the nose shadow flows right along the natural crease from the nose right down to the corner of the mouth. The shadow should stop there.

Remember that the key light will help soften the fill light's nose shadow and vice versa. So, when you're looking at them one at a time, it's okay if the shadow looks a little too pronounced.

When you're happy with each individual light, they should look pretty good when you turn on all three.

Once you've lit your subject, record some tape. Play back your tape in class for evaluation.

# EXERCISE 6a - THE BASIC EDIT  (LINEAR EDITING SYSTEM)

**Purpose:**
To try a simple editing exercise for the first time. To familiarize yourself with assemble and insert edits.

**Needed supplies:**
1) A black source tape or other black source
2) A source footage tape with at least three different shots
3) A record master tape
4) A 2-machine videotape-based linear editing system

*Assignment:*
1) Record black
2) Assemble three shots
3) Assemble black

**Method:**
1) Record black. In a linear editing system using videotape machines, remember that the first edit on a new unrecorded tape cannot actually be an edit. Why? Because there is no video for the machines to pre-roll back over.

a) On the player, put in a black source and push the play button.

b) On the recorder, push the play and record buttons. You are now recording a black signal onto your master tape.

c) Record about 20 to 30 seconds of black. Stop the machines.

2) Assemble three shots:

a) Select the assemble mode. Why? Because you are about to pick up from where you left off at the end of the black and push on into unrecorded video territory. That requires control track which means you must use the assemble mode.

b) Unload the black tape from the player and load a source tape with a variety of shots to choose from.

c) Select a shot in the player and mark an "in point."

d) Select a point on the master tape where you want the shot to occur and select an in point. NOTE: Make sure the in point is located somewhere prior to the end of the control track.

e) Preview your edit if desired. The edit controller gives you the option of previewing, which results in the machines going through all the motions of the edit, displaying the edit, but not actually recording the edit.

f) If you are not happy with the location of the in points, make adjustments on either the source or the record machines. If you are happy with the preview, do the edit by selecting the appropriate edit function on your edit controller.

g) Perform the edit and stop where desired after several seconds.

h) Repeat the process and edit two more shots in a sequence, all in the assemble mode, all starting at in points that are set just before the prior shot runs out.

3) Edit black. After editing three shots, select your black source tape one more time. This time, you will treat the black source just as any other video source. Perform another assemble edit just like the others. The effect will be to edit a curtain—video black—onto the end of the tape. The in point will, again, be just before your last shot ends.

The result will look like this:

| BLACK | SHOT 1 | SHOT 2 | SHOT 3 | BLACK |
|-------|--------|--------|--------|-------|

## Variation:

Now, perform the same sequence of edits as above, but this time, stay in the insert mode after you've blacked a length tape that is longer than your show will be. This is the way most editors prefer to edit. Once the tape is blacked, there is control track throughout. All subsequent edits can be performed without having to switch back and forth between assemble and insert.

## Procedure:

1) Do the dub copy of black just as you did in Step 1 above, but this time, instead of just letting the black go for 20-30 seconds, let it go for several minutes. Thus, you have created a bed of control track and black over which to edit your three shots.

2) Switch to insert mode. Edit the three shots.

3) No need to add black when you're finished. It's already there from your initial blacking.

# EXERCISE 6b - THE BASIC EDIT (NON-LINEAR EDITING SYSTEM)

## Purpose:
To try a simple editing exercise for the first time. To familiarize yourself with digitizing and editing using a non-linear editor.

## Needed Supplies:
1) A source tape with scenes on it
2) A record tape if you wish to record your final product

## Assignment:
1) Edit three or four shots, fading up from black at the beginning and back to black at the end.

## Method:
1) In a non-linear system you must first create a project file.

2) Within that file, establish a bin for storing your digitized clips.

3) Choose a source videotape from which to digitize.

4) Digitize three or four shots.

5) Place scenes on the timeline. Fade up from black to the first scene. After the last shot, fade to black.

6) At this point, the scenes are only on your computer. If you want to put your finished editing project back on videotape, you must tell the system to record your show onto tape. Put a master tape into the VTR. The computer can then play the timeline while recording onto the master tape.

# EXERCISE 7 - PREPARING A ROLL-IN SEGMENT

**Purpose:**
To try two basic ways to prepare the head of a tape for a studio roll-in.

**Supplies:**
1) A source footage tape with various individual numbers ranging from "2" through "5."
2) A source tape with a commercial spot and a news package.
3) Either a linear or non-linear editing system.

**Description:**
VTR roll-ins are segments prepared for insertion in a live broadcast such as a newscast. A roll-in may be a news report, magazine feature, etc. As an editor, you may be asked to prepare roll-ins for a broadcast show. Video roll-ins prepared for broadcast often have countdown leaders at the head end. The countdowns begin anywhere from five to ten seconds prior to the beginning of the show. Studio directors use these countdowns to execute precise roll cues.

VTRs need to come up to speed before the transition occurs. That means the tape has to start rolling a few seconds prior to the actual transition. Typically, a director will cue up a VTR to a spot exactly three seconds prior to the start of the program. The VTR is paused on this three second spot ready to go, awaiting the director's command to "Roll VTR" about two to three seconds prior to the transition. When the command is given, the videotape machine rolls through the remaining countdown. Just before the end of the countdown, the director calls for a transition from the studio to the VTR program. It may be a cut, a wipe, a dissolve, or a fade to black."

There are two ways to prepare a VTR for a studio roll-in:

1) kiss black—black before and after the roll-in allows for a momentary fade to black and fade up again as a transition.

2) cut, wipe, or dissolve—the roll-in begins a little early, allowing time for a cut, wipe, or dissolve as a transition.

## KISS BLACK TRANSITION

In the first case, the effect will be a fade to black from the studio and a fade back up to the first video coming from the VTR. This is typical for transitions to and from TV commercial breaks. It signifies a major departure from the previous scene.

In this case, the numbers on the countdown must stop appearing on the screen during the last two seconds in which the transition occurs. The remainder of the countdown is black only. This two-second period of black allows the director to do a transition from studio to black and up to VTR without accidentally seeing any numbers on the screen.

Thus, the countdown starts at some number from five to ten and ends just a few frames after the "2" appears. The remainder of the final two seconds is black.

## CUT, WIPE, OR DISSOLVE TRANSITIONS

The other method of preparing a VTR roll involves starting the roll-in a few seconds early. This lead-in video is called "pad." During this pad, the director may execute a cut, wipe, or dissolve from studio to roll-in and back again at the end. The pad should precede the important content of the roll-in. In other words, if the roll-in features a reporter saying, "Hello, I'm John Smith," then the pad will consist of three seconds of John Smith standing there ready to speak. During this period, the director has time to make the transition.

*Assignment:*

Create one of each VTR roll-in segment preparations: one designed for a kiss black transition and one designed for a cut, dissolve, or wipe.

After each countdown is prepared, edit at least a couple of scenes to represent the beginning of an actual show.

## METHOD #1: The "Kiss Black" or fade down and up transition (to a commercial or new program).

1) Black a couple of minutes of tape.

2) Starting about 30 seconds into your black, edit a countdown using numbers from your source tape: "5" for a duration of one second, "4" for one second, "3" for one second.

3) Then, edit only five frames of the "2," leaving the remainder of the countdown in black, allowing time to crossfade in blackness.

4) At the zero mark, following the 55 frames of black, edit the commercial break. The edit point on the source tape should be just before the fade up to the commercial.

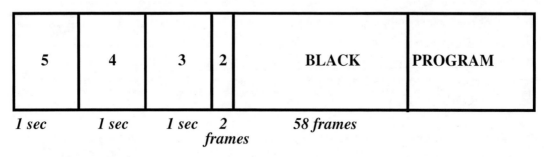

| 5 | 4 | 3 | 2 | BLACK | PROGRAM |

1 sec     1 sec     1 sec    2 frames     58 frames

EXAMPLE #1 - Preparing the leader for a "fade to black" transition

**METHOD #2: The "pad" transition (to a news package or magazine feature).**

1) Black a couple of minutes of tape.

2) Starting about 30 seconds into your black, edit a countdown using numbers from your source tape: "5" for one second, "4" for one second.

3) At the point where the "3" would begin, edit the first shot of your news package. Keep in mind that the in point should be three seconds prior to actual action or beginning of the program. In other words, the first three seconds of the news package are a leader that runs during the final three seconds of the countdown, enabling the director to execute a wipe or dissolve. If the timing works properly, the transition will be complete just before the content of the news package begins. This first three seconds of the package is referred to as "pad."

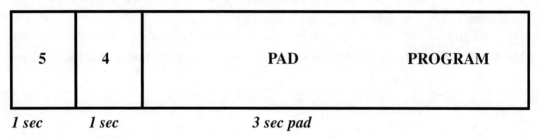

| 5 | 4 | PAD | PROGRAM |

1 sec     1 sec        3 sec pad

EXAMPLE #2 - Preparing the leader for a "pad" transition.

# EXERCISE 8 - THE CHASE (Moving through Time and Space)

## Purpose:
To shoot and edit a chase scene, experimenting with moving people through time and space.

## Description:
As with most chase scenes on TV or films, the chase doesn't stay in one area. The progression of the chase takes the subjects in and out of various locations. The student must make judicious use of: screen direction, entering and exiting scenes, using head-on/tail-away shots, and cutaways to make the action work smoothly and logically.

## Supplies:
A source tape with raw field footage, shot by the student or provided by the instructor.

## Assignment:
Conceive of a chase sequence between two people. Think up a storyline. Cast the actors. You may wish to storyboard the sequences to make sure you know exactly what kinds of shots you want, what screen directions, what camera angles, etc. Plan on using all the tricks from chapter 15: exiting, entering, head-on/tail-away, and cutaways. Shoot the raw footage. Then edit a chase scene. Preferably, use ambient sound on one audio channel and music on the other channel.

## Method:
1) Conceive an idea and consider locations.
2) Storyboard your chase. Consider when and how actors will enter and exit scenes.
3) When shooting, get some cutaways in addition to the main shots. These cutaways will help you bridge jump cuts later in editing.
4) View and log your raw footage. Do a "paper edit." Referring to your log and make a list of the shots you want in the order you want them. Then, when you go into the editing room, you will already have a plan in mind.

# EXERCISE 9 - THE INTERVIEW

**Purpose:**
To learn the technique of shooting and editing the interview format using a single camera. To frame good over-the-shoulder shots and close-ups. To coach talent in an interview setting. To edit interview done with one camera.

**Supplies:**
Source tape provided by student or instructor.

**Description:**
The interview style is pervasive throughout the world of TV and film. Talk shows, news shows, documentaries, sports programs, game shows, dramatic programs and even arts programs use the over-the-shoulder interview format.

The easiest way to do an interview is with two or more cameras in a live multi-camera studio with a switcher. That way, the shots back and forth between guest and host can be selected instantly.

But in the field, with one camera, it's a bit more challenging. Only one angle can be shot at a time. Sometimes, production teams will take two camera along and shoot both angles simultaneously, but that is often a luxury that the budget won't always permit.

**Assignment:**
Conceive of a one-on-one interview between two people: a host and a guest. Pick two people and pick a subject for them to discuss. Shoot the interview. Shoot more material than you will actually use.

Shoot both angles. From each angle, shoot both an over-the-shoulder shot for some questions and a close-up for others. Change framing between questions.

Start with the guest angle, because you want the guest's responses to be fresh and unpracticed. Then move the camera to the other side and shoot the reverse angle of the host asking key questions, reacting, and making opening and closing comments. Do not bother having the guest answer the questions again.

Edit the interview, piecing the opposite angles, both OS and CU shots, together in a sequence that makes it seem as if this were a two-camera interview. In fact, the success of your project will primarily be seen in the smoothness between the cuts back and forth and the way the dialogue flows well from cut to cut.

If the guest talks too much on any given answer and you want to consolidate the time, use cutaways of the host reacting or listening to cover jump cuts that appear as a result of your consolidation.

Matching shots is the key to a good reverse angle over-the-shoulder. The reverse angle should be a mirror image of the other. The same angle. The same level. The same framing of OS and CU shots.

**Method:**
1) Choose host and guest.

2) Choose subject matter to discuss.

3) Work with the host on an opening and closing statement made to the camera.

4) Set up the first OS of the guest. Always start with the guest.

5) Use lights if necessary. In a bright room or outdoors lights may not be needed, but if your class has access to lighting, you may wish to enhance the available light with TV lights.

6) For audio, don't rely on a shotgun mic on your camera. That's too far away. Instead, if you only have one mic channel, place an extension mic between the two subjects. If you have a two channel audio input system, you can put a separate mic on each subject.

**Note:**
If you have a one-channel audio system, you can only use one mic unless you have a mixer. With one mic, place it directly between the host and guest, leaving it there for both angles works better than pinning it on each subject in turn. The reason is simple: If you mic one person at a time, then whenever the other one talks, they sound far away. You want the mic presence to be even.

7) During the interview, get both OS and CU shots.

8) After the interview is over, move the camera to the reverse angle. Have the host do three things:

a) Repeat the opening and closing comments to the camera,

b) ask major questions, and

c) do some reactions for cutaways including straight listening, nodding a little, and smiling. These become a repertoire of resources for various cutaway needs later in the edit room.

9) In the edit room, piece your interview together. You can throw out sections, and condense it to any length.

10) Evaluate your work in class. Look for smooth dialogue and well-framed opposing angles that are well-matched.

# EXERCISE 10 - THE MASTERSCENE

**Purpose:**
To learn to shoot and edit a dramatic scene using the masterscene approach.

**Supplies:**
Source tape provided by instructor or shot by the student.

**Description:**
A dramatic scene between two or more actors is usually shot several times from several angles. This approach is called masterscene shooting. For the first angle, the camera shoots a wide shot, known as the masterscene. This angle shows all the action in the scene. Then, the camera is moved to another angle and the action is repeated. Then another angle and the action is repeated again. Thus, the actors repeat a scene several times.

In the editing room, the editor can choose where and when to cut between angles. The result is an edited scene that looks as if it were shot with multiple cameras.

**Assignment:**
Cast a short dramatic scene using friends or actors. Plan your shots and shoot the scene, starting with a masterscene and follow with as many various angles as seem appropriate. Typical alternate angles include: over-the-shoulders of key subjects engaged in dialogue, close-ups of other people participating in the conversation, reaction shots, close-ups of action or props in the scene.

**Method:**
1) Choose a scene, perhaps an excerpt from a play, something of your own invention, or footage provided by your instructor.

The easiest kind of scene to work with would have all the actors in close proximity, such as all around a table. Don't use too many actors—three or four will do.

2) Cast the actors and rehearse.

3) Choose angles.

4) Consider lighting and audio. The ideal audio would be a shotgun microphone hung off a fishpole over the actors just out of camera view. Try to keep lighting and audio consistent as you shoot the various angles. If you make lighting or audio changes, then the scenes will seem to change back and forth and will look strange.

5) Begin with the masterscene, the cover shot. Follow with all other angles in any order you desire.

6) View and log the raw footage.

7) Edit the scene using any sequence of angles you desire. It's common to begin with the wide shot and move in to closer shots. That gives the viewer a chance to see the relationships between people in the entire scene.

8) Your biggest challenge is to match action between cuts. If one cut ends with the glass half way up to the man's mouth, then the next angle should pick up exactly where the previous one left off. Otherwise you get a jump cut.

9) Evaluate in class for smoothness of editing, matching action, and shot selection.

# Glossary

*The following glossary represents a partial list of terms introduced in this book as well as other useful terms. For a full list of new terms from this book and their locations, please refer to the index.*

**AFTRA** - American Federation of Television and Radio Artists, a talent union.

**AGC** - automatic gain control for sound recording levels.

**ALTERNATING CURRENT** - electrical current that cycles through plus and minus waves.

**AMBIENT SOUND** - natural sound in the environment.

**ANALOG RECORDING** - traditional electronic encoding process that emulates an acoustic or light wave pattern.

**APERTURE** - variable hole or opening in the lens through which light passes.

**ARC** - camera movement in a constant radius to the subject.

**ASPECT RATIO** - TV screen dimensions. TV aspect ratio is 4:3; HDTV is 16:9.

**ASSEMBLE EDIT** - an edit mode that generates new control track.

**ASSISTANT DIRECTOR** - crew position—one who closely assists the director.

**AUDIO IN** - the input on a VTR or audio recorder for an audio signal.

**AXIS OF ACTION** - imaginary line dissecting any action which the camera should not normally cross in order to maintain consistent orientation.

**A/B ROLLING** - in video—using two source machines to create dissolves or wipes. In film, preparing two source films, checkerboarding each scene as preparation for final merging into one film.

**A/C ADAPTER** - a power supply that plugs into an A/C wall outlet and converts power to DC for the camera/VTR.

**BACK LIGHT** - the light placed in back of the subject in three-point lighting.

**BALANCED LINE** - an audio cable with a third wire for grounding.

**BARN DOORS** - metal shades to restrict light spill from a lighting instrument.

**BETAMAX** - a once-popular consumer half-inch videotape format by SONY.

**BETACAM/BETACAM SP** - a half-inch cassette professional videotape format by SONY BetaCam is oxide tape. BetaCam SP is metal tape. Digital BetaCam is digital, however the VTR can play back analog tapes as well.

**BLACK** - video black is the darkest part of the picture and is measured as 7.5 on the waveform monitor.

**BOOM** - a crane used to hold a microphone over the talent.

**BNC CONNECTOR** - a video cable connector consisting of a push-and-twist connector.

**CARDIOID** - a heart-shaped microphone pick-up pattern.

**CHARACTER GENERATOR (CG)** - computer used to create type (words and simple graphics) for the TV screen.

**CHARGE-COUPLED DEVICE (CCD)** - a computer chip in the video camera that converts light to electricity.

**"CHEAT"** - director's call to talent to look a little toward the camera so the viewer can see the face better; "cheat" toward the camera.

**CHROMA-KEY** - a type of electronic key that ignores a prescribed color and replaces it with another image.

**CHROMINANCE** - the color portion of the TV picture.

**CLOSE-UP (CU)** - a close framing of a subject.

**CODEC** - a software algorithm for coding and decoding digital audio or video information. Different companies have marketed their own proprietary codecs under names such as: QuickTime, Cinepak, and Indio.

**COLOR TEMPERATURE** - the color rating of a given light source.

**COMPONENT PROCESSING** - a high quality video process in which parts of the video signal are split into three separate color component signals.

**COMPOSITE PROCESSING** - traditional method of video processing in which no signal separation occurs.

**CONDENSER MICROPHONE** - a particularly sensitive microphone that uses an electret capacitor as a sound pick-up element. Requires additional power supply such as battery.

**CONTRAST RATIO** - the range of brightness and darkness within one picture.

**CUE** - 1) a verbal signal to begin an action; 2) finding a starting point on a tape.

**CUTAWAY** - a shot selection that takes the viewer away from the primary subject.

**CUTS-ONLY EDITING** - editing with only one source machine, hence no dissolves or wipes.

**CUTTING ON ACTION** - an editing transition that takes place during some obvious movement, making the transition less noticeable.

**DECIBEL (DB)** - a unit of sound pressure level or volume.

**DEGREES KELVIN** - the measurement scale for color temperature.

**DEPTH OF FIELD** - the area in front of and behind the focal point that is also in focus.

**DIGITAL SIGNAL** - a signal encoding based on converting all sound or picture information to sequences of binary numbers.

**DIGITAL VIDEO EFFECTS** *(DVE)* - the digital process of manipulating a video image, used for transitions and special effects.

**DIRECT CURRENT** - the type of electrical current found in batteries; no plus-and-minus cycling as in alternating current.

**DIRECTOR** - person responsible for execution of production.

**DIRECTOR'S GUILD OF AMERICA (DGA)** - director's trade union.

**DISSOLVE** - a transition in which one picture fades while another appears.

**DOLLY** - 1) the cart that a camera rides on for moves; 2) the act of moving a camera toward or away from the subject.

**DROPOUT** - a portion of the video signal that is missing due to tape damage, appearing on the TV screen as a small white or black speck or line.

**DROPOUT COMPENSATOR** - circuitry in a VTR that tries to replace missing video information (dropout) with similar information.

**E-TO-E (ELECTRONICS TO ELECTRONICS)** - in VTRs, whenever a tape is not engaged or playing, any signal routed into the VTR's input can be seen as that VTR's output.

**EDIT DECISION LIST (EDL)** - a list of all edits showing source locations, record locations, edit modes, transitions, and notes.

**EDITING** - in film or video, the process of sequencing scenes.

**ELECTRONIC FIELD PRODUCTION (EFP)** - same as ENG but broader, the process of using a single camera on location for any kind of production.

**ELECTRONIC NEWS GATHERING (ENG)** - the use of a single camera in the field to gather news stories.

**ESTABLISHING SHOT** - a wide angle of a scene to show overall physical relationships within a scene.

**FEEDBACK** - electronic distortion caused when any sound or video recorder is attempting to playback and record simultaneously; the signal records itself and creates a distortion.

**FILL LIGHT** - the secondary light source in three-point lighting.

**FILTER** - a gel used for color correction or neutral density.

**FISHPOLE** - a pole used to hold a microphone over the talent.

**FLAG** - a piece of metal or fabric used to restrict the flood of a given light source.

**FLUID HEAD** - a tripod head using fluid to create smooth motion.

**FOCAL LENGTH** - the distance from the optical center of the lens to the focal plane—film, tube, or CCD surface; the longer the focal length, the more telephoto the lens.

**FOCAL PLANE** - the point in the camera on which the focused image lies: film, CCD, or tube surface.

**FOCAL POINT** - the spot out in front of the lens that is perfectly in focus, the subject being photographed.

**FORMAT** - the type of videotape used and the associated VTR to play it.

**FRAME** - one still image—the basic unit of simulated movement in film or video.

**F-STOP** - scale used to measure the size of a lens' aperture opening.

**GEL** - A tinted translucent piece of acetate used to alter the color of a light source.

**GENERATION LOSS** - degradation due to copying of analog tapes.

**GRIP** - a person that handles lights and hardware.

**HEAD** - 1) small electromagnet that makes contact with an audio or video tape to read or play back the signal; 2) the top section of the tripod that does the panning and tilting.

**HEADPHONES** - small speakers worn over the ears to monitor sound.

**HIGH DEFINITION TELEVISION (HDTV)** - a new TV signal standard that doubles the traditional number of scan lines to produce a higher resolution picture and a 16:9 aspect ratio.

**HMI** - Hg (Mercury) Medium Source Iodide. A lighting instrument with bulb balanced for daylight.

**HOT SPOTS** - over-exposed parts of the picture.

**HUE** - color.

**INCIDENT LIGHT** - light that comes directly from the light source.

**INSERT EDIT** - an edit mode that only affects individual tracks, producing no control track.

**INTERLACED SCANNING** - the process by which the TV picture scanning sweeps all even lines followed by odd lines.

**IRIS** - see aperture.

**JUMP CUT** - an illogical or displeasing juxtaposition of shots.

**KEY LIGHT** - the main light source in three-point lighting.

**LAVALIERE MICROPHONE** - a small clip-on style of mic.

**LIGHT** - An energy wave that is the medium by which we see.

**LIGHTING INSTRUMENT** - A bulb mounted in a fixture used for illumination.

**LINEAR EDITING** - traditional mode of editing using videotape machines.

**LONG SHOT** - see establishing shot.

**LOOK SPACE** - a value given to the area in front of a subject's face used to balance the picture by offsetting the face.

**LUMINANCE** - the brightness component of the TV picture. Luminance without chrominance results in a black and white image on the TV screen.

**LUMINANCE KEY** - a type of electronic key that ignores any part of the image below a certain luminance level and replaces it with another image.

**MATCH FRAME EDIT** - an edit that picks up on the very next frame from where the last edit ended.

**MPEG-2** - a compression algorithm for encoding digital video—the format specified for DVD technology. MPEG stands for Motion Pictures Experts Group.

**M-II** - a professional half-inch videotape format marketed by Panasonic.

**NARRATION** - a voice heard as part of the audio track; same as voice over.

**NOISE** - electronically speaking, unwanted audio hiss or snowy quality in picture inherent in analog recording.

**NON-LINEAR EDITING** - newer mode of editing using random access computer environment to arrange scenes.

**NOTCH FILTER** - an audio equalization processor that can isolate, boost, or diminish very narrow frequency ranges.

**NTSC** - National Television Standards Committee, the U.S. standard for television signal processing.

**NEUTRAL DENSITY FILTER** - a filter that does not affect color but cuts down on light level.

**OFFLINE EDIT** - a rough cut edit using a simple editing system, saving time by avoiding fancy transition effects.

**ONLINE EDIT** - a final edit in which all transitions, titles, and effects are added.

**PAINT** - 1) a generic term for computer graphic rendering; 2) adjusting the color output of a camera to achieve an effect.

**PAL** - Phase Alternate Line—a 625 line TV standard found in many European countries.

**PERSISTENCE OF VISION** - the lag time in which the brain retains the image which allows a sequence of frames to simulate movement.

**PICK-UP PATTERN** - the area around the microphone that is most sensitive to sound waves.

**PRESENCE** - the feeling of the sound: close up or far away.

**PRESSURE ZONE MICROPHONE (PZM)** - microphone with hemispheric pick-up pattern.

**PRODUCER** - person responsible for the overall production.

**PRODUCTION ASSISTANT (PA)** - general assistant to the production.

**REACTION SHOT** - shot from opposite angle showing someone's response.

**REFLECTED LIGHT** - light that bounces off something before hitting the subject.

**REVERSE ANGLE** - opposite angle.

**ROLL TAPE** - 1) During field production, the call by director to begin VTR recording; tape should roll for several seconds before action; 2) During studio production, the call by the director to begin a VTR roll-in.

**SATURATION** - in color, how deep or rich the color is.

**SCRIM** - a fire retardant cloth or mylar material placed in the path of a light source in order to diffuse it.

**SECAM** - Sequential Color with Memory—a 625 line TV standard found in France and Russia.

**SEGUE** (seg-way) - transition.

**SHOTGUN MICROPHONE** - a mic with a super cardioid pick-up pattern.

**SHOOTING RATIO** - amount of footage shot compared with amount of footage actually used in final program.

**SIGNAL-TO-NOISE RATIO** - a ratio expressing how much noise is inherent in a recording made by a given camera, VTR, or audio recorder.

**SMPTE** - Society of Motion Picture and Television Engineers, a guild that sets technical standards including the standard for time code.

**SOFT LIGHT** - a reflected light.

**SOUND EFFECTS (SFX)** - sound added in editing.

**SPECIAL** - A light that is added for a specific additional purpose or effect—to light an object, or to create a pattern.

**SPLIT EDIT** - an edit in which the in point of one or more tracks come after the main edit point.

**STEADICAM** - the trademarked name, often used generically, of Cinema Products' spring-loaded camera mount worn on the shoulders for running with the camera.

**STORYBOARD** - a script format composed of sketches or pictures to represent the flow of action.

**SYNC** - 1) part of the video signal required for stabilization 2) an outside electronic pulse fed to various machines for a common timing reference.

**TALENT** - anyone performing for the program: actors, spokespeople, anchors, etc.

**TAPE LOG** - a detailed description of raw footage shot on location.

**THREE-POINT LIGHTING** - basic lighting configuration composed of key, fill, and backlight.

**TELEPROMPTER** - a device that scrolls type over the front of the camera lens for the talent to read so as to maintain camera eye contact.

**TILT** - tripod-based camera rotation up or down.

**TIME CODE** - an encoded clock time on a track on the videotape.

**UNBALANCED LINE** - an audio line with no third line for grounding, more susceptible to interference.

**VECTORSCOPE** - an oscilloscope showing color information.

**VHS** - a half-inch consumer grade videotape format by Panasonic.

**VIDEO IN** - the input on a VTR for a video signal.

**VOICE-OVER (V/O)** - see narration.

**WAVEFORM MONITOR** - an oscilloscope showing luminance information or light level.

**WHITE BALANCE** - a method of calibrating the camera to see recognize the color white under a given light source.

**WIND SCREEN** - a foam or cloth over a mic to cut down on wind disturbance.

**WIPE** - a transition composed of a geometric pattern.

**XLR CONNECTOR** - standard microphone cable connector consisting of three pins.

**Y/C** - a video signal in which the brightness (Y) and the chroma (C) are separated—also known as s-video.

**ZEBRA BARS** - a stripe pattern seen in the camera view finder to indicate hot spots.

# INDEX

shotgun mic, 109, 172
shot sheet/shot list, 94
simplicity, 65
signal-to-noise ratio, 131
single-column format, 88
site survey, 98
soft news/feature, 78
sound effects (SFX), 287
sound pressure level, 289
sound stage, 220
source tape(s), 111, 227
special (light), 217
split edit, 252
split track, 289
spokesperson, 114
sports, 79
stand (lighting), 110
stand-ups, 105
static shot, 136
steadicam, 111
stock footage, 232
storyboard format, 92
super-cardioid, 170
switcher, 248
sync sound, 286
S-video, 23
talent, 201
telephoto, 57
texture, 61
three-point lighting, 157
tilt, 135
time code, 130, 241
timeline, 257
tracking, 252
training/informational, 79
treatment, 81
tripod, 107
truck(s), 108, 136
tungsten, 127, 146
two-column format, 85
two-inch VTR, 18
type, 273
under exposure, 125
unidirectional, 170
U-MATIC, 18
VHS, 297
video file server, 31
video out, 128

video track, 239
videotape formats, 22
videotape recorder/VTR, 106-7, 121, 129
voice over (V/O), 286
volts, 151
VU meter, 287
waist shot, 67
wattage, 150
waveform monitor, 154
white balance, 127, 147
wide angle, 57
wild sound, 286
windscreen, 109, 173
wipe, 248, 262
wireframe animation, 276
wireless, 109
writer, 112
waist shot (WS), 65
Y/C, 23
zebra bars, 155
zoom, 135
zoom lens, 57
3/4 inch cassette, 18
3/4 profile, 69